AGS® Reading Skills for Life

Level E
Teacher's Guide

AGS®

American Guidance Service, Inc.
Circle Pines, Minnesota 55014-1796
1-800-328-2560 www.agsnet.com

Content Reviewers

The publisher wishes to thank the following educators for their helpful guidance and review during the development process for *Reading Skills for Life.* Their assistance has been invaluable.

Jack Cassidy, Ph.D.
Professor of Education
Texas A&M University
Corpus Christi, Texas

James Johnston
Reading Specialist
Portsmouth High School
Portsmouth, New Hampshire

Alva Webb Jones, Ed.S.
Special Education Consultant
Richmond County Board of Education
Augusta, Georgia

Robin Pence
Reading Specialist
Clay High School
Clay County Schools
Green Cove Springs, FL

Ted Stuff
School Psychologist
Special Education
Department Chair
McLaughlin High School
Anchorage, Alaska

Development and editorial services provided by Inkwell Publishing Solutions, Inc.

Level E Student Worktext Photo and Illustration Credits

Page 4, © Jeff Greenberg/PhotoEdit; p. 6, © David Young-Wolff/PhotoEdit; pp. 9, 30, 102, 104, 112, 116, Joel Snyder; pp. 13, 14, © Jimmy S. Baca; p. 22, © Charles Mauzy/Corbis; p. 36, © WLS-TV; pp. 39, 170, © AFP/Corbis; pp. 44, 46, 67, 71, 79, 129, 144, 146, Barbara Counsellor of John Edwards, Inc.; p. 52, © AP/Wide World Photos; p. 54, © Bettman/Corbis; p. 86, © Michael Newman/PhotoEdit; p. 94, © Mark Richards/PhotoEdit; p. 97, © Myrleen Ferguson Cate/PhotoEdit; pp. 132, 136, © Corbis; p. 153, © Joseph Sohm/Visions of America/Corbis; p. 155, © Adam Woolfit/Corbis; p. 157, © 1996 PhotoDisc, Inc.; p. 164, © Black Star; p. 166, © Museum of Flight/Corbis; p. 168, © Flip Schulke/Black Star

Publisher's Project Staff

Director, Product Development: Karen Dahlen; Associate Director, Product Development: Teri Mathews; Senior Editor: Patrick Keithahn; Development Assistant: Bev Johnson; Designer and Cover Illustrator: Denise Bunkert; Design Manager: Nancy Condon; Desktop Publishing Specialist: Jack Ross; Desktop Publishing Manager: Lisa Beller; Purchasing Agent: Mary Kaye Kuzma; Executive Director of Marketing: Matt Keller; Marketing Manager: Brian Holl

Printed in the United States of America

ISBN 0-7854-2646-9

Product Number 91742

A 0 9 8 7 6 5 4 3 2

Contents

Reading Skills for Life Program Overview

What is Reading Skills for Life?

Reading Skills for Life is a comprehensive reading program designed to address the specific needs of students in grades 6–12 who have been unable to achieve reading success through traditional methods of instruction. The goal of *Reading Skills for Life* is to enable these students to achieve a functional level of reading fluency. To accomplish this goal, the program utilizes research-based methods proven to be effective for below-level readers. The program is structured to build on each student's level of literacy. Multiple entry points address a range of reading abilities. *Reading Skills for Life* has six levels.

Levels A–E progress developmentally. Students enter the program at the level that matches their proficiency. New skills are introduced and practiced one at a time, giving students the opportunity to master each skill before going on to the next. Students have multiple opportunities to review and practice the skills they learn. Level A begins with a reading level of approximately 1.5; by the end of Level E, students will be reading at about the sixth grade level and may successfully transition into a mainstream reading and language arts course.

Level P is designed for nonreaders and beginning readers who have gaps in their understanding of basic letter-sound correspondences or limited phonemic awareness. Level P provides prereading instruction in phonemic awareness, the alphabet, basic concepts about print, and the 35 basic letter-sound correspondences.

Evaluation and Placement

Reading Skills for Life offers remediation for struggling readers. Two assessments are available from AGS for use in determining which level is most appropriate for your students. See page 10 of this Teacher's Guide for information about the *Reading-Level Indicator* and GRADE.

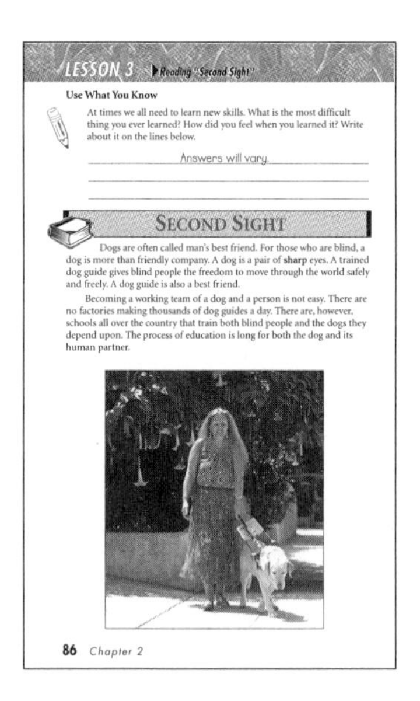

LESSON 3 Reading "Second Sight"

Use What You Know

At times we all need to learn new skills. What is the most difficult thing you ever learned? How did you feel when you learned it? Write about it on the lines below.

Answers will vary.

SECOND SIGHT

Dogs are often called man's best friend. For those who are blind, a dog is more than friendly company. A dog is a pair of **sharp** eyes. A trained dog guide gives blind people the freedom to move through the world safely and freely. A dog guide is also a best friend.

Becoming a working team of a dog and a person is not easy. There are no factories making thousands of dog guides a day. There are, however, schools all over the country that train both blind people and the dogs they depend upon. The process of education is long for both the dog and its human partner.

86 Chapter 2

Student Worktexts

In addition to teaching students the basic skills and strategies required for reading, *Reading Skills for Life* offers students many opportunities to practice reading. High-interest, controlled-vocabulary fiction and nonfiction selections are the center of every lesson and reinforce the skills students have been taught.

Ongoing Assessment

Reading Skills for Life provides teachers and students with timely information about each student's progress. Every lesson concludes with two pages of exercises, reinforcing and extending the skills that have been learned. Summaries of skills and strategies, along with extensive Chapter Reviews offer opportunities for review and re-teaching. Reproducible chapter and end-of-level tests check students' acquisition of skills at each level.

Comprehensive Teacher's Guides

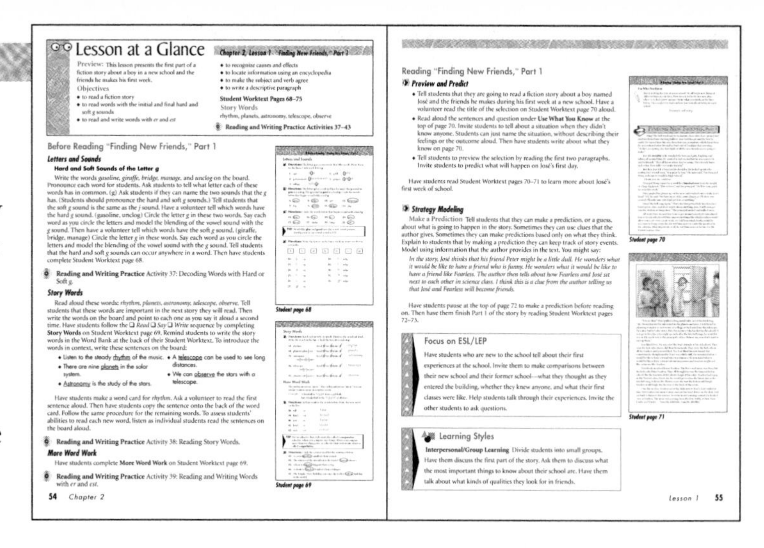
Lesson at a Glance

Before Reading "Finding New Friends," Part 1

Reading "Finding New Friends," Part 1

Focus on ESL/LEP

Learning Styles

54 Chapter 2

Lesson 1 55

Chapter Planning Guides give teachers the tools they need to plan for each student's needs. The consistent three-step teaching plan is easy to use: **Before Reading, Reading, After Reading.** Each annotated Teacher's Guide shows the related Student Worktext pages with all answers at point of use. Reproducible chapter tests, end-of-level tests, and record forms are included for each level.

Reading Skills for Life addresses the needs of a diverse population of students. Lesson-specific activities for students with varying learning styles, learning disabilities, and limited English proficiency are included in each Teacher's Guide.

Learning Styles

- Visual/Spatial
- Auditory/Verbal
- Body/Kinesthetic
- Logical/Mathematical
- Interpersonal/Group Learning

Learning Styles

Body/Kinesthetic Have groups of students role play a scene in which Jamal and one or more teammates conduct an interview with a TV talk show host. First have students choose roles and come up with questions and responses. Then have groups perform for the class.

Focus on ESL/LEP

To access prior knowledge and build vocabulary about basketball, draw or display a picture of a basketball game. Have students name things they see and describe what they know about basketball. List their responses on the board. Have students say new words after you.

Focus on LD

Work with students to complete **More Word Work** on Student Worktext page 81. Write the first word, *patches,* on the board; read it aloud, and ask a volunteer to draw a line between the two syllables. Then have students write the word and divide it in the Student Worktext. Follow a similar procedure for the next four words, and have students work on their own to divide the last two words, *hatchling* and *teething.*

Each Teacher's Guide also offers suggestions for helping students connect the content of the lessons to real-life applications at home, in the community, and the world of work.

Application

Career Connection Students may be interested in finding out about careers that are related to sports but do not require an athlete's skill and stamina. These might include careers in sports reporting, radio or TV broadcasting, camera work, advertising, sports medicine, and administration. Students might invite a person involved with professional sports to the class to talk about career opportunities in sports.

Reading and Writing Practice

Hundreds of reproducible activities on CD-ROM give students additional practice with phonics and word study skills, automatic recognition of story vocabulary and high-frequency words, and the other skills instructed in the program.

Chapter Books

Levels A and B each include three small, easy-to-read chapter books for sustained reading and the opportunity to read for pleasure. Levels C, D, and E recommend selected books at the end of each chapter that closely match students' reading abilities and interests.

Reading Skills for Life Scope and Sequence

Phonemic Awareness	P	A	B	C	D	E
Phonemic Awareness	●	●	○	○	○	○

Phonics and Phonograms	P	A	B	C	D	E
Single Consonants (initial, final)	●	●	○	○	○	○
Double(d) Consonants (medial, final)	●	●	○	○	○	○
Consonant Blends (initial,final)	●	●	●	○	○	○
Consonant Digraphs (initial, final)	●	●	●	●	○	○
Consonant Digraphs (medial)		●	●	●	●	●
Silent Consonants		●	●	●	●	●
Short Vowels: CVC	●	●	●	●	●	●
Long Vowels: CVC*e*	●	●	●	●	●	●
Long Vowels: Digraphs		●	●	●	●	●
Long Vowels: Open Syllable			●	●	●	●
r-controlled Vowels		●	●	●	●	●
l-controlled Vowels		●	●	●	●	●
w-controlled Vowels			●	●	●	●
Vowel Variants			●	●	●	●
Vowel Diphthongs			●	●	●	●
Schwa			●	●	●	●

Word Study	P	A	B	C	D	E
Endings *-s, -es*	●	●	●	●	●	●
Ending *-ies*		●	●	●	●	●
Ending *-ed*	●	●	●	●	●	●
Ending *-ing*	●	●	●	●	●	●
Suffix *-er* (one who)		●	●	●	●	●
Suffix *-or* (one who)				●	●	●
Suffixes *-ar, -ist* (one who)						●
Prefixes *un-, re-*			●	●	●	●
Suffix *-ly*		●	●	●	●	●
Suffix *-ful*			●	●	●	●
Suffixes *-er, -est* (more, most)			●	●	●	●
Prefixes *pre-, dis-*				●	●	●
Suffixes *-less, -ness*				●	●	●
Prefixes *de-, non-*					●	●
Suffixes *-tion, -sion, -ion*					●	●
Prefixes *in-, im-*					●	●
Suffixes *-ment, -y*					●	●
Prefixes *mid-, mis-*						●
Prefixes *sub-, trans-*						●
Suffixes *-able, -ible*						●
Suffixes *-ous, -eous, -ious*						●

Reading Strategies	P	A	B	C	D	E
Make a Prediction	●	●	●	●	●	●
Summarize	●	●	●	●	●	●
Clarify	●	●	●	●	●	●
Reread/Read Ahead	●	●	●	●	●	●
Set a Purpose	●	●	●	●	●	●
Access Prior Knowledge	●	●	●	●	●	●
Use Context Clues	●	●	●	●	●	●

Reading Comprehension Skills	P	A	B	C	D	E
Topic	●	●	●	●	●	●
Main Idea and Supporting Details	●	●	●	●	●	●
Draw Conclusions	●	●	●	●	●	●
Cause and Effect	●	●	●	●	●	●
Note Sequence	●	●	●	●	●	●
Author's Purpose	●	●	●	●	●	●
Summarize	●	●	●	●	●	●
Compare and Contrast	●	●	●	●	●	●
Categorize	●	●	●	●	●	●
Fantasy vs. Realism		●	●	●	●	●

Critical Thinking Skills	P	A	B	C	D	E
Make Judgments	●	●	●	●	●	●
Make Decisions	●	●	●	○	○	○
Problem Solving	●	●	●	○	○	●
Distinguish Fact from Opinion	●	●	●	●	●	●
Evaluate				●	●	●
Synthesize						●
Recognize Point of View and Bias						●

Spelling	P	A	B	C	D	E
Spelling		●	●	●	●	●

Study Skills	P	A	B	C	D	E
Using a Dictionary	●	●	●	○	●	○
Using an Encyclopedia		●	●	●	●	●
Organizing Information		●	●	●	●	●
Using Graphic Aids	●	●	●	●	●	●
Following Directions	●	●	●	●	●	○
Test-Taking Strategies		●	●	●	●	●

Language	P	A	B	C	D	E
Identifying Sentences	●	●	●	●	○	○
Subjects and Predicates	●	●	●	●	●	●
Common and Proper Nouns	●	●	●	●	●	●
Singular and Plural Nouns	●	●	●	●	●	●
Possessive Nouns			●	●	●	●
Action Verbs	●	●	●	●	●	●
Linking Verbs (including forms of *be*)	●	●	●	●	●	●
Subject-Verb Agreement	●	●	●	●	●	●
Main Verbs/Helping Verbs			●	●	●	○
Simple Tenses			●	●	●	●
Perfect Tenses					●	●
Pronouns		●	●	●	●	●
Possessive Pronouns			●	●	●	●
Adjectives		●	●	●	●	●
Adverbs			●	●	●	●
Prepositions			●	●	●	●
Prepositional Phrases				●	●	●
Compound Sentences					●	●
Complex Sentences						●
Contractions		●	●	●	●	●
Troublesome Words		●	●	●	●	○
Fixing Fragments and Run-ons				●	●	●
Capitalization	●	●	●	●	●	●
Punctuation	●	●	●	●	●	●

Writing	P	A	B	C	D	E
Persuasive		●	●	●	●	●
Narrative	●	●	●	●	●	●
Expository		●	●	●	●	●
Descriptive	●	●	●	●	●	●
Expressive		●	●	●	●	●
Functional/Real World	●	●	●	●	●	●

Literary Appreciation	P	A	B	C	D	E
Story Elements	●	●	●	●	●	●
Theme		●	●	●	●	●
Narrative Voice		●	●	●	●	●
Appreciate Poetry		●	●	●	●	●
Literary Forms	●	●	●	●	●	●
Mood		●	●	●	●	●
Figurative Language			●	●	●	●

● Skill is instructed **○ Skill is maintained**

Building a Foundation for Reading Success

Success for Students with Special Needs

The individuals to benefit from *Reading Skills for Life* may include

- middle school or high school students who are not reading or are reading at a first or second grade level;
- students with learning disabilities;
- English language learners;
- students who are experiencing behavior problems or have experienced other risk factors that have interfered with their acquisition of basic reading skills.

Reading Skills for Life builds a foundation for reading success by addressing the needs of this varied population in a number of ways:

- Skills are introduced at a slow and steady pace, giving students an opportunity to master each skill before moving on to the next.
- Multiple opportunities for practice are presented with every skill introduced.
- Teaching methods address a variety of learning styles based on Howard Gardner's theory of multiple intelligences: visual/spatial, auditory/verbal, body/kinesthetic, logical/mathematical, and interpersonal/group learning.
- Activities are designed to help teachers capitalize on students' individual strengths and dominant learning styles. The activities reinforce each lesson by teaching or expanding upon the content in a different way.
- The content of the material is age and developmentally appropriate, high interest, and designed to motivate students to read by appealing to their interests and abilities.
- Teaching tips and activities for making the materials accessible to students with different needs appear throughout each Teacher's Guide.

Sample Teaching Tips

- Give students sufficient time to respond to questions.
- Limit the number or complexity of tasks to complete at one time.
- Narrow the focus of a question.
- Allow a student to answer orally instead of requiring a written response.
- Limit the amount of text a student encounters on a page.
- Identify phonetic elements in English that may pose difficulties for English language learners.

Phonics and Word Study

Reading Skills for Life offers a focused and comprehensive approach to reading instruction that provides explicit instruction in phonics and word attack strategies within the context of reading for meaning.

Phonemic Awareness is the ability to hear individual sounds (phonemes) in spoken words. Research has established that phonemic awareness plays a critical role in the early stages of reading acquisition (Adams 1994; Ehri 1994; Honig et al. 2000). Level P of *Reading Skills for Life* develops essential phonemic awareness skills, including recognizing phonemes and rimes and developing the ability to segment, blend, isolate, match, and manipulate sounds. Levels A–E strengthen students' basic phonemic awareness skills while developing more complex skills in the context of letter-sound relationships.

Systematic and Explicit Instruction in Phonics is central to *Reading Skills for Life*. Instruction proceeds at a slow, sequential pace and is recursive from level to level. Research has provided compelling evidence that explicit, systematic instruction in phonics can help older students who have not achieved reading mastery (Adams 1994; Chall 1996; Honig et al. 2000). The program provides instruction in the 35 basic correspondences by the end of Level P, and reinforces these skills in Levels A and B. *R*-controlled vowels, vowel variants, vowel diphthongs, other spellings for long vowel sounds, and exceptions to the rules are introduced in Level A and beyond. Students are taught the blending principle beginning with Level P, and this skill is practiced and reinforced with all the decodable words students are taught.

Phonograms are patterns of letters common to many words. Words with the same phonogram are often called *word families;* for example, the words *main, rain,* and *pain* all have the phonogram *ain*. Research has shown that nearly 500 primary-grade words can be derived from a set of just 37 phonograms (Adams 1994). *Reading Skills for Life* teaches more than 50 high-utility phonograms in the phonics lessons to which they correspond.

High-Frequency Words are drawn from Fry's *1000 Instant Words* (Fry 1997). Fry points out that just 300 words make up 65 percent of all written material. In addition, these same 300 words account for more than half the text of every newspaper article, textbook, children's story, or novel. The 1,000 words are introduced sequentially at a pace of approximately 100 words per level at Levels P, A, and B, and approximately 200 words per level at Levels C–E. Many of the words in Fry's list are in fact decodable using the basic letter-sound correspondences such as CVC, CVC*e*, CVVC, and *r*-controlled vowel patterns. Therefore, students will be able to decode many of these "sight words" at first occurrence, without introduction prior to the lesson story.

Word Recognition Strategies are taught throughout the program. Students learn a limited number (usually 3–6) of new content words before they read each story in the Student Worktext, practicing a five-step strategy for learning new words: They **hear, see, read, say**, and **write** each new word before it is encountered in a story. Students see and read each new word multiple times in the lesson and in subsequent stories.

Structural Analysis includes recognition of inflected endings, prefixes, suffixes, and certain kinds of structures such as compound words. According to Chall and Popp (1996), when students know prefixes and suffixes, they are better prepared to decode unknown multisyllabic words. Knowing prefixes and suffixes will also help in learning the meaning of a word. *Reading Skills for Life* introduces the most common prefixes, suffixes, and inflected endings, along with the generalizations that accompany them. Students practice forming, reading, and writing many words having each targeted structure.

For a list of phonics and word study skills instructed in *Reading Skills for Life,* see the Scope and Sequence of Skills on page 6 of this Teacher's Guide. On pages 12–13, you'll find the complete scope and sequence of skills instructed at this level of the program.

Integrating Skills and Strategies

Reading Skills for Life offers a comprehensive approach to teaching reading that includes direct instruction in the most useful skills and strategies:

Reading Comprehension and Critical Thinking Skills
Each lesson in the Student Worktext offers multiple opportunities for students to think literally, inferentially, and critically about the text. See the Scope and Sequence of Skills on pages 6–7 for a complete list of reading comprehension and critical thinking skills instructed in the program.

Strategic Reading Skills *Reading Skills for Life* provides explicit, ongoing instruction in reading strategies. Teachers model reading strategies in the context of guiding students as they read each lesson's selection. Students are taught to make predictions about a story before reading it, to check and revise those predictions often while reading, and to use other useful reading strategies to help them get the most out of reading.

Study Skills Functional skills that help students locate and organize information, interpret graphic data, and prepare for tests are woven across the program. At Levels A–E, *Reading Skills for Life* targets the most useful and essential skills for students attaining a basic level of literacy, and for students who are preparing to enter the working world.

Spelling Skills Research (e.g., Adams 1994) has shown that learning how to spell words (encoding) is a companion skill to learning how to read words (decoding). When students write words and word patterns they have learned to read, their visual sense of each word is reinforced kinesthetically. *Reading Skills for Life* teaches spelling patterns in conjunction with phonics skills, and provides practice with regular and irregular words most often needed for writing and words that are frequently misspelled.

Writing and Language The writing strand in *Reading Skills for Life* is developmental, cautious, and practical. Skills and expectations are linked to the reading scope and sequence. They reflect competencies students typically are required to demonstrate on state performance assessments and they emphasize real-life writing forms students will need on the job.

Literary Appreciation Skills Effective readers do not simply apply skills to comprehend text—they also enjoy what they read and appreciate literature. *Reading Skills for Life* introduces students to a variety of genres and literary forms, and helps students appreciate what the various forms have to offer.

Research References and Bibliography

Adams, M. J. 1994. *Beginning to read: Thinking and learning about print.* Cambridge, MA: MIT Press.

Anderson, R. C., E. H. Hiebert, J. A. Scott, and I. A. G. Wilkinson. 1985. *Becoming a nation of readers: The report of the Commission on Reading.* Washington, DC: National Institute of Education.

Chall, J. S. 1996. *Learning to read: The great debate.* 3rd ed. Fort Worth, TX: Harcourt Brace.

Chall, J. S., and H. M. Popp. 1996. *Teaching and assessing phonics: Why, what, when, how.* Cambridge, MA: Educator's Publishing Service.

Crawley, S. J., and K. Merritt. 2000. *Remediating reading difficulties.* 3rd ed. New York: McGraw-Hill.

Ehri, L. 1994. Development of the ability to read words: Update. In R. Ruddell, M. Ruddell, and H. Singer, eds., *Theoretical models and processes of reading.* Newark, DE: International Reading Association.

Fry, E. 1997. *1000 instant words.* Chicago: Contemporary Books.

Fry, E., J. E. Kress, and D. L. Fountoukidis. 2000. *The reading teacher's book of lists.* 4th ed. Paramus, NJ: Prentice Hall.

Honig, B. 2001. *Teaching our children to read: The components of an effective, comprehensive reading program.* 2nd ed. Thousand Oaks, CA: Corwin Press.

Honig, B., L. Diamond, L. Gutlohn, and J. Mahler. 2000. *Teaching reading: Sourcebook for kindergarten through eighth grade.* Novato, CA: Arena Press.

Miller, W. H. 1993. *Complete reading disabilities handbook.* West Nyack, NY: The Center for Applied Research in Education.

Simmons, D. C., and E. J. Kameenui, eds. 1998. *What reading research tells us about children with diverse learning needs: Bases and basics.* Mahwah, NJ: Erlbaum.

For more information on the research that supports the *Reading Skills for Life* instructional approaches outlined here, please go to **www.agsnet.com** or call Customer Service at **1-800-328-2560** to request a summary of research.

Using Reading Skills for Life

Evaluation and Placement

How do you know which level of *Reading Skills for Life* will be most appropriate for your students? Where should you begin? The evaluation and assessment methods described below will help you answer this question.

Teacher Judgment You may already know a general reading level for your students. You may have obtained this information from informal testing or by observation. If you are confident you know the level at which your students are reading, use this guide to determine where to start.

If your students are reading at this grade level	Begin here with *Reading Skills for Life:*
Less than 1.5	Level P
1.5	Level A
2.0	Level B
2.5	Level C
3.0	Level D
4.0	Level E

Reading-Level Indicator

The *Reading-Level Indicator* is a quick screening measure of reading ability available from AGS. Norm-referenced scores are reported as grade equivalents. The screener can be individually or group administered in less than 15 minutes, and it samples both vocabulary and basic comprehension skills. Use the Placement Chart on the right to identify where to place your students in *Reading Skills for Life.*

GRADE/Group Reading Assessment and Diagnostic Evaluation The GRADE is a developmentally-based, group-administered diagnostic reading assessment also available from AGS. Developed for use with individuals ages 4–25, GRADE provides reliable diagnostic results for each student. If you need comprehensive diagnostic information about your students' reading abilities, use GRADE. The GRADE will also provide a grade-equivalent score. Use the chart below for placement in *Reading Skills for Life.*

Using Grade-Equivalent Scores for Placement

To place students in *Reading Skills for Life,* use the grade-equivalent score for the Instructional Reading Level from the *Reading-Level Indicator,* or the grade-equivalent score of the Total Test Score from the GRADE.

Placement Chart

If the grade-equivalent score is	Begin here with *Reading Skills for Life:*
1.0 or lower	Level P
1.1 to 1.9	Level A
2.0 to 2.4	Level B
2.5 to 3.0	Level C
3.1 to 4.0	Level D
4.1 to 6.0	Level E

Note: The grade-equivalent score from the Reading-Level Indicator is the median of the normative group based on two subtests, Vocabulary and Sentence Comprehension. The grade-equivalent score from the GRADE is the median of the normative group based on several subtests of items including Passage Comprehension. Therefore, there may be slight differences between the two grade equivalents. If you have given both assessments to a student, it is recommended that you use the grade-equivalent score from the GRADE.

Sequence of Instruction

Each lesson and chapter in *Reading Skills for Life* follows a predictable sequence. The easy-to-use, three-step teaching plan supports teachers in guiding students through the Student Worktext lessons. In addition to the **Before Reading, Reading,** and **After Reading** sequence, **Reinforce & Extend** at the end of each lesson in the Teacher's Guide includes spelling, study skills, language arts, writing, and literary appreciation activities, along with additional Reading and Writing Practice on CD-ROM.

The chart on the following page summarizes the sequence of instruction in *Reading Skills for Life.*

For more information about the *Reading-Level Indicator* or GRADE, please go to **www.agsnet.com** or call Customer Service at **1-800-328-2560**.

Reading Skills for Life Sequence of Instruction

STEP 1 Before Reading

Letters and Sounds

- Explicit instruction in phonics
- Introduction and practice with phonograms
- Reading and Writing Practice

Story Words

- Five-step strategy for learning new words: **hear, see, read, say, write**
- Addition of new words to the Word Bank at the back of the Student Worktext
- Reading and Writing Practice

More Word Work

- Explicit introduction to a word study (structural analysis) skill
- Review and practice of previously taught word study skills
- Reading and Writing Practice

STEP 2 Reading

Preview and Predict

- Strategy application—Leads students to access prior knowledge about story topic or content, or guides them to make a prediction

Strategy Modeling

- Reading—Students read a high-interest selection with decodable text including high-frequency words previously introduced, new story words, words that contain the lesson's phonic element, and other known and decodable words
- Teacher guides students through the selection and models specific reading strategies

Stop and Think

- Strategy application—Leads students to make a prediction about the rest of the selection

STEP 3 After Reading

Personal Response

- Personal response or critical thinking about the story

Think About the Story: Reading Comprehension

- Review of new story content words and high-frequency words
- Reading comprehension—literal, inferential, critical questions; using context to determine word meaning; written responses

Look Ahead

- Strategy application—Guide students to make a prediction about the next part of a continuing story

Chapter Assessment

Summary of Skills and Strategies

Chapter Review

Chapter Test

Note: Reproducible test pages are found at the back of this Teacher's Guide.

Reading Skills for Life Scope and Sequence-Level E

Chapter	Lesson	Phonics and Phonograms	Word Study	Reading Strategy	Reading Comprehension Skill	Critical Thinking Sk
CHAPTER 1	Lesson 1, "It's Never Too Late," Part 1	Long Vowel Review (All Spellings); One Syllable Words CVC, CVC*e*, CVVC	Endings *-ed, -ing* (no change, dropping *e*, changing *y* to *i*, doubling final consonant)	Access Prior Knowledge	Evaluate	
	Lesson 2, It's Never Too Late," Part 2	Irregular Spellings for Long Vowels: Open and Closed VCV	Plurals: *-s, -es* (change *f* to *v*); *-ies* (drop *y*)	Use Context Clues	Summarize	
	Lesson 3, "Birthday Party"	Unusual Spellings for Long Vowels in Multisyllabic Words; VC/CV	Irregular Plurals; Plurals of Words Ending in *o*	Make a Prediction	Fantasy vs. Realism	
	Lesson 4, "Oprah Winfrey"	Silent Consonants Review (*t, h, n, w, g, k, d, c, b, l*)	Possessives; Possessives with Irregular Plurals	Reread/Read Ahead	Recognize the Topic	
	Lesson 5, "Role Models"	Silent *p*; VC/CCV	Suffixes for People (*-er, -or, -ar, -ist*)	Summarize		Solve Problem
	Lesson 6, "Against All Odds"	Hard and Soft *c* (initial and final); VC/CCCV	Prefixes *un-, re-, pre-, dis-, de-, non-, -im, in-*	Use Context Clues		Synthesize
CHAPTER 2	Lesson 1, "Finding New Friends," Part 1	Hard and Soft *g* (initial and final); V/V	Endings *-er, -est; more, most*	Make a Prediction	Cause and Effect	
	Lesson 2, "Finding New Friends," Part 2	Sounds for *ough* and *augh;* Three-Syllable Words	Suffixes: *-ly, -ful, -less, -ness, -ment, -y*	Summarize	Recognize the Author's Purpose	
	Lesson 3, "Second Sight"	*ei* vs. *ie*	Compound Words	Set a Purpose		Make Judgme
	Lesson 4, "Student Volunteer"	Schwa sound: *el, al, le, er, or, ar, es, is, en, on, ion, ed, id, sion, tion*	Contractions	Clarify	Compare and Contrast	
	Lesson 5, "Blood Brothers," Part 1	Schwa sound Spelled *a, e, o, i*	Suffixes *-able, -ible*	Reread/Read Ahead		Distinguish Fa from Opinion
	Lesson 6, "Blood Brothers," Part 2	Vowel Diphthongs in Longer Words; Four-Syllable Words	Suffixes *-ous, -eous, -ious*	Access Prior Knowledge		Recognize Poi of View and B
CHAPTER 3	Lesson 1, "Lava Spill"	Vowel Variants in Longer Words	Prefixes *mid-, -mis*	Clarify	Recognize the Main Idea and Supporting Details	
	Lesson 2, "Foster Child"	*r*-Controlled Vowels in Longer Words: /ôr/; /ûr/; /âr/; /ir/; /ar/	Prefixes *sub-, trans-*	Set a Purpose	Draw Conclusions	
	Lesson 3, "Our Nation's Capital"	Homophones with *r*-Controlled Vowels	Decoding Multisyllabic Words with Affixes	Access Prior Knowledge	Categorize	
	Lesson 4, "Sally Ride"	Decoding Multisyllabic Words with Unusual Spellings for Consonant Sounds	Adverbs	Summarize	Note Sequence	

Spelling	Study Skill	Language	Writing	Literary Appreciation	
ords with Long *a;* Long *e*		Subject (Complete and Simple)	A Paragraph of Information		CHAPTER 1
ords with Long Vowel ounds		Predicate (Complete and Simple)		Figurative Language	
ords with Long *u*		Common and Proper Nouns		Story Elements (Character, Plot, Setting)	
ords with Silent onsonants (*t, h, n, w, g, k, c, b, l*)		Singular and Plural Nouns		Fiction vs. Nonfiction	
ords with Silent Consonants		Possessive Nouns	Compare and Contrast		
ural Nouns (*s, es, y/ies, s/oes,* Irregular Forms)		Action and Linking Verbs	A Paragraph of Opinion		
	Locating Information in an Encyclopedia	Subject-Verb Agreement	A Descriptive Paragraph		CHAPTER 2
	Organizing Information Using Charts and Timelines	Past, Present, and Future Verb Tense		Theme	
ords with *ei* and *ie*		Perfect Tenses of Verbs	A How-to Paragraph		
ords with the Schwa Sound		Pronouns	A Business Letter		
	Using Diagrams and Maps as Graphic Aids	Possessive Pronouns		Narrative Voice	
owel Diphthongs in Longer ords		Adjectives and Adverbs	A Personal Narrative with Dialogue		
	Test-Taking Strategies	Prepositions and Prepositional Phrases	A Summary		CHAPTER 3
ob-Related Words equently Misspelled		Compound Sentences	A Persuasive Paragraph		
omophones with *r*-ontrolled Vowels		Complex Sentences	A Research Report		
ords with *-able, -ible*		Fixing Fragments and Run-On Sentences	A Job Application		

Chapter 1 Planning Guide

Skills and Learning Objectives

	Student Pages	Phonics and Phonograms	Word Study	Reading Strategy
Lesson 1 It's Never Too Late, Part 1	10–17	One-syllable words CVC, CVCe, CVVC	Endings *-ed, -ing,* (no change, dropping *e,* changing y to *i,* doubling final consonant)	Access Prior Knowledge
Lesson 2 It's Never Too Late, Part 2	18–25	Irregular spellings for long vowels *e, a, o, u;* VCV and V/CCV patterns	Plurals: *-s, -es* (change *f* to *v*); *-ies* (drop *y*)	Use Context Clues
Lesson 3 Birthday Party	26–33	Unusual spellings for long vowels in multisyllabic words; VC/CV pattern	Irregular plurals (man/men); plurals of words ending in *o*	Make a Prediction
Lesson 4 Oprah Winfrey	34–41	Silent consonants review (*t, h, n, w, g, k, d, c, b, l*)	Possessives with *'s* and *s'*; possessives with irregular plurals	Reread/Read Ahead
Lesson 5 Role Models	42–49	Silent *p* (*receipt, raspberry*); VC/CCV (rum/ple, hun/dred)	Suffixes for people (*-er, -or, -ar, -ist*)	Summarize
Lesson 6 Against All Odds	50–57	Hard and soft *c,* (initial and final); VC/CCCV pattern	Prefixes *un-, re-, pre-, dis-, de-, non-, im-, in-*	Use Context Clues

Independent Reading

Independent Reading Lesson:
Teacher's Guide pages 46–47
List of Recommended Books to Read:
- *Crash*
- *Windcatcher*
- *Belle Prater's Boy*
- *Tracker*
- *Beyond the Mango Tree*
- *Taking Sides*
- *Helen Keller's Teacher*
- *Searching for Candlestick Park*
- *Seedfolks*
- *Shadow of a Bull*
- *Hatchet*
- *Slake's Limbo*

Assessment and Review

Chapter 1 Summary of Skills and Strategies:
Student Worktext page 58

Chapter 1 Review:
Student Worktext pages 59–66
Teacher's Guide pages 48–51

Chapter 1 Test:
Teacher's Guide pages 129–131

Reading Comprehension/ Critical Thinking	Spelling	Study Skill	Language	Writing	Literary Appreciation	Learning Styles	Focus on LEP/ESL or LD	Application	Reading and Writing Practice Activities
Evaluate	20		20	20		17, 18	18		1–7
Summarize	25		25		25	23	23	24	8–12
Fantasy vs. Realism	30		30		30	28	28	29	13–17
Recognize the Topic	35		35		35	33		34	18–22
Solve Problems	40		40	40			38	39	23–29
Synthesize	45		45	45			43	44	30–36

Common Reading Errors

If the Student . . .		Then . . .
◆ gives up on unknown words	→	◆ encourage the student to skip the unknown word, finish reading the sentence, and use context clues to figure out the word's meaning.
◆ pronounces silent letters	→	◆ reteach Lessons 4 and 5.
◆ fails to adjust schema when new information is presented	→	◆ reteach the Make a Prediction reading strategy; encourage frequent checking of predictions and revising of predictions to match story content.
◆ confuses the sequence of events in written text	→	◆ suggest that the student read more slowly and note signal words such as *first* and *next*.
◆ is unable to determine important details to summarize	→	◆ reteach the lesson on Summarize in Lesson 5; remind students that a summary is short and leaves out supporting details.

Lesson at a Glance

Chapter 1, Lesson 1 "It's Never Too Late," Part 1

Preview: This lesson presents the first part of a two-part nonfiction selection about Jimmy Santiago Baca, a Mexican-American poet who taught himself to read and to write poetry while in jail.

Objectives

- to read a nonfiction selection
- to read words with a long vowel sound
- to add *ed* and *ing* to words
- to spell words with a long *a* and long *e* sound
- to learn how to evaluate information
- to recognize complete and simple subjects
- to write a paragraph of information

Student Worktext Pages 10–17

Story Words

orphanage, survival, convict, revenge, awkward, savior

Reading and Writing Practice Activities 1–7

Before Reading "It's Never Too Late," Part 1

Letters and Sounds

Long Vowels

Remind students that the letters *a, e, i, o,* and *u* are vowels. Explain that when a vowel sound is the same as its letter name it has a long vowel sound. Sometimes letter pairs such as *ea* in *cheat* and *oa* in *boat* stand for a long vowel sound. Write the words *date, cheat, time, boat,* and *flute* on the board. Read the words and have students repeat them. Underline the long vowel sound in each word. Tell students that the underlined letters have a long vowel sound. Then have students complete Student Worktext Page 10.

Review with students the CVC, CVCe, and CVVC patterns in one-syllable words. Remind them that a single vowel in a word usually takes the short sound (hat). If there are two vowels in a word and the second is final *e*, the first vowel usually stands for a long vowel sound and the *e* is silent (cape). Finally, in the case of vowel teams, the first vowel usually takes the long sound, and the second is silent (bait).

Reading and Writing Practice Activity 1: Long Vowel Review: CVC, CVC*e*, CVVC.

Story Words

Read aloud the words: *orphanage, survival, convict, revenge, awkward, savior.* Tell students that these words are important in the next story. Then write the words on the board and point to each one as you say it aloud a second time. Next, have students follow the ❑ *Read* ❑ *Say* ❑ *Write* sequence by completing **Story Words** on Student Worktext page 11. To introduce the words in context write these sentences on the board:

- Jimmy lived in an <u>orphanage</u> when he was a child.
- The <u>survival</u> of the passengers of the car crash was amazing.
- The <u>convicts</u> served long prison sentences.
- The man wanted <u>revenge</u> against those who had wronged him.
- After he had injured his leg, his movements were <u>awkward</u>.
- Words and poetry are the <u>saviors</u> that kept Jimmy from returning to prison.

Reading and Writing Practice Activity 2: Reading Story Words.

More Word Work

Have students work in pairs to complete **More Word Work** on Student Worktext page 11.

Reading and Writing Practice Activity 3: Reading and Writing Words with Endings *ed, ing.*

LESSON 1 ▸ Before Reading "It's Never Too Late," Part 1

Letters and Sounds

TIPS: ▸ Words like **cane** and **fine** have a consonant-vowel-consonant silent **e**, or CVC**e** pattern.
▸ Words like **team** and **meet** have a consonant-vowel-vowel-consonant, or CVVC pattern.

Directions: Write the word on the line. Circle the letter or letters that create the long vowel sound in the words below.

1. crate crate
2. meat meat
3. crime crime
4. coat coat
5. mute mute

Directions: Here are some more words that have long vowel sounds. Read each word, rewrite it, then circle the letter or letters that make the long vowel sound.

6. trait trait
7. greet greet
8. life life
9. home home
10. mule mule

Directions: Write each word in the box where it belongs.

tube kite boast lame feet
mole cute lime treat great
dime dome dame dune dean

long *a* sound	long *e* sound	long *i* sound	long *o* sound	long *u* sound
11. dame	14. treat	17. dime	20. mole	23. tube
12. lame	15. feet	18. kite	21. dome	24. cute
13. great	16. dean	19. lime	22. boast	25. dune

Directions: Write the letters on the lines. How many words can you make?

a e i o u

26. ca or op e
27. h a t e
28. h e a t
29. ma or od e
30. b ai,ea, or oa t
31. m a i d

Student page 10

Story Words

Directions: Read each word to yourself. Then say the word out loud. Write the word on the line. Check the box after each step.

32. orphanage (or|phan|age) Read ☑ Say ☑ Write ☑ orphanage
33. survival (sur|viv|al) Read ☑ Say ☑ Write ☑ survival
34. convict (con|vict) Read ☑ Say ☑ Write ☑ convict
35. revenge (re|venge) Read ☑ Say ☑ Write ☑ revenge
36. awkward (awk|ward) Read ☑ Say ☑ Write ☑ awkward
37. savior (sav|ior) Read ☑ Say ☑ Write ☑ savior

More Word Work

Directions: You can add **ed** to many verbs. Do this to make a verb tell about the past. Circle the correct **ed** word and rewrite it on the line.

38. dip diped dipped dipped
39. hire hired hird hired
40. toss tossed tosed tossed
41. carry carryed carried carried

TIP: For words that end in a silent **e,** just add **d.** For words that end in a consonant, you can often double the final letter and then add **ed.** For words that end in **y**, change the **y** to an **i,** then add **ed.**

Directions: You can add **ing** to many verbs. Do this to make a verb tell about the present. Circle the correct **ing** word and rewrite it on the line.

42. run runing running running
43. hurry hurrying hurriing hurrying
44. help helpping helping helping
45. file filling filing filing

TIP: For words that end in a silent **e,** drop the **e,** then add **ing.** For words that end in a consonant, you can often double the final letter and then add **ing.** For words that end in a **y,** just add **ing.**

Student page 11

Reading "It's Never Too Late," Part 1

Preview and Predict

- Tell students they are about to read a story about the Mexican-American poet Jimmy Santiago Baca. Have a volunteer read aloud the title on Student Worktext page 12. Point out the pictures of Baca throughout the selection.
- Explain that Baca had a very difficult childhood and that at the age of 17 he went to jail. Ask students if they know of people who have faced great challenges in life.
- Read aloud the introductory questions under **Use What You Know**. Have students work in small groups to make a list of ways that people make changes in their lives.
- Have students share their responses. Then ask them to predict how Baca went from being a prison convict to becoming a poet.

Learning Styles

Auditory/Verbal Locate poems by Jimmy Santiago Baca for students to read, or skip ahead to Lesson 2 and show students the excerpts of Baca's poems in the selection. Have volunteers read selected poems to the class to give students an idea of what his poetry sounds like.

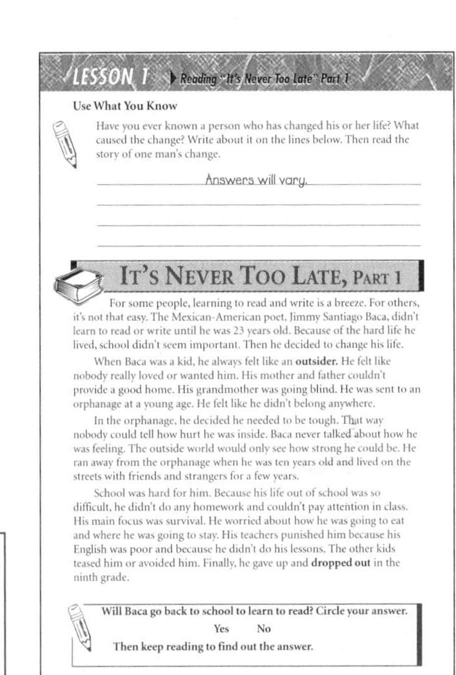
LESSON 1 ▸ Reading "It's Never Too Late" Part 1

Use What You Know

Have you ever known a person who has changed his or her life? What caused the change? Write about it on the lines below. Then read the story of one man's change.

Answers will vary.

IT'S NEVER TOO LATE, PART 1

For some people, learning to read and write is a breeze. For others, it's not that easy. The Mexican-American poet, Jimmy Santiago Baca, didn't learn to read or write until he was 23 years old. Because of the hard life he lived, school didn't seem important. Then he decided to change his life.

When Baca was a kid, he always felt like an **outsider.** He felt like nobody really loved or wanted him. His mother and father couldn't provide a good home. His grandmother was going blind. He was sent to an orphanage at a young age. He felt like he didn't belong anywhere.

In the orphanage, he decided he needed to be tough. That way nobody could tell how hurt he was inside. Baca never talked about how he was feeling. The outside world would only see how strong he could be. He ran away from the orphanage when he was ten years old and lived on the streets with friends and strangers for a few years.

School was hard for him. Because his life out of school was so difficult, he didn't do any homework and couldn't pay attention in class. His main focus was survival. He worried about how he was going to eat and where he was going to stay. His teachers punished him because his English was poor and because he didn't do his lessons. The other kids teased him or avoided him. Finally, he gave up and **dropped out** in the ninth grade.

Will Baca go back to school to learn to read? Circle your answer.

Yes No

Then keep reading to find out the answer.

Student page 12

Baca needed money. The only kinds of work he could get were low-paying jobs that no one else wanted to do. He turned to small crimes to make money. It seemed as if he didn't have a choice. He was sad and alone, but he didn't have the skills to express his feelings. He knew he deserved a better life, but what could he expect? His life on the streets was the only life he knew.

His first trip to jail was when he was 17. Life in jail made him worse. He and the other convicts were not treated well. Even though it was a terrible place to be, he did get one good thing. He heard the prisoners read poetry and tell stories to each other. He heard the power of **finely-tuned language.** It was like a song or a sunset. It stirred something deep inside him that had been locked away for a long time. When he listened to another prisoner read, he felt alive.

After he was released, he quickly landed back in jail. He saw that this was how most convicts lived their lives, **like the jail had a revolving door.** He imagined that this was how his life was going to continue. His second trip behind bars began no better than the first. Little did he know that his life was about to change.

One day, Baca got so angry at one of the guards, he decided to get revenge. He reached through the bars and stole a book from the guard's desk. When he later returned to his cell, he opened the book and tried to read. He sounded out the letters. He practiced until he could understand some of the lines. What he had stolen was a book of poetry! As he read the lines over and over again, something electric happened. It was as if

Student page 13

◆ *Strategy Modeling*

Access Prior Knowledge Read aloud the first paragraph of the selection on Student Worktext page 12 and model using prior knowledge. You might say:

Baca didn't learn to read until he was 23. My experience tells me that people who learn things late in life are often determined to improve themselves.

Then read aloud the first two sentences in the second paragraph on page 13 beginning "His first trip to jail . . .". You might say:

I've read about people who have gone to jail. I know it sometimes makes people hard and bitter.

Have students pause after finding out that Baca went to jail. Ask them how their own experience of hardship helps them understand Baca's life. Then have students continue reading the selection on their own.

Focus on ESL/LEP

Explain and discuss the following terms used in the story:

- is a breeze (is easy)
- dropped out (stopped doing something)
- behind bars (in jail)
- turn his life around (make a positive change)

Learning Styles

Interpersonal/Group Learning Baca practiced his reading skills by reading aloud to others. Divide students into small groups. Instruct students to take turns reading portions of the selection to each other.

his heart and his mind grew wings and began to fly! The beauty of language and of the world broke open for him again. This time he would never trade it for anything. Just a few days later, he wrote his first poem.

Baca knew it would be hard to learn how to read and write well. His reading was slow and awkward. He made up his own way to spell words. But he began to fill up notebooks with his new language. He read everything he could. He begged his jailers to help him go back to school, but they refused. He then refused to work, and they threw him in a locked cell for many years. He continued to teach himself and learned what he could from the supply of books he could find to read. He became serious about his studies.

For Baca, the beauty of language helped him see the beauty of the world. What used to be a dark, ugly, and hard place now held great wonder. Through his writing and reading, Baca began to notice small and good things: the shapes of clouds in a stormy sky, the patterns of sand, or the colors of a sunset.

While he was still in prison, he practiced his new skills. He wrote letters for the other prisoners and read poems and stories to them. Many of them were touched by words the same way he was. They could see he was serious about changing his life, and they respected him for it. The people who worked at the prison saw how Baca was changing. A few of them even helped him get books to read. After serving his long prison term, he was released.

Student page 14

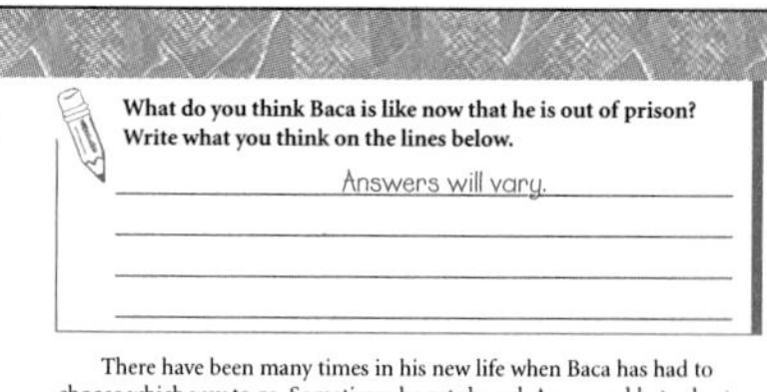

What do you think Baca is like now that he is out of prison? Write what you think on the lines below.

Answers will vary.

There have been many times in his new life when Baca has had to choose which way to go. Sometimes he gets bored. Anger and hatred get the better of him. But Baca has listened to the beat, tone, and music of words. They are his saviors. Because of them, Baca has not been in jail for many years. He has earned a college degree. His poetry is known all around the country for its powerful images and strong emotions. He has won many awards and has been an inspiration to all kinds of people.

Baca's life story is a perfect example of the saying "It's never too late." As a teenager and a young man, even he thought he was doomed to a life of prison and crime. It took a lot of hard work and faith in himself to turn his life around, but he did it. Today he lives a happy life with his wife and children. He continues to write poetry and other books. Learning to read and write made him a free man. ▶

Student page 15

After Reading "It's Never Too Late," Part 1

Personal Response: What Do You Think?

Explain that in the course of a lifetime every person changes in many different ways. Ask students how they have changed. Then have students form small groups and answer the questions presented in **What Do You Think?** on Student Worktext page 16.

Think About the Story: Reading Comprehension

Have students complete the remaining items on Student Worktext pages 16–17 independently or in pairs. Check their responses to help you assess their comprehension of the story. If students' responses indicate that they did not understand the story events, have them reread the story in small groups.

Critical Thinking Skill: Evaluate

Tell students that one of the ways to get the most out of what they read is to evaluate the information or story. Explain the following points:

- *Evaluate* means to give an opinion about a story.
- Evaluations tell what a reader thinks about a story.
- Evaluations answer questions such as *Was the story interesting? accurate? meaningful?*

Tell students to think about "It's Never Too Late," Part 1. Ask them what they would say about the story in an evaluation. Use the following questions to help guide students:

- Do you think the topic is covered well enough?
- Can you relate the information to movies you have seen or other stories you have read?
- Were you surprised about any of the information in the article?

Look Ahead

Tell students that they will learn more about Baca in Part 2 of the selection. Ask students to form small groups and use the question in **Look Ahead** to help them predict what will happen next.

LESSON 1 **After Reading "It's Never Too Late" Part 1**

What Do You Think?

1. Jimmy Santiago Baca sometimes has to fight off his old ways of thinking and acting. How do you think he does this?
   Answers will vary.
2. Is Baca's story an inspiration to you? Why or why not?
   Answers will vary.

Think About the Story

Use Story Words

Directions: Look at your list of story words on page 11. Write a story word on each line

3. Baca felt that words and language were his saviors.
4. In the beginning, his reading and writing were awkward.
5. In order to get revenge on the guard, Baca stole a book.
6. An orphanage is a home for children who don't live with their parents.
7. Some of the other convicts read poetry and told stories to each other.
8. When he lived on the streets, his main concern was survival.

How Did They Feel?

Directions: Circle the word that best describes how the character in the story felt.

9. How did Baca feel when he was put in the orphanage?
   (worried) alive lucky
10. How did Baca feel when he heard poetry read out loud?
    worried (alive) lucky

Student page 16

Write Sentences About the Story

Directions: Use words from the story to answer these questions.

11. Why did Baca feel so hopeless?
    Baca's parents couldn't provide a good home. He was sent to an orphanage at a young age.
12. How did reading and writing make Baca feel alive again?
    Discovering the beauty of language helped Baca see the beauty of the world: the shapes of clouds, the patterns of sand, and the colors of a sunset.

Words and Meanings

Directions: Think about how the **bold** words are used in the story. Then circle the words that show the meaning of each word or phrase.

13. **Finely-tuned language** is ____.
    a. (words and sounds that are carefully chosen)
    b. lyrics to a song
    c. a kind of story
14. When Baca **dropped out** in the ninth grade he ____.
    a. fell down
    b. (quit school)
    c. got into a fight
15. The words **like the jail had a revolving door** mean ____.
    a. (convicts are in and out of jail often)
    b. convicts go through revolving doors often
    c. convicts escape from prison
16. When Baca felt like an **outsider,** he felt like ____.
    a. he was out of doors
    b. (he didn't belong)
    c. he liked nature

Look Ahead

17. Do you think Baca's poetry would be soft and polite, or would it be strong and forceful? Write what you think on the lines below. Then read on to find out.
    Answers will vary.

Student page 17

Reinforce & Extend

SPELLING: Words with Long *a* and *e* Vowel Sounds

1. payment **2.** eagerly **3.** laid **4.** favor **5.** need **6.** late **7.** because **8.** receive **9.** tray **10.** feast

The letters *a, ai,* and *ay* can stand for the long *a* sound as in the word *ray.* The letters *e, ea, ee,* and *ei* can stand for the long *e* sound as in the word *seed.* Have students number a sheet of paper 1–10. Dictate the words above one at a time. Ask students to write each word down. Then have students circle the letter or letters that make the long *a* or long *e* sounds.

Reading and Writing Practice Activity 4 provides additional practice spelling words with long *a* and *e* vowel sounds.

LANGUAGE: Complete and Simple Subjects

Write this sentence on the board:

The tall thin boy ate hungrily.

Underline the complete subject in the sentence. (complete subject: *The tall thin boy*)

Once again, write the sentence on the board. Underline the simple subject. (simple subject: *boy*)

Explain:

- All sentences have a subject.
- The subject of the sentence mentions whom or what the sentence is about.
- All the words that identify a person, place, or thing make up the complete subject.
- The one word that can identify a person, place, or thing is the simple subject.

Write this sentence on the board:

Young Jimmy lived in an orphanage.

Call on a volunteer to underline the complete subject of the sentence .(Young Jimmy) Once again, write the sentence on the board. Have a volunteer underline the simple subject in the rewritten sentence. (Jimmy) Then ask students to copy three sentences from the story. Have them underline the complete subject and circle the simple subject in each sentence. If the sentence has only a simple subject, have students rewrite the sentence with added words to make a complete subject.

Reading and Writing Practice Activity 5 provides additional practice with complete and simple subjects.

WRITING: A Paragraph of Information

Read aloud the paragraph beginning "Baca knew it would be hard to learn how to read and write well . . ." on Student Worktext page 14. Tell students this paragraph gives information about how Baca taught himself to read. Explain:

- A paragraph of information consists of one or more sentences about a particular subject.
- Many paragraphs of information are organized around a main idea and its supporting details.
- A paragraph of information usually begins with a topic sentence that tells the reader the subject of the paragraph and presents a specific idea or viewpoint.
- Other sentences add details to support or clarify the idea or viewpoint.
- The last sentence sums up the main idea of the paragraph.

Reading and Writing Practice Duplicate and distribute Activities 6 and 7, the Writing Model of a paragraph of information. Help students identify the topic sentence and supporting details in the paragraph. Then have students write their own paragraph of information in response to one of these prompts.

- Why didn't Baca learn to read until he was 23 years old?
- Explain how you eventually learned to do something very difficult.

Lesson at a Glance

Chapter 1, Lesson 2 "It's Never Too Late, Part 2

Preview: This lesson presents the second part of a story about Jimmy Santiago Baca, a poet who uses words to express his thoughts and feelings.

Objectives
- to read nonfiction
- to read and spell words with irregular spellings for long vowels
- to write the plural form of words
- to summarize information
- to identify simple and complete predicates
- to recognize figurative language

Student Worktext Pages 18–25

Story Words
poverty, experience, impression, duality, recipient

Reading and Writing Practice Activities 8–12

Before Reading "It's Never Too Late," Part 2

Letters and Sounds

Words with irregular spellings for long vowels

Remind students that different combinations of letters can produce the same sound. Write *few* on the board, read it aloud, and circle the *ew*. Tell students that this word ends with the sound of long *u*, which is produced by *ew*. Explain that many words have long vowel sounds produced by different combinations of letters. Then write *key, piano, weight,* and *my* on the board. Read the words aloud. Have students circle the letters that form each long vowel sound.

Write the words *pilot* and *planet* on the board. Remind students that an open syllable ends with a vowel and has a long sound. Point out the VCV pattern of pi/lot. Then point out the short vowel sound in the first syllable of plan/et and note that the division is made after the consonant (VCV). Then have students complete Student Worktext page 18.

Reading and Writing Practice Activity 8: Irregular Spellings for Long Vowels.

Story Words

Read aloud these words: *poverty, experience, impression, duality, recipient.* Tell students that these words are important in the next story they will read. Then write the words on the board and point to each one as you say it aloud a second time. Have students follow the ❑ *Read* ❑ *Say* ❑ *Write* sequence by completing **Story Words** on Student Worktext page 19. Remind students to write the story words in the Word Bank at the back of their Student Worktext. To introduce these words in context, write these sentences on the board:

- Juan's childhood was filled with poverty and hardship.
- Having my mother for a substitute teacher is an experience I want to forget.
- Tom shook the principal's hand to make a good impression.
- Duality happens when something has more than one side to it.
- Leah just found out she is this year's recipient of the Outstanding Student award.

Read the sentences aloud. To assess students' ability to read each new word, listen as students read the sentences on the board. Have students make a word card for *poverty.* Have students write another sentence using *poverty* on the back of their card. Follow the same procedure for the remaining words.

Reading and Writing Practice Activity 9: Reading Story Words.

More Word Work

Have students complete **More Word Work** on Student Worktext page 19.

Reading and Writing Practice Activity 10: Reading and Writing Plural Words.

LESSON 2 ▸ Before Reading "It's Never Too Late," Part 2

Letters and Sounds

Directions: These words have long vowel sounds made with unusual, or **irregular,** combinations of letters. Write the word on the line. Then circle the letters that make the long vowel sound.

1. neigh neigh
2. prey prey
3. donkey donkey
4. dough dough
5. though though
6. greyhound greyhound

Directions: These words have long vowel sounds made with **irregular** letter combinations. Read each word. Rewrite it on the line. Then circle the letters that make the long vowel sound.

7. sleigh sleigh
8. grey grey
9. monkey monkey
10. although although
11. flakey flakey

Directions: The following words have the vowel-consonant-vowel (VCV) or the vowel-consonant-consonant-vowel (V/CCV) pattern. Write the word on the line. Put a slash between the two syllables of the word.

12. pilot pi|lot
13. planet pla|net
14. matrix ma|trix
15. machine ma|chine
16. April A|pril
17. hatred ha|tred
18. program pro|gram
19. replace re|place
20. trophy tro|phy

TIP: Many words have more than one **syllable.** A syllable is a section of a word. The word **boy** has one syllable. **Biplane** has two. To show the syllables, you can write the word **bi | plane.**

Student page 18

Story Words

Directions: Read each word to yourself. Then say the word out loud. Write the word on the line. Check the box after each step.

21. poverty (pov|er|ty) Read ☑ Say ☑ Write ☑ poverty
22. experience (ex|per|i|ence) Read ☑ Say ☑ Write ☑ experience
23. impression (im|pres|sion) Read ☑ Say ☑ Write ☑ impression
24. duality (du|al|i|ty) Read ☑ Say ☑ Write ☑ duality
25. recipient (re|cip|i|ent) Read ☑ Say ☑ Write ☑ recipient

More Word Work

Directions: You can add **s** or **es** to many words to show that they mean more than one of something. Words that mean more than one are also called **plurals.** Read the word. Make it plural and write the new word on the line.

26. puppy puppies
27. game games
28. shelf shelves
29. branch branches
30. bush bushes
31. half halves
32. country countries

TIP: To change a word that ends in **f** from single (one thing) to plural (more than one thing), change the **f** to **v** and add **es.** To change a word that ends in **y,** change the **y** to **i** and add **es.**

Directions: Circle the correct plural ending for each word and write the plural word on the line.

33. self selfs (selves) selves
34. patty (patties) pattys patties
35. fly flyes (flies) flies
36. elf (elves) elfs elves

Student page 19

Reading "It's Never Too Late," Part 2

Preview and Predict

- Tell students that they are going to continue reading about Jimmy Santiago Baca and his poetry. Have a volunteer read aloud the title of the story on Student Worktext page 20.
- Read aloud the introductory sentences and question from **Use What You Know** at the top of page 20. Have small groups of students brainstorm ways they can express their thoughts and feelings. Then have the students record their answers on page 20.
- Ask students to preview the story by reading the first paragraph and looking at the photo on page 22. Then have them draw upon their observations to explain how a poet makes pictures with words.
- Explain that a poet uses words that appeal to the senses. As a large group activity, brainstorm phrases that describe what a person might think, smell, taste, hear, and feel about love. Record all responses on the board. Then have pairs of students work together to incorporate the phrases in a poem titled "Love."
- Tell students that a person's view of an event depends on their own experience. Have students reflect on the childhood story "The Three Little Pigs." Ask students to identify the point of view from which the events are described. (the pigs) Then ask them to identify the villain of the story from this perspective. (Big Bad Wolf) Encourage students to consider how the story might change if told from the wolf's point of view. Then have small groups of students retell the story from this point of view.

LESSON 2 *Reading "It's Never Too Late," Part 2*

Use What You Know

Jimmy Santiago Baca writes poetry to express his thoughts and feelings. Do you have a way to express what you're thinking and feeling? Write about it on the lines below. Then read on to learn more about Baca's poetry.

Answers will vary.

IT'S NEVER TOO LATE, PART 2

A poet and a painter have a lot in common. Both want to make people feel deeply. Both make pictures. The only difference is that a painter makes pictures with paints. A poet makes pictures with words. How do poets like Baca do this? How do they use words to make us feel and to see things with **fresh eyes?** By looking at Baca's poetry, we can learn a lot about what **inspires** him.

Baca was a troubled young man when he first found poetry. His life had been filled with poverty and hardship. At the age of 18, he found himself in a world where he did not belong, where he did not **fit in.** He was in prison and his future looked bleak. Baca knew that life wasn't supposed to be like this.

He now believes that poetry saved his life. He said it was his "discovery of the possibilities of language that transformed what appeared to be a doomed life."

His poem "Like an Animal" describes how Baca felt while he was locked up in prison. It expresses the fears he had about his future. It is a good example of how poets use language to change feelings into words.

In his poem, Baca doesn't just tell us he is scared. He shows us scary things. He describes bloody fingernails and chalk white scars. He speaks of a part of himself that has died, and of prison walls. As we see these things, perhaps we also feel scared. In addition to pictures, Baca uses sound in his poem. He writes of running those bloody fingernails across his eyes, which are as hard as a blackboard. Think about the sound that would make. The sound of fingernails scraping against a blackboard is a horrible sound. It makes us want to shudder, just as we shudder when we are afraid.

Student page 20

The poet's use of all the senses is important for making pictures with words. A poet writes of the soft clink of ice cubes against a glass. A poet describes the ring of water left on a porch floor when a glass is picked up. A poet tells of the sweet sugar and the tart lemon on the tongue. A poet recalls the smell of roses in the warm, bright air. These words place us on a porch in the summer sunshine drinking lemonade. We see, hear, taste, smell, and feel the experience.

Sense impressions are just one kind of detail found in poetry. Poets like Baca know that the better their description is, the more powerful the image will be. In Baca's poem, "Martin," he describes the first home he and his wife shared:

> House furnished with second-hand furniture,
> frayed wicker rocking chair,
> leaning bookshelves, woolen wall hangings,
> wood and wool stitched blinds,
> oak wood couch, and phone ringing constantly
> you answered to console, comfort, and talk with friends.

In this poem, Baca gives us details that tell us what his life is like. He doesn't live in a shiny, modern house. His house is filled with second-hand furniture. The bookshelves lean. The phone is always ringing because he and his family have many friends. They have friends that they console, comfort, and joke with. These details help to create a clear picture in the reader's mind.

Baca's poem "El Sapo" is about a man who loves life. El Sapo is a big man who works hard and laughs deeply. He uses a coffin for a living room table. He wears a blue baseball cap. His jacket smells like hay. He has worked outdoors all his life. His skin is as tough as a turtle's shell. The details Baca uses to describe El Sapo paint a portrait of this character.

Baca compares El Sapo to a turtle a few times in his poem. In poetry, to compare one thing to another is called a simile or metaphor. The use of metaphor is one of the ways that poets help us to see things in a new way. This is what Baca is doing when he tells us that El Sapo's feet are swollen and have puffy veins. He calls them **turtle feet.** To compare them to a turtle gives us a clearer picture. We see feet so swollen they are rounded like a turtle's feet. We see feet so beaten they are cracked and rough like the skin of a turtle. We see feet so tired they move slowly, just as a turtle moves. We get the feeling that El Sapo is a man who is tired all the way down to his bones. A straight description gives us a picture, but a metaphor makes us want to look again.

Student page 21

◆ *Strategy Modeling*

Use Context Clues Tell students that when they come to a word that looks new, or a word that has more than one meaning, they can try using context clues to figure out the word's meaning. Explain that context clues are the words and phrases around the word in question. Then read aloud the first five paragraphs of the selection and model using context clues to figure out the meaning of a multiple-meaning word. You might say:

The word chalk *in the fifth paragraph can have more than one meaning. It can be a noun that describes a tool used for writing on a board. It can also be an adjective to describe the color of something. Which meaning is used here? I'll see if there are other words nearby that can help me figure out the meaning. I see the words* white *and* scars *next to it, so here,* chalk *is being used to describe the color of the scars.*

Have students use context clues to help them figure out other words that look new, or words that have more than one meaning, as they continue to read.

Focus on ESL/LEP

Explain and discuss the following terms used in the story:

- second-hand furniture (previously used by someone else)
- fresh eyes (observing something for the first time)

Learning Styles

Logical/Mathematical Have pairs of students make a graphic organizer that illustrates the steps Baca follows when writing a poem.

Learning Styles

Body/Kinesthetic Reinforce story content by having small groups of students role play a question and answer session between Baca and the members of a creative writing class.

What kind of person do you think El Sapo is? Circle your answer.

1. **A tiny, fearful man.**
2. **A large, happy farmer.**
3. **A stubborn, mean person.**

Baca's poem "Into Death Bravely" centers on one metaphor. The character in the poem is the winter season. He never uses the word "winter", but Baca portrays Winter as a soldier carrying a white shield. Winter is powerful and causes great destruction. He laughs a deep, fearless laugh as he breaks the branches of trees. He crushes the world with white. Like many soldiers, Winter dies. However, also like a soldier, he faces death bravely. He does not run away like a dog with his tail between his legs. However, as Spring finally takes over the land, Winter limps off to die.

There is another strange thing about "Into Death Bravely." In the poem, Winter is presented as having at least two features. He is strong and destructive, but he also has a short life. The two things is what poets call "duality." It means that all things and beings have more than one side to them. Life is both happy and sad. People are both weak and strong. Things that are new become old. You will find duality in many poems. Perhaps this is what Baca means when trying to explain the creative process. He says, "Writing is a form of mourning in which you sing happy songs."

Student page 22

Baca is happy to have found poetry. He values words and the worlds they create. In "I Am Offering This Poem," he expresses how meaningful he believes poetry can be. Baca offers the poem to someone he loves. He says it will provide warmth like a coat. The poem will give food like a pot full of yellow corn. If the person is lost, the poem can point out the right direction. No wonder he tells the recipient to treasure the poem. Its powers seem magical. Even though he says the poem is all that he has to offer, he believes it is a wonderful gift. Here are the last lines of the poem:

It's all I have to give,
and all anyone needs to live,
and to go on living inside,
when the world outside
no longer cares if you live or die;
remember,
I love you.

Poets like Baca appeal to all our senses: sight, sound, touch, taste, and smell. They use metaphor to explain the new, and to make us understand the old with fresh eyes. They show us the many sides of life. Though poets use words instead of paints, they create pictures. There is another thing that poets and painters have in common. When they move us their works become part of us. A painting or a poem is not just yours or mine. It belongs to the world, to be enjoyed again and again.

◆

Student page 23

After Reading "It's Never Too Late," Part 2

Personal Response: What Do You Think?

Read aloud the questions under **What Do You Think?** on Student Worktext page 24. Ask students to describe how they felt when reading Jimmy Santiago Baca's poems. Then have groups discuss the **What Do You Think?** questions and record their responses.

Think About the Story: Reading Comprehension

Have students complete the remaining items on Student Worktext pages 24–25 independently or in pairs. Check their responses to help you assess their comprehension of the story. If students' responses indicate that they did not understand story events, reread the story aloud, pausing to discuss key events.

Reading Comprehension Skill: Summarize

Remind students that to summarize a story or article is to retell the important events or ideas. Explain:

- A summary is short—much shorter than the story.
- A summary includes main ideas or events, not details.
- A summary does not include the reader's opinions.

Guide students in listing events on the first page of "It's Never Too Late," Part 2. The list might look like this:

1. A poet creates pictures with words.
2. Baca did not fit in as a child. He thinks poetry saved his life.
3. Baca uses language to make readers see, hear, taste, smell, and touch things in his poems.

Have students work in pairs to write a four- or five-sentence summary for each of the other pages in the story. Give partners a chance to read their summaries aloud.

Application

In the Community Have small groups of students research places in your community that a struggling poet could turn to for support and skill development. Suggest that group members begin their search by contacting local schools and libraries. Compile all results in a booklet titled "Developing Your Writing Skills." You may even choose to share the finished product with the school's guidance counselors or other staff members who act as career advisors.

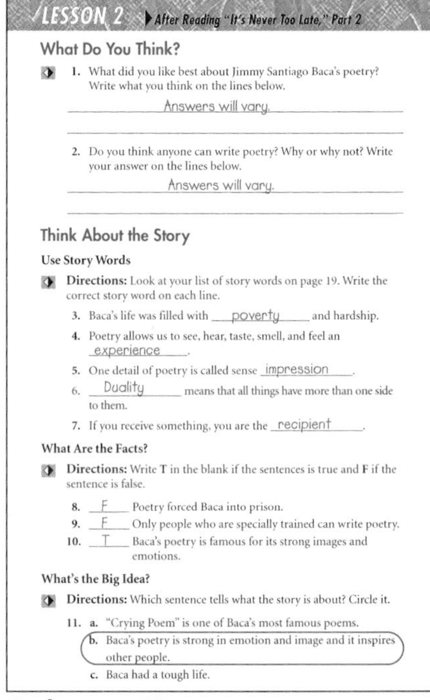

LESSON 2 ▸ After Reading "It's Never Too Late," Part 2

What Do You Think?

1. What did you like best about Jimmy Santiago Baca's poetry? Write what you think on the lines below.
   Answers will vary.

2. Do you think anyone can write poetry? Why or why not? Write your answer on the lines below.
   Answers will vary.

Think About the Story

Use Story Words

Directions: Look at your list of story words on page 19. Write the correct story word on each line.

3. Baca's life was filled with poverty and hardship.
4. Poetry allows us to see, hear, taste, smell, and feel an experience.
5. One detail of poetry is called sense impression.
6. Duality means that all things have more than one side to them.
7. If you receive something, you are the recipient.

What Are the Facts?

Directions: Write T in the blank if the sentences is true and F if the sentence is false.

8. F Poetry forced Baca into prison.
9. F Only people who are specially trained can write poetry.
10. T Baca's poetry is famous for its strong images and emotions.

What's the Big Idea?

Directions: Which sentence tells what the story is about? Circle it.

11. a. "Crying Poem" is one of Baca's most famous poems.
    b. Baca's poetry is strong in emotion and image and it inspires other people. (circled)
    c. Baca had a tough life.

Student page 24

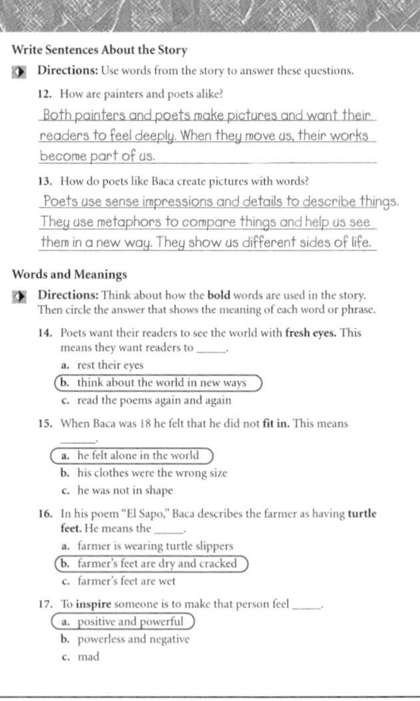

Write Sentences About the Story

Directions: Use words from the story to answer these questions.

12. How are painters and poets alike?
    Both painters and poets make pictures and want their readers to feel deeply. When they move us, their works become part of us.

13. How do poets like Baca create pictures with words?
    Poets use sense impressions and details to describe things. They use metaphors to compare things and help us see them in a new way. They show us different sides of life.

Words and Meanings

Directions: Think about how the **bold** words are used in the story. Then circle the answer that shows the meaning of each word or phrase.

14. Poets want their readers to see the world with **fresh eyes.** This means they want readers to ____.
    a. rest their eyes
    b. think about the world in new ways (circled)
    c. read the poems again and again

15. When Baca was 18 he felt that he did not **fit in.** This means ____.
    a. he felt alone in the world (circled)
    b. his clothes were the wrong size
    c. he was not in shape

16. In his poem "El Sapo," Baca describes the farmer as having **turtle feet.** He means the ____.
    a. farmer is wearing turtle slippers
    b. farmer's feet are dry and cracked (circled)
    c. farmer's feet are wet

17. To **inspire** someone is to make that person feel ____.
    a. positive and powerful (circled)
    b. powerless and negative
    c. mad

Student page 25

Reinforce & Extend

SPELLING: Words with Long Vowel Sounds

1. glue
2. through
3. although
4. tie
5. wrote
6. donkey
7. weigh
8. prey
9. thorough
10. hope

Write *dough* on the board. Tell students that the long *o* sound in *dough* can be spelled in various ways. Then write *apply* on the board. Tell students that the long *i* sound in *apply* can be spelled in various ways. Have students number a sheet of paper 1–10. Dictate the words above, one at a time, pausing for students to write them. Next, write the words on the board. Have students check each word, making corrections as needed.

Reading and Writing Practice Activity 11 provides additional practice with words containing the sound of long *i* or long *o*.

LANGUAGE: Predicate (Complete and Simple)

Write these sentences on the board:

The frightened puppy ran under the bed.

Many tropical plants grow along the west coast of Florida.

Tell students that a predicate is the part of a sentence that describes the action of a subject. Explain:

- A simple predicate is the verb of a sentence.
- A complete predicate is the verb and all its modifiers.

Have a volunteer read the first sentence aloud. Ask students to name the simple predicate. (ran) Note that this verb describes the action of the subject or puppy. Then ask students to name the complete predicate. (ran under the bed) Note that this complete predicate includes the verb and a prepositional phrase that describes it. Follow the same procedures with the second sentence on the board. Stress that a simple predicate is part of a complete predicate.

Have students identify the simple and complete predicates in the following sentences:

Tom didn't arrive until after the late bell. (simple predicate: didn't arrive; complete predicate: didn't arrive until after the late bell)

The substitute teacher went directly into the main office. (simple predicate: went; complete predicate: went directly into the main office)

Reading and Writing Practice Activity 12 provides additional practice identifying simple and complete predicates.

LITERARY APPRECIATION: Figurative Language

Remind students that poets use figurative language to paint pictures with words. Tell them that two types of figurative language are similes and metaphors. Both devices compare items. Explain:

- A *simile* is a comparison between two different things using the words *like* or *as*.
- A *metaphor* is a comparison that lacks the clue words *like* or *as*. A metaphor states that one thing *is* another thing.

Write the following examples of figurative language on the board:

The farmer's wheelbarrow looked as if it had been run over by a tractor. (simile)

Friendship is a cup of hot chocolate in front of a fire. (metaphor)

The storm was a fire-breathing dragon that destroyed the picnic. (metaphor)

Huge raindrops fell like tears from the dark clouds. (simile)

Have students classify each as a simile or metaphor. Then discuss the image each conveys.

Lesson at a Glance

Chapter 1, Lesson 3 "Birthday Party"

Preview: This lesson describes the conflict a teen faces when choosing how to spend a free afternoon.

Objectives

- to read drama
- to read multisyllabic words with unusual spellings for long vowels
- to read words with the long *u* sound
- to correctly spell irregular plurals
- to distinguish between fantasy and realism
- to recognize common and proper nouns
- to recognize character, plot, and setting

Student Worktext Pages 26–33

Story Words

elements, princess, troop, saluting, courage, memories

Reading and Writing Practice Activities 13–17

Before Reading "Birthday Party"

Letters and Sounds

Multisyllabic words with unusual spellings for long vowels

Remind students that different combinations of letters can produce the same sound. Write *melody* on the board, read it aloud, and circle the *y.* Tell students that this word ends with the sound of long *e,* which is produced by *y.* Explain that many words have long vowel sounds produced by different combinations of letters. Then write *eighty, buying, toenail,* and *beautiful* on the board. Read the words aloud. Have students circle the letters that form each long vowel sound.

Remind students that many words contain the sound of long *u.* Write *new* and *use* on the board. Have a student read the words aloud and circle the letters that make the sound of long *u.* Then write *neighborhood* and *fulfill* on the board. Tell students that both words contain the same vowel sound as *foot.* Have a volunteer circle the letters that make this sound. Then have students complete Student Worktext page 26.

Reading and Writing Practice Activity 13: Words with Unusual Spellings for Long Vowels.

Story Words

Read aloud these words: *elements, princess, troop, saluting, courage, memories.* Tell students that these words are important in the next story they will read. Then write the words on the board and point to each one as you say it aloud a second time. Have students follow the ❑ *Read* ❑ *Say* ❑ *Write* sequence by completing **Story Words** on Student Worktext page 27. Remind students to write the story words in the Word Bank at the back of their Student Worktext. To introduce these words in context, write these sentences on the board:

- Every story has basic elements.
- Hannah wrote a story about a princess.
- A long line of customers began to troop into the store.
- The photograph showed hundreds of soldiers saluting the president.
- It took courage for Tia to admit it.
- The old school yearbook triggered many fond memories.

Read the sentences aloud. To assess students' ability to read each new word, listen as students read the sentences on the board. Have students make a word card for *elements.* Have students write another sentence using *elements* on the back of their card. Follow the same procedure for the remaining words.

Reading and Writing Practice Activity 14: Reading Story Words.

More Word Work

Have students complete **More Word Work** on Student Worktext page 27.

Reading and Writing Practice Activity 15: Irregular Plurals.

LESSON 3 ▶ Before Reading "Birthday Party"

Letters and Sounds

Directions: Below are words that have long vowel sounds made with **irregular** letter combinations. Read the word. Write it on the line. Then circle the letters that make the long vowel sound.

1. neighborhood neighborhood
2. neutral neutral
3. boastful boastful
4. osprey osprey
5. seamy seamy

Directions: The vowel sound of the letter **u** in **pupil** is the long **u.** Read the word. Write it on the line. Circle the letters that make the long **u** sound.

6. human human
7. future future
8. communicate communicate
9. usual usual

Directions: The **u** sound in **put** is the same as the **oo** vowel sound in **foot.** Read the word. Write it on the line. Circle the letters that make this vowel sound.

10. book book
11. push push
12. soot soot
13. sugar sugar

TIP: Words like **pewter** and **cuckoo** have the vowel-consonant/consonant-vowel, or VC/CV pattern.

Directions: The **u** sound in **use** is the same vowel sound as the **oo** in **fool** or the **ew** in **view.** Read the word. Write it on the line. Circle the letters that make this vowel sound.

14. fuse fuse
15. pool pool
16. review review
17. duty duty
18. pewter pewter
19. cuckoo cuckoo

Directions: These words all have a **u** sound. Write them on the lines beneath the word that has the same **u** sound.

prune football junior loose cookie bugle pudding igloo unit wooden universe toolbox butcher

pupil	foot	fool
20. unit	23. football	28. prune
21. universe	24. cookie	29. junior
22. bugle	25. wooden	30. loose
	26. pudding	31. igloo
	27. butcher	32. toolbox

Student page 26

Story Words

Directions: Read each word to yourself. Then say the word out loud. Write the word on the line. Check the box after each step.

33. elements (el|e|ments) Read ☑ Say ☑ Write ☑ elements
34. princess (prin|cess) Read ☑ Say ☑ Write ☑ princess
35. troop Read ☑ Say ☑ Write ☑ troop
36. saluting (sa|lut|ing) Read ☑ Say ☑ Write ☑ saluting
37. courage (cour|age) Read ☑ Say ☑ Write ☑ courage
38. memories (mem|o|ries) Read ☑ Say ☑ Write ☑ memories

More Word Work

Some words ending in **o** use **es** to become plural.

Example: echo + es = echoes

Directions: Add **es** to the following words to make them plural. Write the plural form on the line.

39. potato potatoes
40. domino dominoes
41. veto vetoes
42. hero heroes
43. tomato tomatoes

Student page 27

Reading "Birthday Party"

Preview and Predict

- Tell students that they are going to read a play about a teen who must make a difficult decision. Have a volunteer read aloud the title of the story on Student Worktext page 28.
- Ask a volunteer to read aloud the **Use What You Know** at the top of page 28. Have small groups of students discuss ways of handling conflicts between family members. Then have the students record a personal response on page 28.
- Ask students to preview the story by reading about the time and setting, and by looking at the illustration on page 30. Then have them draw upon their observations to predict how Shaquana decides to spend her afternoon.
- Explain that the selection is classified as a drama. Guide students in recognizing that a drama is a piece of literature that is written to be performed in front of an audience. Tell them that dramas, which are also called plays, can be read as well as acted out. Discuss the traits of a drama that are different from a fiction story. (Plays identify a character's name and then his or her words and actions, begin with a description of the setting, and note a character's feelings by words enclosed in parentheses.)
- Then ask students to work in groups to identify similarities that exist between plays and fiction stories. (Both have a title, setting, characters, plot, conflict or problem, and resolution or how the problem is solved.) Invite students to share their answers.

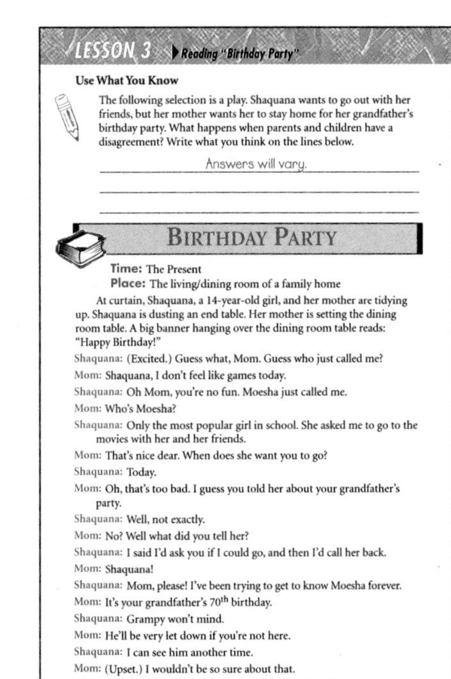

LESSON 3 ▶ Reading "Birthday Party"

Use What You Know

The following selection is a play. Shaquana wants to go out with her friends, but her mother wants her to stay home for her grandfather's birthday party. What happens when parents and children have a disagreement? Write what you think on the lines below.

Answers will vary.

BIRTHDAY PARTY

Time: The Present
Place: The living/dining room of a family home

At curtain, Shaquana, a 14-year-old girl, and her mother are tidying up. Shaquana is dusting an end table. Her mother is setting the dining room table. A big banner hanging over the dining room table reads: "Happy Birthday!"

Shaquana: (Excited.) Guess what, Mom. Guess who just called me?
Mom: Shaquana, I don't feel like games today.
Shaquana: Oh Mom, you're no fun. Moesha just called me.
Mom: Who's Moesha?
Shaquana: Only the most popular girl in school. She asked me to go to the movies with her and her friends.
Mom: That's nice dear. When does she want you to go?
Shaquana: Today.
Mom: Oh, that's too bad. I guess you told her about your grandfather's party.
Shaquana: Well, not exactly.
Mom: No? Well what did you tell her?
Shaquana: I said I'd ask you if I could go, and then I'd call her back.
Mom: Shaquana!
Shaquana: Mom, please! I've been trying to get to know Moesha forever.
Mom: It's your grandfather's 70th birthday.
Shaquana: Grampy won't mind.
Mom: He'll be very let down if you're not here.
Shaquana: I can see him another time.
Mom: (Upset.) I wouldn't be so sure about that.
Shaquana: Of course I can. What are you talking about?

Student page 28

Mom: Nothing. I am not talking about anything because you are not going anywhere with a **crowd** of girls. You are going to your grandfather's party and you will enjoy it.
Shaquana: But Mom!
Mom: Didn't I just tell you what I want you to do?
Shaquana: It's not fair! Grampy would let me go.
Mom: Shaquana! Not one more word. Your father is picking up your grandparents and they'll be here any minute. I want you to call that girl back and tell her you can't go.
Shaquana: Yes, Mother.
Mom: I wrapped the photo album you got Grampy in the blue paper. It's on the table with the other presents.
Shaquana: Thank you.
(Mom exits. Shaquana picks up the phone and dials.)
Shaquana: Hello, Moesha? . . . Hi, it's Shaquana. Listen, I asked my mom if I could go to the movies today, but she said no. I'm sorry, I really wanted to go, but today is my grandfather's birthday and we're having a party for him. My mom is making a big deal out of it. The really stupid thing is that I know my grandfather would let me go. I just bet if he heard me talking right now he'd say get out of here and ask what I'm waiting for . . . oh wow. Moesha, that's it! You call me back in about an hour and ask me again. My grandfather will hear me talking to you and tell me to go. I just know it. Great, I'll talk to you later.

Do you think Shaquana's plan will work? Write what you think on the lines below. Then keep reading to find out what takes place.

Answers will vary.

(Shaquana hangs up the phone. From off stage we hear the front door open.)
Dad: Hello everybody!
Shaquana: (Calling out.) Mom! They're here.
(Shaquana's father and grandmother enter. They are holding her grandfather by the arms.)
Grandmother: Hello Shaquana, dear. Get him into the chair.
Grandfather: Stop worrying about me. I feel better now.
Mom: (Entering.) Dad? What's wrong?

Student page 29

Strategy Modeling

Make a Prediction Tell students that a prediction is a statement about a future event based on known facts. To make a prediction about how Shaquana decides to spend her afternoon, they should think about what they already know about the story. Ask them to reflect on the title, **Use What You Know,** the first page of the drama, and the illustration. Modeling this process, you might say:

The title of the story tells me that the main idea of the drama focuses on a birthday party. From ***Use What You Know,*** *I know that Shaquana would rather go out with her friends than attend the party. The illustration shows Shaquana spending time with her grandfather. So it seems that she is spending time with him. Maybe Shaquana attended the party for a little while and then went out with her friends. Or, she might have chosen to stay home for the entire party.*

Have students read Student Worktext pages 28–31 to learn about Shaquana's decision. Tell students to pause at the Mid-Story Question on page 29 and predict how Shaquana spends the afternoon.

Focus on ESL/LEP

Explain and discuss the term *present* as used in the following sentences:

- This drama takes place in the *present.* (happening now)
- Grandfather couldn't wait to open his birthday *present.* (gift)

Learning Styles

Visual/Spatial Have each student create a list of characters in the play and a short description of each. Students can then refer to the list when reading and rereading the play.

Learning Styles

Body/Kinesthetic Reinforce story content by having pairs of students role play the following scenes:

- Shaquana telling her mother about Moesha's call and their plans to go out
- Moesha's second call to Shaquana to find out if she can go to the movies

Grandfather: I'm fine now sweetie. My stomach was just bothering me.
Dad: He was sick in the car.
Grandmother: He was out walking in the rain the other day with no hat. I've told him time and again he can't go out in the elements that way.
Grandfather: James, I'm sorry about your car.
Dad: Don't you worry about it. Can I get you anything?
Grandfather: A glass of water would be nice.
Dad: You've got it.
(He exits.)
Shaquana: (Concerned.) Grampy?
Grandfather: There's my princess. Come over here and give your grampy a kiss.
Shaquana: (Kisses him.) Are you all right?
Grandfather: I am now that I've seen you. Look at that face, **it's a poem.**
(Dad enters with water and some paper towels.)
Dad: Some water for the birthday boy.
Grandfather: Thank you. Why don't you all troop out of here so I can visit with my granddaughter?
Grandmother: Well I guess we can take a hint.
Dad: I'll be outside cleaning up the car.
Mom: Okay dear. Mother, why don't you help me finish icing the cake?
(As they exit.)
Grandmother: Did you use sweet butter like I told you?
Mom: Yes, Mother.
(Shaquana is alone with her grandfather.)
Shaquana: How are you?
Grandfather: I am **dying to find out** what you got me for my birthday.
Shaquana: You want to open it now?
Grandfather: Why not? It's my birthday, isn't it?
(Shaquana brings the gift.)
Grandfather: You open it for me.
Shaquana: (Opens it.) See, it's a photo album.
Grandfather: It's beautiful.
Shaquana: Oh, I guess Mom put these pictures inside. They're photos of you and me.
Grandfather: How nice. Look at this one. You must have been about three years old then.

Student page 30

Shaquana: What am I doing with my hand?
Grandfather: You're saluting me. We used to play soldiers. It was a favorite game of yours. We were like a couple of old war heroes.
Shaquana: I can't believe I can't remember that. I guess you were the general.
Grandfather: Oh no, I was a private. You were the general. You always did like being in charge.
(They laugh.)
Shaquana: Look at this one! This was the first summer I spent with you and Grandma. You taught me to fish. I always cried because I was afraid to put the worm on the hook. But you never laughed at me or got angry. You just put it on for me.
Grandfather: Until one day you got the courage to do it yourself. I never put another worm on a hook again. Not your hook or mine either. You insisted on baiting them all.
(Again they laugh.)
Shaquana: You were always there for me Grampy.
Grandfather: We had fun.
Shaquana: Grampy, is there something wrong with you?
Grandfather: Yes, princess.
Shaquana: But you're going to be all right?
Grandfather: Maybe I will. But it's all right if I'm not, we'll still have each other and all our memories. We have wonderful memories. I wouldn't trade them for all the money in the world.
Shaquana: I wouldn't either.
(The phone rings.)
Shaquana: Oh, that's for me.
(She picks up the phone.)
Shaquana: Hello? Oh, hi Moesha. Gee Moesha, I'd really like to do that but my grandfather is here. It's his birthday. Maybe we can go another time. Goodbye.
Grandfather: What was all that?
Shaquana: My friend Moesha wanted me to go to the movies with her.
Grandfather: Wouldn't you rather spend the day with your friend?
Shaquana: Grampy, how can you compare the movies to spending time with you?
Grandfather: So long as you're sure.
Shaquana: I'm sure. Happy birthday Grampy.
(They look at photos, laugh, and talk as the curtain falls.)

Student page 31

After Reading "Birthday Party"

Personal Response: You Be the Judge

Read aloud the question under **You Be the Judge** on Student Worktext page 32. Have small groups of students discuss the merits of Shaquana's decision. Then have each student record a personal response to the **You Be the Judge** question.

Think About the Story: Reading Comprehension

Have students complete the remaining items on Student Worktext pages 32–33 independently or in pairs. Check their responses to help you assess their comprehension of the story. If students' responses indicate that they did not understand story events, reread the story aloud, pausing to discuss key events.

Reading Comprehension Skill: Fantasy vs. Realism

Remind students that they have learned about different kinds of fiction stories. Explain:

- In a realistic fiction story, all the events and characters could exist in real life.
- In a fantasy story, one or more story elements cannot exist or happen in real life.

Ask students if "Birthday Party" is a realistic fiction story, and why or why not. (Students should reply that it is realistic.) Then discuss what kinds of things would need to be in a story for it to be fantasy. (Possible answers might include: supernatural events, characters doing things beyond their natural abilities, etc.)

Application

At Home Have each student reflect on a family member with whom he or she shares fond memories. Ask the students to write a brief letter to that family member, thanking him or her for being such a strong presence in the student's life. Have students in groups discuss whether to actually mail their letters to family members.

LESSON 3 ▶ After Reading "Birthday Party"

You Be The Judge

1. Shaquana changed her mind. She decided she would rather stay with her grandfather than go to the movies with friends. Did she make the right decision? Why or why not? Write what you think on the lines below.
Answers will vary.

Think About the Story

Use Story Words

Directions: Look at your list of story words on page 27. Write a story word on each line.

2. Shaquana's grandmother told Grampy not to go out in the elements without his hat.
3. Shaquana got the courage to bait her own fishing hook.
4. Shaquana and her grandfather have many good memories.
5. Grampy told the family to troop out of the living room so he could talk to Shaquana.
6. In the photograph, Shaquana is saluting her grandfather.
7. Grampy likes to say that Shaquana is a princess.

When Did It Happen?

8. Write a number from 1 to 4 in front of each event to show when it happened.
2 Shaquana and her grandfather look at pictures.
1 Shaquana calls Moesha.
4 Shaquana decides to stay at the party.
3 Moesha calls Shaquana.

Student page 32

What Were the Facts?

9. Why does Shaquana decide to stay for her grandfather's birthday party? Circle the reasons.
a. Her mother told her to stay.
b. Her grandfather is sick and she might not see him again.
c. She doesn't like Moesha.
d. Shaquana remembers how nice her grandfather was to her.
e. Shaquana doesn't like the movie Moesha wants to see.

Write Sentences About the Story

Directions: Use words from the story to answer these questions.

10. Why is Shaquana dusting an end table as the play begins?
Her family is having a seventieth birthday party for her grandfather, and he will be there any minute.
11. Why is Shaquana sure that she wants to spend the day with her grandfather after all?
Even if her grandfather is not going to get better, they share wonderful memories that can't compare with the movies.

Words and Meanings

Directions: Think about how the **bold** words are used in the story. Then circle the words that show the meaning of each word or phrase.

12. Shaquana wants to go to the movies with a **crowd** of girls. Here crowd means ____.
a. a large number of girls in a tight space
b. a group of girls
c. a party
13. When Grampy says that he is **dying to find out** what Shaquana got him for his birthday, he means ____.
a. he is worried sick that he'll be disappointed
b. he is eager to see her present
c. his face is changing colors because of the excitement
14. When her grandfather says Shaquana's face **is a poem,** he means ____.
a. her face is beautiful, like a poem is beautiful
b. she has a poem written on her face
c. her face rhymes

Student page 33

Reinforce & Extend

SPELLING: Words with the Long *u* Sound

1. music	**3.** fuse	**5.** human	**7.** value	**9.** root
2. mood	**4.** tube	**6.** particular	**8.** preview	**10.** usually

Write *future* and *boot* on the board. Tell students that both words contain the long *u* sound. Have students number a sheet of paper 1–10. Dictate the words above, one at a time, pausing for students to write them. Next, write the words on the board. Have students check each word, making corrections as needed.

Reading and Writing Practice Activity 16 provides additional practice with words containing the long *u* sound.

LANGUAGE: Common and Proper Nouns

Write the following words on the board:

office   singer   White House   Angela

Point out that these words are all nouns. Remind students that a noun names a person, place, or thing. Tell them that nouns are classified as common nouns or proper nouns. Explain:

- A common noun names any person, place, or thing.
- A proper noun names a particular person, place, or thing. Proper nouns begin with a capital letter.

Write the following nouns on the board. Have students classify each as either a common noun or proper noun. Then ask them to identify a similar common noun for each proper noun or proper noun for each common noun.

Florida (proper noun; state)
date (common noun; October 29, 1954)
person (common noun; Chris)
Friday (proper noun; day)
Wilson High School (proper noun; school)

Reading and Writing Practice Activity 17 provides additional practice identifying common and proper nouns.

LITERARY APPRECIATION: Story Elements (Character, Plot, Setting)

Explain that every story, just like every human body, has a basic skeleton. Draw an analogy between bones that form the human skeleton and story elements that form a story's skeleton. Tell students that three kinds of story elements are setting, characters, and plot. Explain:

- Setting is where and when the events of a story take place.
- Characters are the individuals who perform the main actions of the story.
- Plot is the sequence of events that occur during a story.

Have volunteers identify the setting and characters of "Birthday Party." (The setting is a suburban location in present time. The characters are Shaquana, Grampy, Shaquana's mother, father, grandmother, and Moesha.) Then have students work cooperatively in small groups to list the main events of the story or its plot.

Lesson at a Glance

Chapter 1, Lesson 4 "Oprah Winfrey"

Preview: This lesson describes the early hardships Oprah Winfrey overcame to become one of the most successful businesswomen in America.

Objectives

- to read a biography
- to read and spell words with silent consonants
- to correctly spell the possessive form of words
- to identify the topic of a paragraph
- to read and spell singular and plural nouns
- to distinguish between fiction and nonfiction

Student Worktext Pages 34–41

Story Words

television, humble, celebrated, rural, audience, scholarship

Reading and Writing Practice Activities 18–22

Before Reading "Oprah Winfrey"

Letters and Sounds

Words with silent consonants

Remind students that some words contain letters that are not pronounced. These silent consonants may appear in the beginning, middle, or end of a word. Write *straight* on the board. Have students read the word aloud. Explain that the consonants *gh* are silent. Then write *knife* on the board and have a volunteer read it aloud. Explain that this word begins with a silent consonant, *k*, which is not pronounced. Then write *answer, ghastly,* and *handsome* on the board. Read the words aloud. Have students circle the silent consonant or consonants in each word. (w, h, d, e) Then have students complete Student Worktext page 34.

Remind students that they know the VC/CV division of *magnet.* Then explain that when the same letter pattern contains a digraph, the digraph stays together (VCC/V).

Reading and Writing Practice Activity 18: Words with Silent Consonants.

Story Words

Read aloud these words: *television, humble, celebrated, rural, audience, scholarship.* Tell students that these words are important in the next story they will read. Write the word *wither* on the board. Then write the words on the board and point to each one as you say it aloud a second time. Have students follow the ❑ *Read* ❑ *Say* ❑ *Write* sequence by completing **Story Words** on Student Worktext page 35. Remind students to write the story words in the Word Bank at the back of their Student Worktext. To introduce these words in context, write these sentences on the board:

- Zack once appeared in a <u>television</u> commercial.
- Rose owns a <u>humble</u> little cottage by the seashore.
- The joyous team <u>celebrated</u> their championship season.
- My cousin lives in a <u>rural</u> part of New York state.
- At the end of the play, the <u>audience</u> burst into applause.
- Mykia is attending college on an athletic <u>scholarship</u>.

Read the sentences aloud. To assess students' ability to read each new word, listen as students read the sentences on the board. Have students make a word card for *television.* Have students write another sentence using *television* on the back of their card. Follow the same procedure for the remaining words.

Reading and Writing Practice Activity 19: Reading Story Words.

More Word Work

Have students complete **More Word Work** on Student Worktext page 35.

Reading and Writing Practice Activity 20: Reading and Writing Possessives.

LESSON 4 ▸ Before Reading "Oprah Winfrey"

Letters and Sounds

TIP: The consonants **t, h, n, w, g, k, d, c, b,** and **l** can be silent. These silent letters are not pronounced.

Directions: The words below begin with a silent consonant. Read the word. Then write it on the line. Circle the silent consonant.

1. know ___know___
2. psalm ___psalm___
3. write ___write___
4. knot ___knot___
5. gnat ___gnat___

Directions: The second consonant in the words below is silent. Read the word. Then write it on the line. Circle the silent consonant.

6. ghost ___ghost___
7. science ___science___
8. rhyme ___rhyme___
9. scene ___scene___

Directions: Write the word on the line. Then circle the silent consonant in these words.

10. fasten ___fasten___
11. reign ___reign___
12. debt ___debt___
13. scepter ___scepter___
14. wring ___wring___
15. knife ___knife___
16. doubt ___doubt___
17. soften ___soften___
18. autumn ___autumn___
19. nestle ___nestle___
20. Wednesday ___Wednesday___
21. hour ___hour___
22. corps ___corps___
23. half ___half___
24. column ___column___

TIP: Silent consonants can also appear in the middle or at the end of a word. Examples are the **t** in **often** and the **n** in **condemn.**

Student page 34

Story Words

Directions: Read each word to yourself. Then say the word out loud. Write the word on the line. Check the box after each step.

25. television (tel|e|vi|sion) Read ☑ Say ☑ Write ☑ ___television___
26. humble (hum|ble) Read ☑ Say ☑ Write ☑ ___humble___
27. celebrated (cel|e|brat|ed) Read ☑ Say ☑ Write ☑ ___celebrated___
28. rural (ru|ral) Read ☑ Say ☑ Write ☑ ___rural___
29. audience (au|di|ence) Read ☑ Say ☑ Write ☑ ___audience___
30. scholarship (schol|ar|ship) Read ☑ Say ☑ Write ☑ ___scholarship___

More Word Work

To indicate the possession of someone or something, add an apostrophe (') and an **s** to the word.

Example: Sally + 's = Sally's   <u>Sally</u> has red hair. Sally's hair is red.

Directions: Make the underlined word possessive. Rewrite each sentence on the line using the possessive.

31. The <u>woman</u> has a green car. ___The woman's car is green.___
32. The <u>dog</u> has a large bone. ___The dog's bone is large.___
33. <u>Tom</u> has an interesting book. ___Tom's book is interesting.___

TIP: Nouns that change their form when they become plural are called **irregular plurals.** To indicate possession for the irregular plurals that end in **s,** add an apostrophe ('). For irregular plurals that do not end in **s,** add an apostrophe (') and an **s.**

Directions: Make the irregular plural possessive by adding an apostrophe (') or **'s** to the word. Then write the new word on the line.

34. women ___women's___
35. elves ___elves'___
36. feet ___feet's___
37. thieves ___thieves'___

Student page 35

Reading "Oprah Winfrey"

Preview and Predict

- Tell students that they are going to read about Oprah Winfrey's childhood and the hardships she faced. Have a volunteer read aloud the title of the story on Student Worktext page 36.
- Ask students to preview the story by reading the first paragraph and by looking at the photos on pages 36 and 39. Then have them draw upon their observations to predict the skills Oprah used to overcome her childhood hardships.
- Explain that the selection is classified as a biography. Guide students to recognize that a biography is a piece of literature that tells a person's life story. Ask them to explain the difference between a biography and an autobiography. (A biography is written by someone other than the main character. An autobiography is the story of a person's life written by that person.)
- Encourage students to realize that each of them has a unique life story to tell. Have pairs of students make a list of questions one might ask a person when gathering information for a biography. Then have the pairs use their questions to interview each other. Finally, have each student use the interview information to write a one-page biography of his or her partner.

LESSON 4 ▸ *Reading "Oprah Winfrey"*

Use What You Know

This story is about a famous person. There are many famous people in the world. What do you think it would be like to be famous? Write what you think on the lines below.

Answers will vary.

OPRAH WINFREY

Oprah Winfrey is famous for her acting, her television talk show, and her magazine. However, her life hasn't always been so good. Oprah comes from a background of poverty. As a child, she was moved from family member to family member. Her early life was filled with hardships. In spite of her humble beginnings, Oprah is one of the wealthiest, most celebrated women in the world today.

Oprah was born in rural Mississippi on January 29, 1954. While she was still a baby, her mother left her in the care of her grandmother, Hattie Mae. The church was important to Hattie Mae. Oprah remembers speaking before the members of the church. She was good at telling stories, and she could hold an audience's attention. Oprah was already a big hit at age three. Hattie Mae was very proud. She praised Oprah for her speaking and performing talents. As Oprah grew older, she continued to speak and to act in church plays. Oprah enjoyed being in the spotlight. Church wasn't the only place she performed. One of Oprah's jobs on the family farm was feeding the pigs. If no one was around, Oprah read stories aloud to the animals.

Student page 36

Life on the farm was hard work. The family was poor and there were many daily chores to be done. Oprah's family lived in a very simple house. They did not have all the helpful things we take for granted today. Despite the hard life, Oprah still loved the natural beauty around her.

Hattie Mae was difficult and strict. She expected Oprah to do as she was told without asking questions. Any time Oprah disobeyed, her grandmother would whip her. Oprah was even forced to select the switch for her own punishment. She would be sent into the nearby woods to bring back a strong tree switch for Hattie Mae. Needless to say, Oprah did not enjoy this task at all.

Even though Hattie Mae was strict, she did believe in giving Oprah a good education. By the time Oprah was three, her grandmother had taught her to read and do math. Oprah has always been grateful to her grandmother for teaching her to love books and reading. Oprah enjoys books to this day.

When Oprah was six, she went to Milwaukee to live with her mother, Vernita Lee. It was a big change. In Mississippi she was used to running free on a large farm. In Milwaukee, she found herself in a noisy city where her mother worked as a maid for little pay. Oprah lived with her mother and baby sister in one room. When Oprah started going to a new school, she liked it at first. She was a good student, and her teachers were fond of her. The other students made fun of her for being smart. A few times, the children threatened to beat her up. Each time Oprah had to talk her way out of a fight. But she was always frightened. The older she got, the worse it became.

When Oprah was 14, her teacher, Gene Abrams, took an interest in her. He noticed that she was often alone and tried to help her. Because Oprah was such a good student, Mr. Abrams was able to get her a scholarship to a private school. Once again, she had a big change in her life. Oprah was now the only African-American student in an all-white school. She didn't let this bother her though, and she made many friends. Still, there were a few problems. The school was far from where she lived. Oprah had to travel a long way to get there. Also, most of her new friends came from rich families. They didn't understand that Oprah didn't have a lot of money. In her desire to fit in, she began to steal from her mother. She went so far as to fake home robberies to cover her thefts. This caused so much conflict at home that Oprah began to run away from home.

After a while, Oprah's mother couldn't handle her anymore. She decided to put Oprah in a home for girls. Oprah was very scared. She couldn't believe the bad turn her life was taking. It was a stroke of luck for Oprah that the home was full. Her mother was told to bring her back in two weeks. However, Vernita was fed up. She was a single mother and at her **wit's end.** She couldn't wait another two weeks. She called Oprah's father.

Student page 37

Strategy Modeling

Reread/Read Ahead Ask students to name some of the things they can do if they come to something that confuses them while they are reading. Point out that often a reader can clear up confusion by rereading. A reader can also read ahead to see if something later on in the story clears up the confusion. To model rereading, you might say:

I am confused about the different places Oprah lived when she was growing up. I think that she lived in more than one place, but I'm not sure. I will go back and reread the selection. I found out that Oprah first lived with her grandmother, Hattie Mae. Then she went to live with her mother, Vernita Lee. Then she went to live with her father and stepmother, Vernon and Zelma.

If students have trouble grasping other details while reading the story, have students pause. Suggest applicable parts of the story for students to reread. Before rereading, have students pinpoint specific details that are confusing to them. Then have them figure out those details by rereading. If students are still confused, have them read ahead to see if details are made clearer later in the story.

Have students read pages 36–39 to find out more about Oprah Winfrey.

Learning Styles

Visual/Spatial Have each student create a flow chart that illustrates the major events in the life of Oprah Winfrey.

Learning Styles

Body/Kinesthetic Reinforce story content by having pairs of students role play the following scenes:

- Oprah reciting a story to the family's pigs
- Oprah's father and stepmother explaining their rules to her

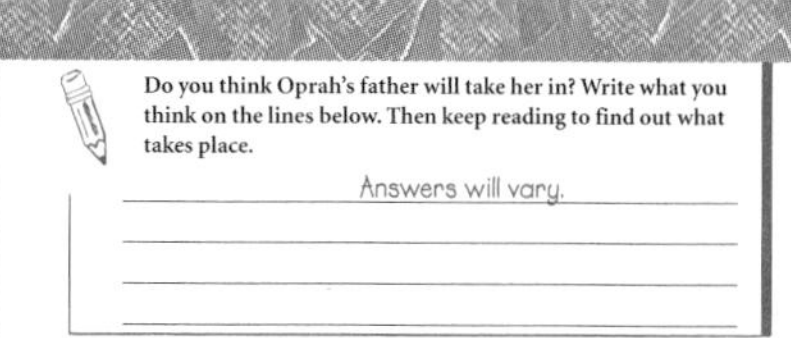

Do you think Oprah's father will take her in? Write what you think on the lines below. Then keep reading to find out what takes place.

Answers will vary.

Vernon Winfrey and his wife Zelma were happy to have Oprah come live with them. She went to Tennessee to live with her father and stepmother in Nashville. She lived with them for over seven years. Oprah knew this was a chance she didn't want to ruin. Her parents' rules were strict, but she now knew what to expect. Like her grandmother, Oprah's father made her go to church. He had a long list of rules for her to obey. She was expected to behave like a lady and was not allowed to wear tight clothes or heavy makeup. Most importantly, she was expected to get good grades at school. Her stepmother made her read books and report on them every two weeks.

The good home and strict rules had a great impact on Oprah. She became an excellent student once more. She got involved in drama classes and was elected president of her school's student council. Oprah also began to participate in beauty contests. In the Elks Club beauty contest, she won a four-year scholarship to Tennessee State University.

Oprah landed a part-time job at a local radio station while she was still in high school. She had gone to the radio station to collect money for a charity. The man at the radio station took a liking to her voice. It had a nice quality that made her sound warm and interesting. He asked Oprah to record her voice on a tape. Everyone at the station loved the tape. Afterwards, Oprah was given a job reading news reports after school and on the weekends.

Oprah knew that fulfilling her dreams would take a lot of focus and hard work. In fact, she decided to break up with her high school boyfriend. She knew she would be very busy and did not want to **string him along.**

After Oprah started college, another big break came her way. In 1973, a television station offered her a job. She became the first woman and the first African-American newscaster in Nashville. Throughout this period, Oprah lived with her father and stepmother. Even though she was a television reporter, she still had to be home early. Soon it was time to step out on her own. In 1976, when she was offered a job with a television station in Baltimore, she jumped at the chance. Oprah was finally a young woman on her own.

Student page 38

In the mid-1980s, Oprah started her own national talk show. Later, she became both the producer and owner of the show. Even though much daytime television was poor, Oprah did not follow the trend. Instead, she made shows she thought audiences would like. Her ideas paid off, as people loved the show.

Oprah left behind a life of poverty to become a wealthy, successful woman. As she got older, Oprah soared on the wings of common sense and dreams. Her love of reading, her self-discipline, and hard work have taken Oprah far and made her life rewarding.

Student page 39

After Reading "Oprah Winfrey"

Personal Response: You Be the Judge

Read aloud the question under **You Be the Judge** on Student Worktext page 40. Have small groups of students discuss the effect that living with her father and stepmother had on Oprah. Then have each student record their response to the **You Be the Judge** question.

Think About the Story: Reading Comprehension

Have students complete the remaining items on Student Worktext pages 40–41 independently or in pairs. Check their responses to help you assess their comprehension of the story. If students' responses indicate that they did not understand story events, reread the story aloud, pausing to discuss key events.

Reading Comprehension Skill: Recognize the Topic

Ask volunteers to share their answers to the questions listed in **What Are the Facts?** and **Write Sentences About the Story** on Student Worktext pages 40–41. Guide students in recognizing that each of these facts is connected to the topic of the selection, or to the success of Oprah Winfrey. Explain:

- A topic is a general statement or idea discussed in a passage.
- All the sentences in the passage are connected to the topic in some way.

Application

Career Connection Explain that the host is just one member of a team of professionals who work together to produce a talk show program. Have students work in pairs to learn more about careers in the television industry. Challenge each pair to identify five different broadcasting occupations and the requirements needed for each. Have pairs report their findings to the class.

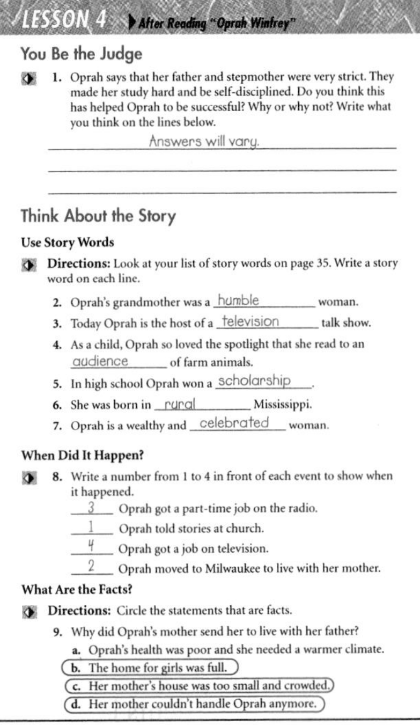

LESSON 4 ▸ After Reading "Oprah Winfrey"

You Be the Judge

1. Oprah says that her father and stepmother were very strict. They made her study hard and be self-disciplined. Do you think this has helped Oprah to be successful? Why or why not? Write what you think on the lines below.
   Answers will vary.

Think About the Story

Use Story Words

Directions: Look at your list of story words on page 35. Write a story word on each line.

2. Oprah's grandmother was a humble woman.
3. Today Oprah is the host of a television talk show.
4. As a child, Oprah so loved the spotlight that she read to an audience of farm animals.
5. In high school Oprah won a scholarship.
6. She was born in rural Mississippi.
7. Oprah is a wealthy and celebrated woman.

When Did It Happen?

8. Write a number from 1 to 4 in front of each event to show when it happened.
   3 Oprah got a part-time job on the radio.
   1 Oprah told stories at church.
   4 Oprah got a job on television.
   2 Oprah moved to Milwaukee to live with her mother.

What Are the Facts?

Directions: Circle the statements that are facts.

9. Why did Oprah's mother send her to live with her father?
   a. Oprah's health was poor and she needed a warmer climate.
   b. The home for girls was full.
   c. Her mother's house was too small and crowded.
   d. Her mother couldn't handle Oprah anymore.

Student page 40

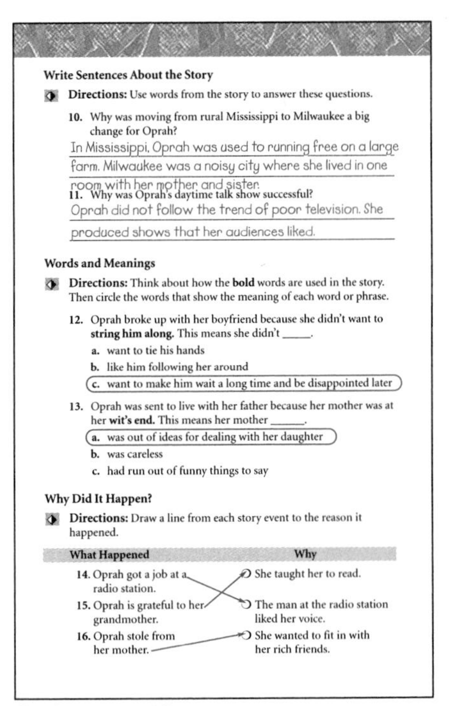

Write Sentences About the Story

Directions: Use words from the story to answer these questions.

10. Why was moving from rural Mississippi to Milwaukee a big change for Oprah?
    In Mississippi, Oprah was used to running free on a large farm. Milwaukee was a noisy city where she lived in one room with her mother and sister.
11. Why was Oprah's daytime talk show successful?
    Oprah did not follow the trend of poor television. She produced shows that her audiences liked.

Words and Meanings

Directions: Think about how the **bold** words are used in the story. Then circle the words that show the meaning of each word or phrase.

12. Oprah broke up with her boyfriend because she didn't want to **string him along.** This means she didn't _____.
    a. want to tie his hands
    b. like him following her around
    c. want to make him wait a long time and be disappointed later
13. Oprah was sent to live with her father because her mother was at her **wit's end.** This means her mother _____.
    a. was out of ideas for dealing with her daughter
    b. was careless
    c. had run out of funny things to say

Why Did It Happen?

Directions: Draw a line from each story event to the reason it happened.

What Happened	Why
14. Oprah got a job at a radio station.	She taught her to read.
15. Oprah is grateful to her grandmother.	The man at the radio station liked her voice.
16. Oprah stole from her mother.	She wanted to fit in with her rich friends.

Student page 41

Reinforce & Extend

SPELLING: Words with Silent Consonants

1. lighten **2.** written **3.** Wednesday **4.** answer **5.** wrestle **6.** Rhode Island **7.** handsome **8.** ghost **9.** scent **10.** drawer

Write *knife* on the board. Tell students that the *k* is silent and not pronounced. Have students number a sheet of paper 1–10. Dictate the words above, one at a time, pausing for students to write them. Next, write the words on the board. Have students check each word, making corrections as needed.

Reading and Writing Practice Activity 21 provides additional practice with words containing silent consonants.

LANGUAGE: Singular and Plural Nouns

Write these words on the board:

day tree shelf man

Tell students that a singular noun names one person, place, or thing. The words *day, tree, shelf,* and *man* are all singular nouns. Point out that plural nouns refer to more than one person, place, or thing. Ask students to write their plural forms, then write them on the board. Explain:

- Most singular words form their plurals by adding *s*. (days, trees)
- Irregular plurals, however, change their forms. (shelves, men)

Have students identify singular and plural nouns by writing the following on the board: *chief, buses, cities, child, highway, roof.* Have students classify the words into two groups, singular nouns and plural nouns. Have them write down the corresponding plurals or singulars (chiefs, bus, city, children, highways, roofs) and note any irregular plurals (children).

Reading and Writing Practice Activity 22 provides additional practice using singular and plural nouns.

LITERARY APPRECIATION: Fiction vs. Nonfiction

Remind students that stories may be classified as nonfiction or as fiction. Review with them that nonfiction is based on real people and real events. Fiction depicts invented characters and made-up events that may seem believable enough to be real. Invite students to discuss "Oprah Winfrey," and to suggest why they can identify the selection as nonfiction. (Most students will be familiar with the name. Others may mention the photographs or use of dates and factual details.)

Lesson at a Glance

Chapter 1, Lesson 5 "Role Models"

Preview: This lesson is about a teenager's discovery that ordinary people can do extraordinary things.

Objectives

- to read realistic fiction
- to read and spell words with a silent *p*
- to decode words containing the suffixes *er, or, ar,* and *ist*
- to learn how to solve problems
- to use possessive nouns correctly
- to write a descriptive paragraph comparing and contrasting

Student Worktext Pages 42–49

Story Words

admire, assignment, emulate, tomorrow, ballet, library

Reading and Writing Practice Activities 23–29

Before Reading "Role Models"

Letters and Sounds

Words with silent *p*

Remind students that in some words containing the letter *p*, the *p* is not pronounced. The silent *p* may appear in the beginning, middle, or end, of a word. Write *psalm* on the board. Have students read the word aloud. Explain that the consonant *p* is silent. Then write *psychology, raspberry,* and *corps* on the board. Read the words aloud. Have students circle the silent *p* in each word. Then have students complete Student Worktext page 42.

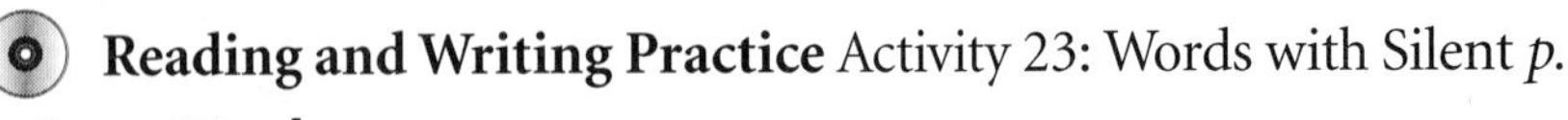

Reading and Writing Practice Activity 23: Words with Silent *p*.

Story Words

Read aloud these words: *admire, assignment, emulate, tomorrow, ballet, library.* Tell students that these words are important in the next story they will read. Then write the words on the board and point to each one as you say it aloud a second time. Have students follow the ❑ *Read* ❑ *Say* ❑ *Write* sequence by completing **Story Words** on Student Worktext page 43. Remind students to write the story words in the Word Bank at the back of their Student Worktext. To introduce these words in context, write these sentences on the board:

- What traits do you admire in a friend?
- Zelda interviewed the mayor for a school assignment.
- Which person do you like to emulate?
- Does the team have a game tomorrow?
- Laurel has studied ballet since she was a young girl.
- Due to his bad behavior, Ted was asked to leave the library.

Read the sentences aloud. To assess students' ability to read each new word, listen as students read the sentences on the board. Have students make a word card for *admire.* Have students write another sentence using *admire* on the back of their card. Follow the same procedure for the remaining words.

Reading and Writing Practice Activity 24: Reading Story Words.

More Word Work

Have students complete **More Word Work** on Student Worktext page 43.

Reading and Writing Practice Activity 25: Reading and Writing Words with *er, or, ar,* and *ist.*

LESSON 5 ▶ Before Reading "Role Models"

Letters and Sounds

Directions: These words have a **silent p.** Read the words. Write them on the lines.

1. receipt receipt
2. raspberry raspberry
3. corps corps

Directions: These words have the VC/CCV pattern. Read the words. Write them on the lines.

4. crumble crumble
5. hundred hundred
6. griddle griddle

TIP: Words that end in **le** often form the **VC/CCV** pattern.

Directions: Write the words below on the lines and then divide them into syllables.

7. stumble stum|ble
8. riddle rid|dle
9. haggle hag|gle
10. jumble jum|ble
11. teamster team|ster
12. wiggle wig|gle
13. unskilled un|skilled
14. straddle strad|dle
15. purple pur|ple
16. sample sam|ple
17. humble hum|ble
18. bubble bub|ble

Directions: Write the letters on the lines. See how many words you can make.

c f g gr h m n p qu s

19. c uddle
20. h uddle
21. m uddle
22. p uddle
23. f umble
24. gr umble
25. h umble
26. m umble
27. n ibble
28. qu ibble
29. f iddle
30. gr iddle
31. m iddle
32. p imple
33. s imple
34. g amble
35. g iggle

Student page 42

Story Words

Directions: Read each word to yourself. Then say the word out loud. Write the word on the line. Check the box after each step.

36. admire (ad|mire) Read ☑ Say ☑ Write ☑ admire
37. assignment (as|sign|ment) Read ☑ Say ☑ Write ☑ assignment
38. emulate (em|u|late) Read ☑ Say ☑ Write ☑ emulate
39. tomorrow (to|mor|row) Read ☑ Say ☑ Write ☑ tomorrow
40. ballet (bal|let) Read ☑ Say ☑ Write ☑ ballet
41. library (li|brar|y) Read ☑ Say ☑ Write ☑ library

More Word Work

Directions: The suffixes **er, or, ar,** and **ist** are found at the end of nouns that refer to people. Write the words below on the lines and circle the **er, or, ar,** or **ist** suffixes in the words.

42. worker worker
43. scholar scholar
44. cyclist cyclist
45. actor actor
46. teacher teacher
47. dentist dentist

TIP: The suffixes **er, or, ar,** and **ist** mean **one who does** or **one who is.**

Directions: Add **er, or, ar,** or **ist** to the word parts below. Then write the word you have made.

48. help + er = helper
49. harp + ist = harpist
50. li + ar = liar
51. auth + or = author

Student page 43

Reading "Role Models"

Preview and Predict

- Tell students that they are going to read about the difficulty a student has when asked to name her role models. Have a volunteer read aloud the title of the story on Student Worktext page 44.
- Ask students to preview the story by reading the first paragraph and by looking at the illustration on page 44. Then have them draw upon their observations to predict actions the student will take to determine her personal role models.
- Ask a volunteer to read aloud the introductory sentence and questions under **Use What You Know** on page 44. Ask students to discuss the questions with a partner and then to record their answers. Invite students to share their answers.
- Point out that their role models usually change over time. Have volunteers identify their childhood role models while explaining why they had high regard for these individuals. Ask these students if they still consider these individuals as their personal role models. Encourage them to provide reasons for their responses.
- Explain that each student in the class acts as a role model to a younger person they know. Have each class member consider who that younger person might be. Then have small groups of students discuss the responsibilities associated with serving as a role model.

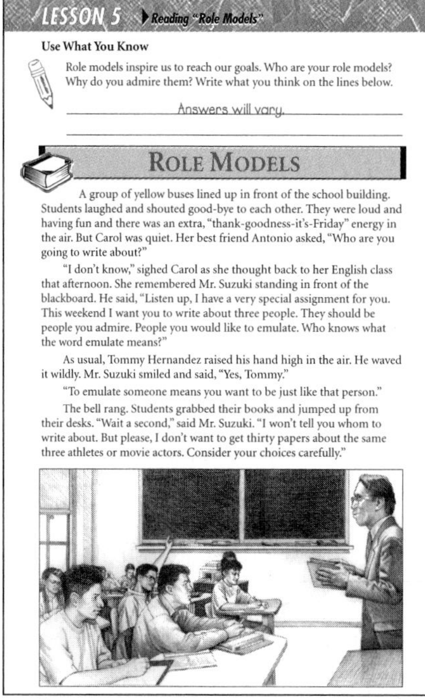

LESSON 5 ▸ Reading "Role Models"

Use What You Know

Role models inspire us to reach our goals. Who are your role models? Why do you admire them? Write what you think on the lines below.

Answers will vary.

ROLE MODELS

A group of yellow buses lined up in front of the school building. Students laughed and shouted good-bye to each other. They were loud and having fun and there was an extra, "thank-goodness-it's-Friday" energy in the air. But Carol was quiet. Her best friend Antonio asked, "Who are you going to write about?"

"I don't know," sighed Carol as she thought back to her English class that afternoon. She remembered Mr. Suzuki standing in front of the blackboard. He said, "Listen up, I have a very special assignment for you. This weekend I want you to write about three people. They should be people you admire. People you would like to emulate. Who knows what the word emulate means?"

As usual, Tommy Hernandez raised his hand high in the air. He waved it wildly. Mr. Suzuki smiled and said, "Yes, Tommy."

"To emulate someone means you want to be just like that person."

The bell rang. Students grabbed their books and jumped up from their desks. "Wait a second," said Mr. Suzuki. "I won't tell you whom to write about. But please, I don't want to get thirty papers about the same three athletes or movie actors. Consider your choices carefully."

Student page 44

"Cool choice," squealed Kim Reynolds. She and Maria Chun were standing by the school's front steps.

Maria said, "Sandy Starr is my favorite. Mr. Suzuki said he didn't want us to write about movie stars, but he didn't say anything about fashion models." The two girls laughed and ran past Carol and Antonio.

Carol looked around. Many of her classmates were nearby. They all seemed to be talking about the assignment. Some were writing about sports stars or movie actors. Others were writing about singers or models. It seemed to Carol that no one had listened to Mr. Suzuki's instructions.

Chris Fisher ran up to Carol and Antonio. "Hi guys. Antonio, do you want to play ball with us tomorrow?"

"I can't," said Antonio. "I've got Big Brothers. We're taking the kids to the petting zoo."

"Tell them you got sick."

"I can't lie to them, Chris."

"Just **skip** it then."

"Stop **putting him on the spot,** Chris," Carol jumped in.

Antonio said, "The kids have been looking forward to this for a long time. I promised that I would go."

As he ran to get his bus, Chris called out, "You're going to miss a great game."

Carol said good-bye to Antonio. She got on the bus and took a seat. She looked out the window and saw Antonio jumping up and down. He was making funny faces. Despite her worries about the homework, Carol laughed. Antonio always knew how to cheer her up.

When Carol got home, the house smelled great. She followed her nose to the kitchen. Her mother was cooking soups and good, thick stews. It looked like she was planning to feed an army.

"Hi, Mom."

"Hi, sweetie."

"What's all the food for?"

"My psychology exam is on Monday. I want to spend a lot of time studying this weekend. So I thought I'd make everything today."

Carol asked, "Does this mean I have to miss my dance class tomorrow morning?"

"Absolutely not!" said Mom. "What if a talent scout comes to class tomorrow and you're not there? I won't have you miss out on that." She smiled at Carol.

Carol watched her mom cook and told her about her day. She asked her mother who she should write about.

"Why don't you write about someone you know?"

"Like who?"

Student page 45

Strategy Modeling

Summarize Tell students that summarizing is one way to keep track of each character and his or her actions in the story. Have students read the first two paragraphs of the story silently. Then show them how to summarize the main ideas of these paragraphs. Modeling this process, you might say:

The first paragraph of the story tells me that Carol is the main character. Antonio is her best friend. It seems that they both have a writing assignment.

In the second paragraph, I learn that Mr. Suzuki is their English teacher. He has given the class a writing assignment. They must write about three people they admire.

Have students continue reading pages 44–45. Ask them to stop and summarize this part of the story. Tell students that their summaries should describe each of the following characters: Tommy Hernandez, Kim Reynolds, Maria Chun, Sandy Starr, and Chris Fisher. Then ask students to read the rest of the selection.

Focus on ESL/LEP

Explain and discuss the meaning of the term *cool* as used in the following sentences.

- Kim thought Maria's role model was *cool.* (attractive, suitable)
- Carol enjoyed a sip of *cool* water. (somewhat cold)
- Chris remained *cool* throughout the interview. (calm)

Focus on LD

Encourage students to organize their summaries in a two-column chart that identifies each character and his or her position in the story.

"Who was the last person you talked to at school today?"

"Antonio. You think I should write about Antonio?"

"What do you think of him?"

"He's my best friend. I think he's great, he always wants to help people. He gets involved in programs like Big Brothers and recycling. He's really caring. He's a good person."

"It sounds to me like Antonio is someone you admire."

"I can't believe I didn't think of him. Thanks, Mom, I'm going up to my room to start writing."

The next morning, Carol went to dance class. Ms. King, the teacher, called out, "And bend your knees, one, two, three, four. And straighten your knees, one, two, three, four."

Babette Miller was standing next to Carol. "Psst," she whispered. "Ms. King is going to hand out parts for the recital today. It's so exciting, I just know I'm going to get the role of the princess."

"How do you know that?" asked Carol.

"Well she has to give the lead to a good dancer. And the princess should be beautiful. So who else can she give it to? Certainly not the new girl," Babette giggled.

Carol looked at Kia, the new girl. Carol thought she was a good dancer. But she **looked like a pole.** She wore shorts instead of a leotard and sneakers instead of ballet slippers. Her hair was always a mess and falling out of its clip. Babette, in her pink leotard and slippers, looked more like a princess.

Ms. King called out, "No talking." Carol was glad the teacher had told them to be quiet. She didn't like talking to Babette.

After class Ms. King announced the roles for the recital. She said, "The princess will be Kia."

Everyone got quiet. Then Babette put on a fake smile and started clapping. Everyone else started clapping, too. Carol looked at Kia, and watched her shy smile get bigger and bigger. "Why, she really is pretty," thought Carol.

Student page 46

On the ride home Carol was quiet. She thought about Ms. King. It was nice that she had given the new girl a chance. Ms. King always did things like that. When you didn't understand a dance, she always said the right thing to help you. And she never yelled at anyone. Ms. King is a good teacher and a nice person. "I admire her," thought Carol.

Suddenly Carol sat up straight in her seat. "Mom, I just thought of another person to write about!"

On Sunday morning the first thing Carol thought about was her paper for English class. She needed to write about one more person. Carol thought and thought. Finally she decided to write about a famous woman scientist. But she had to go to the library to do some research. Her mom didn't want to put off studying, but she said she would take Carol to the library.

When they got back home they heard the phone ringing. Carol's mother ran to answer it. She heard her mom say, "I'll be right there."

"What's wrong?" asked Carol.

"Your Great-Aunt Sarah broke her arm. I have to pick her up at the hospital and take her home. I'm going to go visit with her for a while."

"Mom, what about your test?"

Carol's mother sighed, "I'll take my textbook. Maybe I'll get a chance to study."

She kissed Carol and walked out the door. Carol watched her from the window. She saw her mom push away the branches of a tree they hadn't gotten around to trimming yet. Her mother got in the car and sat still for a moment, and then she drove off. "She looks tired," thought Carol as she picked up her notebook to begin her homework. She started writing about the woman scientist, but she couldn't think. She kept thinking about her mom. Suddenly, Carol crossed out what she had written. She started over. This is what she wrote:

The person I most admire is my mother. I don't know anyone who works harder. She works all day long in an office. Then she goes to school at night. Yet she still manages to keep the house and our clothes clean, and to cook our meals. My mom didn't finish college because she had to take care of me when I was a baby. I am glad she is going back to school now. She is doing it for herself because she likes to learn and wants to get an interesting job. But she is also doing it for us. She wants me to have a better future. My mom is a good person. She is the best person I know. I love her.

Carol read what she had just written. She liked it. She decided to show it to her mother when she got home. "No," Carol changed her mind. "I'll show it to her tomorrow, after she's taken her test."

Student page 47

After Reading "Role Models"

Personal Response: You Be the Judge

Read aloud the questions under **You Be the Judge** on Student Worktext page 48. Have small groups of students discuss whether most people fully appreciate their family and friends. Then have the students each complete the **You Be the Judge** question.

Think About the Story: Reading Comprehension

Have students complete the remaining items on Student Worktext pages 48–49 independently or in pairs. Check their responses to help you assess their comprehension of the story. If students' responses indicate that they did not understand story events, reread the story aloud, pausing to discuss key events.

Critical Thinking Skill: Solve Problems

Ask students to name the problem Carol faced in this story. (She had to decide who her role models are.) Discuss the actions Carol took to solve her problem. (She gathered information through a discussion with her mom and by making observations. Then she analyzed the information and made a decision.) Explain to students that a good problem-solver takes certain steps:

- Identifies the problem.
- Generates a list of possible solutions.
- Analyzes the list of solutions.
- Selects the best solution.

Point out that Carol could have solved her problem in many different ways. For example, she could have written about the first three people she spoke with after English class. She could have put all of her friends' names in a hat and selected three. Carol also could have not made a decision—or not completed the assignment. Have students share their experiences with problem-solving. Ask what steps they took to solve their problems.

Application

In the Community Have small groups of students research Big Brothers to determine the purpose of this organization. The groups should also determine whether Big Brothers, or a similar program, exists in your community. Ask the groups to share their results in an oral report to the class.

LESSON 5 ▸ After Reading "Role Models"

You Be The Judge

1. Carol was surprised to realize how much she admired the people closest to her. Do you think most people fully appreciate their family and friends? Why or why not? Write what you think on the lines below.

Answers will vary.

Think About the Story

Use Story Words

Directions: Look at your list of story words on page 43. Write a story word on each line.

2. In dance class Carol wore ballet slippers.
3. Carol went to the library to do research.
4. Many students admire athletes and movie actors.
5. To emulate someone is to be just like that person.
6. The homework assignment was to write about a role model.
7. Carol worried she would miss her dance class tomorrow.

When Did It Happen?

8. Write a number from 1 to 5 in front of each event to show when it happened.

2 Chris asked Antonio to play ball with him.
1 Mr. Suzuki told the class to write about three people they admire.
4 Carol's mom left to take care of a sick aunt.
3 Kia was given the role of the princess.
5 Carol decided to write about her mother.

Student page 48

Write Sentences About the Story

Directions: Use words from the story to answer these questions.

9. What did Mr. Suzuki hope his students would not do for their writing assignment?
Mr. Suzuki hoped that not all his students would write about the same athletes or movie actors.

10. Who teaches Carol's dance class?
Ms. King teaches Carol's dance class.

11. Why did Carol's mom make enough food to feed an army?
Carol's mom made food ahead of time for the weekend because she wanted to study for a psychology exam.

12. For which group does Antonio do volunteer work?
Antonio does volunteer work for Big Brothers.

Words and Meanings

Directions: Think about how the **bold** words are used in the story. Then circle the words that show the meaning of each word or phrase.

13. When Chris tells Antonio to **skip** Big Brothers, he means Antonio should ____.
a. hop up and down at Big Brothers
(b. not go to Big Brothers)
c. throw Big Brothers away

14. When Carol tells Chris he is **putting Antonio on the spot,** she means Chris is ____.
a. putting spots on Antonio's face
b. moving Antonio to a spot on the ground
(c. putting pressure on Antonio)

15. When Carol says Kia **looks like a pole,** she means Kia ____.
(a. is very thin)
b. reaches from the floor to the ceiling
c. is in the way

Student page 49

Reinforce & Extend

SPELLING: Words with Silent Consonants

1. writer	**3.** scholar	**5.** teacher	**7.** lawyer	**9.** driver
2. actor	**4.** typist	**6.** doctor	**8.** harpist	**10.** director

Write *cleaner, author, liar,* and *dentist* on the board. Explain that the suffixes *er, or, ar,* and *ist* mean "one who does" or "one who is." Have students number a sheet of paper 1–10. Dictate the words above, one at a time, pausing for students to write them. Next, write the words on the board. Have students check each word, making corrections as needed.

Reading and Writing Practice Activity 26 provides additional practice with suffixes *er, or, ar,* and *ist.*

LANGUAGE: Possessive Nouns

Tell students that an apostrophe indicates a possessive noun, a noun that has something that belongs to it. Tell students that with singular nouns, *s* is placed after an apostrophe only if the word that shows ownership does not end in *s.* Then explain:

- Possessive nouns show ownership.
- Most singular nouns end with *'s.*
- Plural nouns end with *s'.*

Write on the board:

Mack *students* *fishes* *reporter*

Invite volunteers to write the possessive form of each term.

Reading and Writing Practice Activity 27 provides additional practice using possessive nouns.

WRITING: Compare and Contrast

Tell students that writers often compare and contrast items to present an image to a reader. Explain:

- When you compare items, you note how they are alike.
- When you contrast items, you note how they are different.

Show students a common classroom object, such as a piece of chalk. As a large group, have students brainstorm how the chalk is similar to other objects. (shaped like a crayon, shatters like seashell, glides like an ice skater) Then brainstorm another list that notes how the chalk is different from other items. (cannot be used on light colored surfaces like a pencil can, lacks the pleasant scent of cologne, does not work like an eraser) Then ask students to use their entries from these lists to write a descriptive paragraph about the item.

Reading and Writing Practice Activities 28 and 29 provide additional practice writing a descriptive paragraph that compares and contrasts.

Lesson at a Glance

Chapter 1, Lesson 6 "Against All Odds"

Preview: This lesson describes what can happen when a person focuses on his abilities rather than his disabilities.

Objectives

- to read a biography
- to read and spell words with the hard and soft *c*
- to correctly spell plural nouns
- to decode words containing the prefixes *pre, re, in, im, dis, de, un,* and *non*
- to identify action and linking verbs
- to learn how to synthesize information
- to write a paragraph of opinion

Student Worktext Pages 50–57

Story Words

baseball, league, improve, athlete, disabled, inspired

Reading and Writing Practice Activities 30–36

Before Reading "Against All Odds"

Letters and Sounds

Words with hard and soft *c*

Write *calendar* and *citizen* on the board. Ask students to read the terms aloud. Tell them that the letter *c* can sound like *k* in *calendar*. The letter *c* can also sound like an *s* as in the word *citizen*. Point out that the same hard and soft *c* sounds are found in many words. Follow a similar procedure for *compare, cents, cells,* and *count.* Then have students complete Student Worktext page 50.

Reading and Writing Practice Activity 30: Words with Hard and Soft *c*.

Story Words

Read aloud these words: *baseball, league, improve, athlete, disabled, inspired.* Tell students that these words are important in the next story they will read. Then write the words on the board and point to each one as you say it aloud a second time. Have students follow the ❑ *Read* ❑ *Say* ❑ *Write* sequence by completing **Story Words** on Student Worktext page 51. Remind students to write the story words in the Word Bank at the back of their Student Worktext. To introduce these words in context, write these sentences on the board:

- Ryan knows all the team averages in baseball.
- Sam has scored more points than any other player in our mayor's basketball league.
- Rose is taking a class to improve her computer skills.
- Joel hopes to become a professional athlete.
- Walt is disabled due to a car accident.
- Many listeners were inspired by the speech.

Have students read the sentences on the board aloud. Listen as individual students read the sentences to assess students' ability to read each new word. Then have students make a word card for *baseball.* Ask students to write another sentence using *baseball* on the back of their card. Follow the same procedure for the remaining words.

Reading and Writing Practice Activity 31: Reading Story Words.

More Word Work

Have students work in pairs to complete **More Word Work** on Student Worktext page 51.

Reading and Writing Practice Activity 32: Reading and Writing Words with Prefixes.

LESSON 6 ▸ Before Reading "Against All Odds"

Letters and Sounds

Directions: The letter **c** can sound like a **k**, as in the word **can.** It can also sound like an **s**, as in the word **city.** Read the words out loud. Write a **k** or an **s** after the word to tell which sound it begins with.

1. coop k
2. circus s
3. cook k
4. cemetery s
5. cite s
6. college k
7. ceiling s
8. care k
9. cement s
10. clean k

TIP: When a **c** makes a **k** sound it is called a **hard c.** When a **c** makes an **s** sound it is called a **soft c.**

Directions: A **hard** or **soft c** can also occur at or near the end of a word. Write a **k** or **s** to tell which sound appears at the end of these words.

11. rice s
12. force s
13. circle k
14. spice s
15. trick k
16. significant k
17. pierce s
18. mosaic k
19. rice s
20. price s

Directions: These words have a **VC/CCCV** pattern. Write the word on the line and divide it into syllables.

21. construct con|struct
22. subscribe sub|scribe
23. enthrall en|thrall
24. instruct in|struct
25. unscramble un|scram|ble
26. enthrone en|throne
27. prescribe pre|scribe
28. instrument in|stru|ment
29. constrict con|strict

Student page 50

Story Words

Directions: Read each word to yourself. Then say the word out loud. Write the word on the line. Check the box after each step.

30. baseball (base|ball) Read ☑ Say ☑ Write ☑ baseball
31. league Read ☑ Say ☑ Write ☑ league
32. improve (im|prove) Read ☑ Say ☑ Write ☑ improve
33. athlete (ath|lete) Read ☑ Say ☑ Write ☑ athlete
34. disabled (dis|a|bled) Read ☑ Say ☑ Write ☑ disabled
35. inspired (in|spired) Read ☑ Say ☑ Write ☑ inspired

More Word Work

Directions: The letters **pre, re, in,** and **im** form prefixes at the beginning of many words. Circle the correct word for each prefix. Then write the word.

36. im (press / take) impress
37. pre (please / pare) prepare
38. in (done / direct) indirect
39. re (union / pare) reunion
40. pre (tend / go) pretend

TIP: The prefix **non** means **not.**

Directions: The letters **dis, de, un,** and **non** also form prefixes at the beginning of many words. Circle the correct word for each prefix. Then write the word.

41. non (descript / good) nondescript
42. dis (here / appear) disappear
43. un (often / usual) unusual
44. de (fool / sign) design
45. dis (look / ease) disease

Student page 51

Reading "Against All Odds"

Preview and Predict

- Tell students that they are going to read about a person who concentrates on his abilities rather than his disabilities. Then have a volunteer read aloud the title of the story on Student Worktext page 52.
- Ask students to preview the story by reading the first paragraph and by looking at the photos on pages 52 and 54. Then have them draw upon their observations to predict how Jim Abbott overcame his disability and achieved his dream.
- Have a volunteer read aloud the introductory sentence and questions under **Use What You Know** on page 52. Then ask students to reflect on a time when they faced an obstacle. Have pairs of students describe their goals, the obstacles they encountered, and the actions they took to overcome these difficulties.
- Have students consider who they would turn to for aid in overcoming an obstacle. As a large group activity, brainstorm a list of such support groups. (Possible resources include family members, friends, teachers, teammates, school staff, coaches, and neighbors.) Explain to students that no one has to face a problem alone.

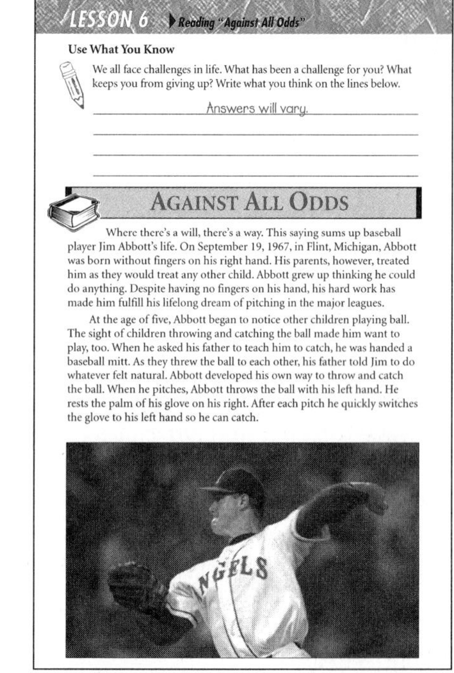

LESSON 6 ▸ Reading "Against All Odds"

Use What You Know

We all face challenges in life. What has been a challenge for you? What keeps you from giving up? Write what you think on the lines below.

Answers will vary.

AGAINST ALL ODDS

Where there's a will, there's a way. This saying sums up baseball player Jim Abbott's life. On September 19, 1967, in Flint, Michigan, Abbott was born without fingers on his right hand. His parents, however, treated him as they would treat any other child. Abbott grew up thinking he could do anything. Despite having no fingers on his hand, his hard work has made him fulfill his lifelong dream of pitching in the major leagues.

At the age of five, Abbott began to notice other children playing ball. The sight of children throwing and catching the ball made him want to play, too. When he asked his father to teach him to catch, he was handed a baseball mitt. As they threw the ball to each other, his father told Jim to do whatever felt natural. Abbott developed his own way to throw and catch the ball. When he pitches, Abbott throws the ball with his left hand. He rests the palm of his glove on his right. After each pitch he quickly switches the glove to his left hand so he can catch.

Student page 52

As a child Abbott practiced throwing and catching for many hours every day. Pretending he was pitcher in a baseball game, he would send the ball exactly where he wanted it. As he practiced, Abbott would throw the ball against a brick wall. He would move closer and closer to the wall. That way he would have less time to catch the ball as it bounced back. Abbott did this to improve his speed. All of his hard work has paid off. As a thin boy of 11 he joined a little league team. In his very first game, he pitched a no-hitter.

Little league was just the beginning for Abbott. When he entered high school he became a star athlete. He was the starting quarterback for his high school football team. He helped the team get to the Michigan state finals. But his heart still belonged to baseball. After all, baseball was the national pastime. Also, it was a game that Abbott was very good at. While still in high school, he showed great promise as a pitcher. In fact, he showed so much promise that the Toronto Blue Jays drafted him. However, Abbott decided to go to college before becoming a pro. After he graduated from high school, Abbott accepted a baseball scholarship to the University of Michigan, where he continued to be a great player. At Michigan, he had a career record of 26 wins and 8 losses.

In addition to school teams, Abbott played ball as a member of Team USA. In 1987, he and the team went to Cuba. Abbott became the first American pitcher in 25 years to beat a Cuban team on their own field. Team USA won a silver medal in the Pan-American Games. Abbott won the U.S. Baseball Federation's Golden Spikes award as the best new player in the country. He wasn't through yet. In 1988, he played on the U.S. Olympic baseball team. Abbott pitched a 5–3 victory over the Japanese. This helped the U.S. win its first gold medal in baseball.

Jim Abbott believes that success is due to hard work and a little bit of luck. Do you agree? Why or why not? Write what you think on the lines below. Then keep reading to find out more about him.

Answers will vary.

Abbott is one of a group of great pitchers. His fastball **clocks in** at over 90 miles an hour. Abbott is unlike most professional players, because he never played in the minor leagues. Right after college Abbott went straight into the majors. In the first round of the 1988 draft, he was chosen by the California Angels to pitch for their team. He pitched for the Angels

Student page 53

Strategy Modeling

Use Context Clues Review with students how to use context clues to figure out the meaning of a new word. Explain that context clues are the words and phrases around the word in question. Then read aloud the first two paragraphs of the selection and model using context clues to figure out the meaning of a new word. You might say:

> *I do not know what the word* mitt *means. I will look at the sentences and words around it to see if I can figure out the word's meaning. The sentence in which the word appears says "When he asked his father to teach him to catch, he was handed a baseball mitt." This says to me that* mitt *is related to baseball. I think it is the same thing as glove. A mitt is a glove.*

Have students use context clues when reading Student Worktext 52–55 to help them figure out other words that look new, or words that have more than one meaning.

Focus on ESL/LEP

Explain and discuss the meaning of the term *major* as used in the following sentences.

- Jim Abbott dreamed of pitching in the *major* leagues. (professional)
- Chris is a *major* in the Air Force. (officer)
- A *major* snowstorm is expected to hit tomorrow. (significant)

Focus on LD

To encourage students to understand the key ideas of the story, have students make a timeline that highlights the sequence of major events in Jim Abbott's life.

for four years. But it was as a pitcher for the New York Yankees that Abbott had the best game of his career. On September 4, 1993, he pitched a no-hitter against the Cleveland Indians.

Sportswriters described the day as a muggy afternoon. A stream of hot air rolled over the stadium. Abbott amazed the crowd and Cleveland's players with his **sinking** fastballs. After striking out players 23 times, Abbott had pitched a no-hitter.

In his usual way, Abbott said, "Every no-hitter takes a bit of luck."

It is surprising to learn that some people told Abbott he would not go far in sports. Abbott says he never agreed with the people who tried to hold him back. He knew that with enough hard work he could reach his dreams. He thinks others should work for their dreams every day. Even if you are tired and **feeling low,** Abbott says, don't give up. He believes you should stick it out to the end. Believe in yourself even when you have doubts and worries.

Perhaps this is why today Abbott speaks up for other disabled athletes. In a recent newspaper article, he stated his position about the Professional Golf Association's appeal to the Supreme Court. They wanted to bar disabled golfers from using carts during events. Abbott said that he respects the rules of sports, but he thinks sports should include everyone. He doesn't think that excluding athletes with disabilities helps any game. Abbott said that Major League Baseball never changed any rules for him. However, he feels that rules should help players with disabilities. He added that such rules should not change the nature of the game.

Student page 54

How do you think someone like Abbott inspires all people? Write what you think on the lines below.

Answers will vary.

For Abbott, his work as an athlete has given greater rewards than mere dollars. He feels rich because he has been able to reach his dream. He explains, "I was born without any fingers on my right hand. Doesn't seem like much, but it brings some extra challenges. Sports were my way of feeling I was just like everyone else."

Abbott is a great athlete. He doesn't consider himself disabled. He doesn't think his hand is as big an issue as some people make it out to be. As a result, Abbott doesn't really enjoy the attention he gets. However, he doesn't try to run away from it, either. He accepts it because he knows his successes mean a lot to many people. He gets hundreds of letters a week from people telling him how he has inspired them to work hard to reach a goal. He knows how much his experience can mean to a disabled child. If he can serve as a role model to help people to follow their dreams, he believes it is worth the fuss. Abbott likes to tell people, "I believe you can do anything you want if you put your mind to it."

Student page 55

After Reading "Against All Odds"

Personal Response: You Be the Judge

Read aloud the question under **You Be the Judge** on Student Worktext page 56. Have small groups of students compare the benefits and disadvantages of Abbott's decision to go to college rather than into the major leagues. Then have each student record their personal response to the **You Be The Judge** question.

Think About the Story: Reading Comprehension

Have students complete the remaining items on Student Worktext pages 56–57 independently or in pairs. Check their responses to help you assess their comprehension of the story. If students' responses indicate that they did not understand story events, reread the story aloud, pausing to discuss key events.

Critical Thinking Skill: Synthesize

Point out to students that sometimes complex information must be sorted out or eliminated to reach a certain conclusion. This skill is called synthesizing. Explain that people use this skill every day, whether it is deciding what notes to write down during a class or listening to a friend explain directions to a park. The information must be sorted out, organized, and sometimes dropped completely if it is not important to the main idea. Explain that this skill is especially important when reading a story or answering questions about it. Go over these tips with students:

- When reading, it might help to take down notes. Include only the main details in an organized way. Decide which details are less important, and leave those out.
- When reading, ask "Why is this part important to the whole story? How does it affect the main idea?"
- When answering a question, decide which things are not true about the question, and do not include them in your answer. Create a list of the things that remain, then include them in your answer.

Guide students to synthesize the information in "Against All Odds." Have students look at the selection again and sort out which information is critical to the story. Students can then deduce the story's purpose and main idea.

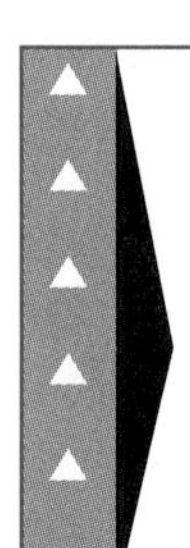

Application

In the Community Divide the class into small groups. Have the groups make direct observations of your community to identify accommodations that have been made for disabled individuals. Ask the groups to share the results of their research in an oral report to the class.

LESSON 6 ▸ After Reading "Against All Odds"

You Be the Judge

1. After high school, Jim Abbott could have gone straight into professional baseball, but he decided to go to college first. Do you think he made a good decision? Why or why not? Write what you think on the lines below.
Answers will vary.

Think About the Story

Use Story Words

Directions: Look at your list of story words on page 51. Write a story word on each line.

2. Abbott was born disabled.
3. Abbott was a star athlete in high school.
4. Abbott played both football and baseball in school.
5. Abbott worked hard to improve his pitching.
6. Abbott played ball for the major leagues.
7. Abbott has inspired many people.

When Did It Happen?

8. Write a number from 1 to 5 in front of each event to show when it happened.
5 Abbott pitched a no-hitter against the Cleveland Indians.
3 Abbott pitched a no-hitter in his first little league game.
1 Abbott was born with no fingers on his right hand.
4 Abbott played on the U.S. Olympic baseball team.
2 Abbott's father taught him to play catch.

Write Sentences About the Story

Directions: Use words from the story to answer these questions.

9. How did Abbott improve his speed while throwing his ball against a brick wall?
He would move closer and closer, so that he had less time to catch the ball as it bounced back.

Student page 56

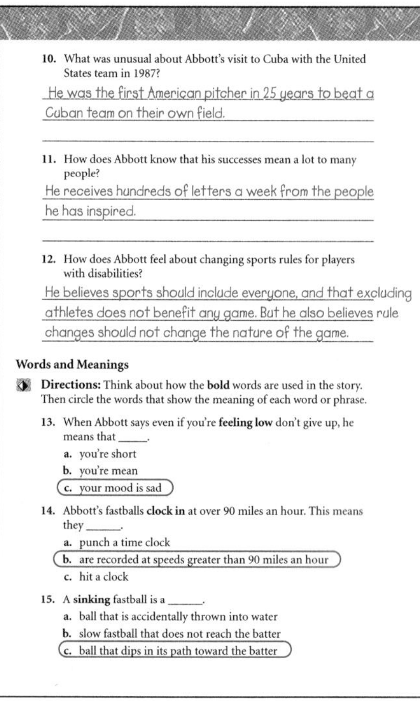

10. What was unusual about Abbott's visit to Cuba with the United States team in 1987?
He was the first American pitcher in 25 years to beat a Cuban team on their own field.

11. How does Abbott know that his successes mean a lot to many people?
He receives hundreds of letters a week from the people he has inspired.

12. How does Abbott feel about changing sports rules for players with disabilities?
He believes sports should include everyone, and that excluding athletes does not benefit any game. But he also believes rule changes should not change the nature of the game.

Words and Meanings

Directions: Think about how the **bold** words are used in the story. Then circle the words that show the meaning of each word or phrase.

13. When Abbott says even if you're **feeling low** don't give up, he means that ____.
a. you're short
b. you're mean
c. your mood is sad (circled)

14. Abbott's fastballs **clock in** at over 90 miles an hour. This means they ____.
a. punch a time clock
b. are recorded at speeds greater than 90 miles an hour (circled)
c. hit a clock

15. A **sinking** fastball is a ____.
a. ball that is accidentally thrown into water
b. slow fastball that does not reach the batter
c. ball that dips in its path toward the batter (circled)

Student page 57

Reinforce & Extend

SPELLING: Plural Nouns

1. branches	**3.** planets	**5.** women	**7.** heroes	**9.** knives
2. crops	**4.** businesses	**6.** parties	**8.** pianos	**10.** ladies

Write *elements* and *wives* on the board. Tell students that both terms are plural nouns. Remind students that many plural nouns, such as *elements,* are formed by adding *s* to the singular form. Irregular plural nouns, such as *wives,* require additional changes to the singular form of the noun. Have students number a sheet of paper 1–10. Dictate the words above, one at a time, pausing for students to write them. Next, write the words on the board. Have students check each word, making corrections as needed.

Reading and Writing Practice Activity 33 provides additional practice spelling plural nouns.

LANGUAGE: Action and Linking Verbs

Write the following sentences on the board:

Jim threw a fastball toward the batter.

He felt better after the game.

Ask a volunteer to read the first sentence. Point to *threw.* Tell students this action verb describes the actions of the subject, *Jim*. Then have another volunteer read the second sentence. Point to *felt.* Tell students this linking verb connects the subject of the sentence with words that describe the subject or the subject's state of being. Explain:

- Action verbs show action and describe what a subject does.
- Linking verbs connect the subject with words describing the subject or the subject's state of being.

Have pairs of students scan the story to find examples of these verbs in two sentences, one sentence that contains an action verb and another that contains a linking verb.

Reading and Writing Practice Activity 34 provides additional practice classifying verbs as action or linking verbs.

WRITING: A Paragraph of Opinion

Tell students that the purpose of a paragraph of opinion is to state the writer's ideas or opinions and to give the writer's reasons for thinking that way.

- A paragraph of opinion clearly identifies the writer's ideas or opinions on a topic.
- A paragraph of opinion contains facts that support the writer's ideas or opinions.

Have students consider the following question: Should students attend school for twelve months rather than ten? Then divide the class into two groups. Have one group brainstorm a list of reasons why students should attend school all year long. Have the other group brainstorm a list of reasons why students should not attend school all year long. Then have group members use their lists to write a paragraph of opinion on the issue.

Reading and Writing Practice Activities 35 and 36 provide additional practice writing one kind of paragraph of opinion, the editorial.

Lesson at a Glance

Objectives

- to complete a trade book successfully
- to practice the word study and phonics skills learned in Chapter 1
- to practice reading the high-frequency and content words learned in Chapter 1
- to build reading fluency

Recommended Books

Crash by Jerry Spinelli
Windcatcher by Avi
Belle Prater's Boy by Ruth White
Tracker by Gary Paulsen
Beyond the Mango Tree by Amy Bronwen Zemser
Taking Sides by Gary Soto
Helen Keller's Teacher by Margaret Davidson
Searching for Candlestick Park by Peg Kehret
Seedfolks by Paul Fleishman
Shadow of a Bull by Maia Wojciechowska
Hatchet by Gary Paulsen
Slake's Limbo by Felice Holman

Before Reading

Introduce the Book

Display some of the books from the recommended trade book list. (Or, if the whole class will read the same book, display just that book.) Tell students that they will read a chapter book. Explain that these books use words that are the same as or similar to the words in Chapter 1, and that they will read the book for fun; they will not be expected to learn new skills.

Access Prior Knowledge

Remind students that prior knowledge is information readers have about a topic before they begin to read a story or book. Ask for volunteers to share what they know about the book topic.

Topic

Remind students that the topic is the subject of the story and the main thing that the story is about. Tell them that by identifying the topic, they can better remember the story.

Reading

Compare and Contrast

Remind students that comparing items notes how they are alike. Contrasting items notes how they are different. Have students think about some books they have read in the past or movies they have seen. Ask students to generate a list of the titles and then determine the titles' similarities and differences. Students can complete a chart like this one:

Title	Alike	Different

Identify Cause and Effect

Ask students to complete a chart like this one:

What Happened?	Why Did It Happen?

After Reading

Evaluate/Make Judgments

Tell students to choose an action by a character in the story. Ask them to tell if they think the character made the right choice and to explain why or why not.

In nonfiction, tell students to choose a topic in the story and give their evaluation of the topic.

Author's Purpose

Ask students to try to put themselves in the author's shoes and to think why the author wrote the story. (For example: To entertain? To inform? To surprise? To prove a point? To scare?)

Extension Activities

Reading

For their own personal interests, suggest that students read other books from the recommended list.

Writing

Suggest that students complete one of these activities:

- Write a ten-sentence summary of the book. Use at least 20 words with the letter patterns studied in the chapter. Circle the targeted words.
- Create a book jacket for the book.

Research

Suggest that students choose a topic that relates to the book and do an Internet search on that topic. They should report their findings to the class.

Chapter 1 Review

The Chapter Review on Student Worktext pages 58–66 will help students review and practice the skills presented in Chapter 1. The review is divided into four parts, A–D.

Suggestions to help students complete the Chapter Review:

- Make sure the students understand that the Chapter Review is not a test. You may have students work in pairs and then compare responses, or you may work through the review as a class.
- Read the instructions for each part aloud.
- Have students complete one part of the review at a time. Pause to go over the answers and have students mark corrections using a second color.

Chapter Test

Reproducible blackline masters of the Chapter 1 Test can be found on pages 129–131 of this book. Use the test to assess students' comprehension of the skills taught in the chapter.

Additional Practice

Reading and Writing Practice Activities 1–36 can be used to reinforce the skills taught in Chapter 1.

Part A

Part A reviews the phonics skills taught in the chapter. Read aloud the summaries presented in the tip boxes before each exercise. Then have the students complete the items. If students show difficulty understanding and using the new letters and sounds, review individual lessons or assign the corresponding Reading and Writing Practice Activities: 1, 8, 13, 18, 23, and 30.

Part A

Summing It Up: Letters and Sounds

The letters **a, e, i, o,** and **u** sometimes have a long vowel sound.

Directions: Write the word on the line. Circle the letters that make the long vowel sound.

1. tame tame
2. comb comb
3. she she
4. wife wife
5. boat boat
6. cute cute
7. gave gave
8. dime dime
9. me me
10. grate grate

Long vowel sounds are sometimes made with **irregular** combinations of letters, such as **eigh, ough, ey,** and **ay.**

Directions: Write the word on the line. Circle the letters that make the long vowel sound.

11. sleigh sleigh
12. key key
13. though though
14. tray tray
15. grey grey

The consonants **b, c, d, g, h, k, l, n, p, t,** and **w** are sometimes silent.

Directions: Circle the silent consonants in these words.

16. night
17. ghost
18. raspberry
19. half
20. write
21. fasten
22. wrong
23. knowledge
24. scenery
25. receipt
26. hasten
27. knife
28. calf
29. column
30. debt

Student page 59

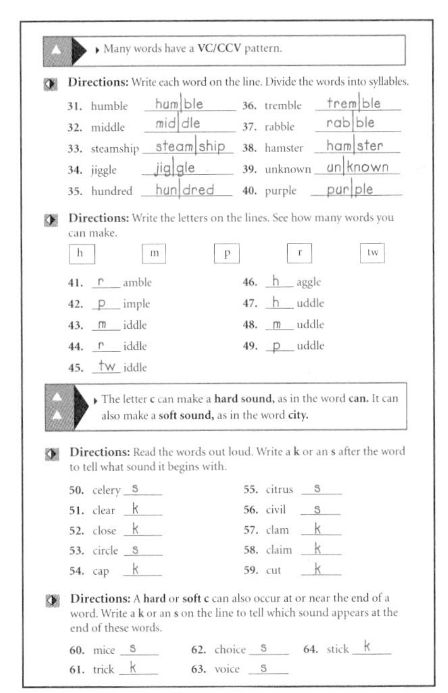

Many words have a **VC/CCV** pattern.

Directions: Write each word on the line. Divide the words into syllables.

31. humble hum|ble
32. middle mid|dle
33. steamship steam|ship
34. jiggle jig|gle
35. hundred hun|dred
36. tremble trem|ble
37. rabble rab|ble
38. hamster ham|ster
39. unknown un|known
40. purple pur|ple

Directions: Write the letters on the lines. See how many words you can make.

h m p r tw

41. r amble
42. p imple
43. m iddle
44. r iddle
45. tw iddle
46. h aggle
47. h uddle
48. m uddle
49. p uddle

The letter **c** can make a **hard sound,** as in the word **can.** It can also make a **soft sound,** as in the word **city.**

Directions: Read the words out loud. Write a **k** or an **s** after the word to tell what sound it begins with.

50. celery s
51. clear k
52. close k
53. circle s
54. cap k
55. citrus s
56. civil s
57. clam k
58. claim k
59. cut k

Directions: A **hard** or **soft c** can also occur at or near the end of a word. Write a **k** or an **s** on the line to tell which sound appears at the end of these words.

60. mice s
61. trick k
62. choice s
63. voice s
64. stick k

Student page 60

Part B

Part B reviews the word study and structural analysis skills taught in the chapter. Read aloud the summaries presented in the tip boxes before each exercise. Then have the students complete the items. You may want to review the skills by looking back at individual lessons, presenting examples on the board, or assigning the corresponding Reading and Writing Practice Activities: 3, 10, 15, 20, 25, and 32.

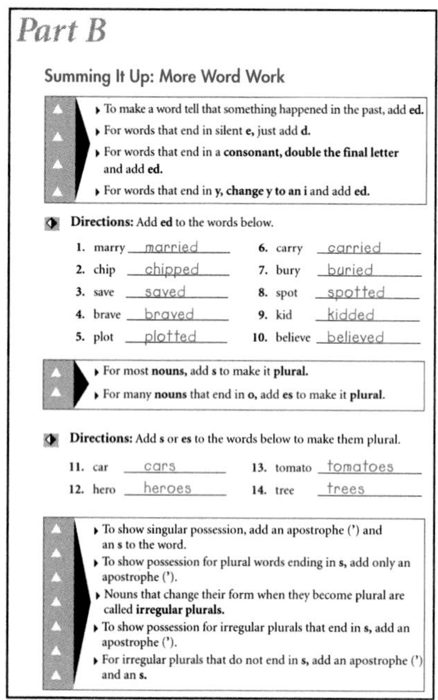

Part B

Summing It Up: More Word Work

- To make a word tell that something happened in the past, add **ed**.
- For words that end in silent **e**, just add **d**.
- For words that end in a **consonant, double the final letter** and add **ed**.
- For words that end in **y, change y to an i** and add **ed**.

Directions: Add **ed** to the words below.

1. marry married
2. chip chipped
3. save saved
4. brave braved
5. plot plotted
6. carry carried
7. bury buried
8. spot spotted
9. kid kidded
10. believe believed

- For most **nouns**, add **s** to make it **plural**.
- For many **nouns** that end in **o**, add **es** to make it **plural**.

Directions: Add **s** or **es** to the words below to make them plural.

11. car cars
12. hero heroes
13. tomato tomatoes
14. tree trees

- To show singular possession, add an apostrophe (') and an **s** to the word.
- To show possession for plural words ending in **s**, add only an apostrophe (').
- Nouns that change their form when they become plural are called **irregular plurals.**
- To show possession for irregular plurals that end in **s**, add an apostrophe (').
- For irregular plurals that do not end in **s**, add an apostrophe (') and an **s.**

Student page 61

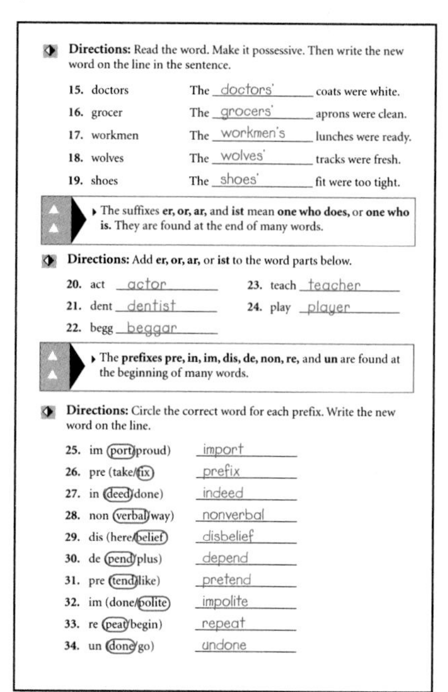

Directions: Read the word. Make it possessive. Then write the new word on the line in the sentence.

15. doctors The doctors' coats were white.
16. grocer The grocers' aprons were clean.
17. workmen The workmen's lunches were ready.
18. wolves The wolves' tracks were fresh.
19. shoes The shoes' fit were too tight.

- The suffixes **er, or, ar,** and **ist** mean **one who does,** or **one who is.** They are found at the end of many words.

Directions: Add **er, or, ar,** or **ist** to the word parts below.

20. act actor
21. dent dentist
22. begg beggar
23. teach teacher
24. play player

- The **prefixes pre, in, im, dis, de, non, re,** and **un** are found at the beginning of many words.

Directions: Circle the correct word for each prefix. Write the new word on the line.

25. im (port/proud) import
26. pre (take/fix) prefix
27. in (deed/done) indeed
28. non (verbal/way) nonverbal
29. dis (here/belief) disbelief
30. de (pend/plus) depend
31. pre (tend/like) pretend
32. im (done/polite) impolite
33. re (peat/begin) repeat
34. un (done/go) undone

Student page 62

Part C

Part C reviews the story words from each story in the chapter. Students are asked to recognize story words and their meanings, and to place them in sentences. Have students review the story words in the Word Bank at the back of their Student Worktext or refer to the stories in the chapter to help them complete the review. For additional practice and word recognition, assign the corresponding Reading and Writing Practice Activities: 2, 9, 14, 19, 24, and 31.

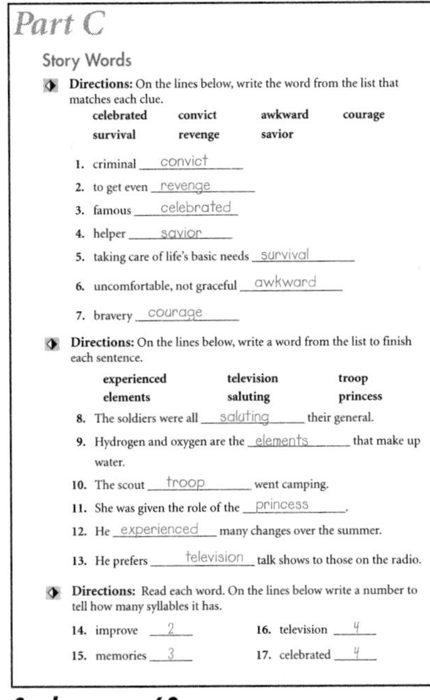

Part C

Story Words

Directions: On the lines below, write the word from the list that matches each clue.

celebrated **convict** **awkward** **courage**
survival **revenge** **savior**

1. criminal convict
2. to get even revenge
3. famous celebrated
4. helper savior
5. taking care of life's basic needs survival
6. uncomfortable, not graceful awkward
7. bravery courage

Directions: On the lines below, write a word from the list to finish each sentence.

experienced **television** **troop**
elements **saluting** **princess**

8. The soldiers were all saluting their general.
9. Hydrogen and oxygen are the elements that make up water.
10. The scout troop went camping.
11. She was given the role of the princess.
12. He experienced many changes over the summer.
13. He prefers television talk shows to those on the radio.

Directions: Read each word. On the lines below write a number to tell how many syllables it has.

14. improve 2
15. memories 3
16. television 4
17. celebrated 4

Student page 63

Directions: On the lines below, write the word from the list that matches each clue.

humble **audience** **tomorrow** **ballet** **rural**
scholarship **library** **admire** **emulate**

18. a place to borrow a book library
19. a dance ballet
20. the people who watch a performance audience
21. to be modest humble
22. an award of money to go to school scholarship
23. not in the city rural
24. not yesterday or today tomorrow
25. to like someone or something admire
26. to be like someone else emulate

Directions: On the lines below, write a word from the list to finish each sentence.

assignment **disabled** **baseball** **inspired**
league **athlete** **memories**

27. The homework assignment was interesting.
28. She was chosen for the high school baseball team.
29. He was inspired by poetry.
30. She was president of the bowling league.
31. A disabled person is often talented in many other ways.
32. He was a good athlete.
33. Her memories of school were happy ones.

Directions: On the lines below, write a word from the list that matches each clue.

orphanage **poverty** **impression** **duality** **recipient**

34. the state of being poor poverty
35. all things have more than one side duality
36. one who receives recipient
37. home for children without parents orphanage
38. poetry uses senses to make this impression

Student page 64

Part D

Part D reviews the content of the stories in the chapter. Students are asked to identify fiction and nonfiction, story characters, details, and cause and effect. If students are having difficulty remembering story details, have them reread stories they have trouble recalling and work in pairs or as a class to complete Part D again.

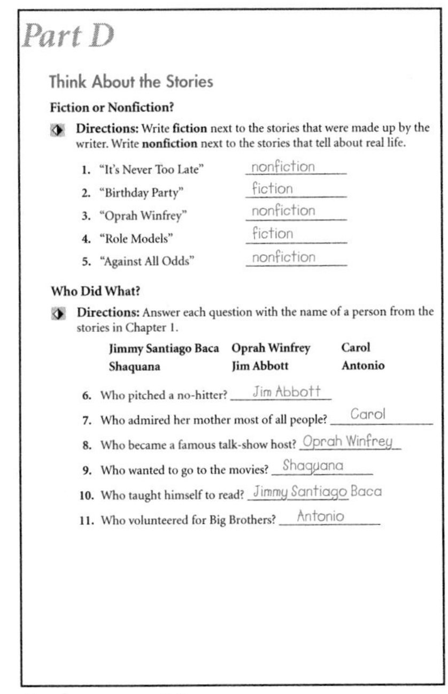

Part D

Think About the Stories

Fiction or Nonfiction?

Directions: Write **fiction** next to the stories that were made up by the writer. Write **nonfiction** next to the stories that tell about real life.

1. "It's Never Too Late" nonfiction
2. "Birthday Party" fiction
3. "Oprah Winfrey" nonfiction
4. "Role Models" fiction
5. "Against All Odds" nonfiction

Who Did What?

Directions: Answer each question with the name of a person from the stories in Chapter 1.

Jimmy Santiago Baca **Oprah Winfrey** **Carol**
Shaquana **Jim Abbott** **Antonio**

6. Who pitched a no-hitter? Jim Abbott
7. Who admired her mother most of all people? Carol
8. Who became a famous talk-show host? Oprah Winfrey
9. Who wanted to go to the movies? Shaquana
10. Who taught himself to read? Jimmy Santiago Baca
11. Who volunteered for Big Brothers? Antonio

Student page 65

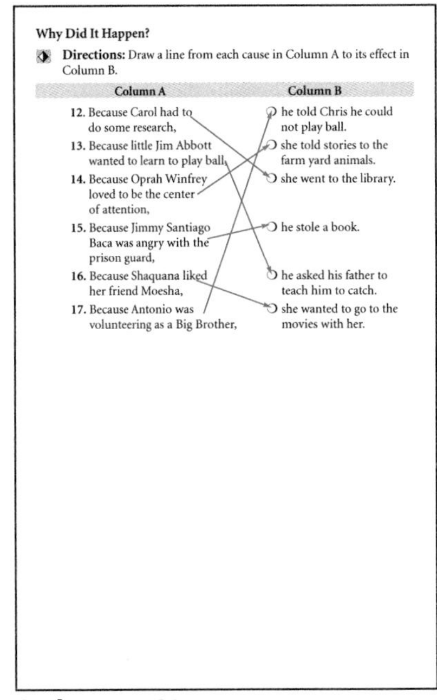

Why Did It Happen?

Directions: Draw a line from each cause in Column A to its effect in Column B.

Column A	Column B
12. Because Carol had to do some research,	he told Chris he could not play ball.
13. Because little Jim Abbott wanted to learn to play ball,	she told stories to the farm yard animals.
14. Because Oprah Winfrey loved to be the center of attention,	she went to the library.
15. Because Jimmy Santiago Baca was angry with the prison guard,	he stole a book.
16. Because Shaquana liked her friend Moesha,	he asked his father to teach him to catch.
17. Because Antonio was volunteering as a Big Brother,	she wanted to go to the movies with her.

Student page 66

Chapter 2 Planning Guide

Skills and Learning Objectives

	Student Pages	Phonics and Phonograms	Word Study	Reading Strategy
Lesson 1 Finding New Friends, Part 1	68–75	Hard and soft *g* (initial and final); V/V pattern	Endings *-er, -est; more, most*	Make a Prediction
Lesson 2 Finding New Friends, Part 2	76–83	Sounds for *ough* and *augh;* three-syllable words	Suffixes *-ly, -ful, -less, -ness, -ment, -y*	Summarize
Lesson 3 Second Sight	84–91	*ei* vs. *ie*	Compound words (*reindeer*)	Set a Purpose
Lesson 4 Student Volunteer	92–99	Schwa sound: as spelled *el, al, le, er, or, ar, es, is, en, on, ion, ed, id, sion, tion*	Contractions (review all)	Clarify
Lesson 5 Blood Brothers, Part 1	100–109	Schwa sound: as spelled *a, e, o, i*	Suffixes *-able, -ible*	Reread/Read Ahead
Lesson 6 Blood Brothers, Part 2	110–119	Vowel dipthongs in longer words	Suffixes *-ous, -eous, -ious*	Access Prior Knowledge

Independent Reading

Independent Reading Lesson:
Teacher's Guide pages 86–87
List of Recommended Books to Read:

- *Dogsong*
- *Scorpions*
- *Tangerine*
- *Do Bananas Chew Gum?*
- *The Ear, the Eye, and the Arm*
- *Bud, Not Buddy*
- *Four Perfect Pebbles*
- *Joey Pigza Swallowed the Key*
- *Racing the Sun*
- *Sing Down the Moon*
- *Song of the Trees*
- *Stonewords, A Ghost Story*
- *Summer Soldiers*

Assessment and Review

Chapter 2 Summary of Skills and Strategies:
Student Worktext page 120

Chapter 2 Review:
Student Worktext pages 121–128
Teacher's Guide pages 88–91

Chapter 2 Test:
Teacher's Guide pages 132–134

Reading Comprehension/ Critical Thinking	Spelling	Study Skill	Language	Writing	Literary Appreciation	Learning Styles	Focus on LEP/ESL or LD	Application	Reading and Writing Practice Activities
Recognize Cause and Effect		58	58	58		55	55, 56		37–43
Recognize the Author's Purpose		63	63		63		60, 61		44–48
Make Judgments	68		68	68		66	65, 66		49–55
Compare and Contrast	73		73	73		70, 71	71		56–62
Distinguish Fact from Opinion		79	79		79	75, 77	75, 76, 77		63–67
Recognize Point of View and Bias	85		85	85		81, 83	81, 82	85	68–74

Common Reading Errors

If the Student . . .		Then . . .
◆ has difficulty making syllable breaks in compound words	→	◆ reteach compound words in Lesson 3; have students make syllable breaks in compound words.
◆ has difficulty reading longer words or words with inflected endings.	→	◆ reteach the lessons on word endings, and model how to identify base words and endings; model breaking words into syllables for decoding.
◆ has difficulty recognizing author's purpose	→	◆ reteach Lesson 2; explain that writers use supporting details to convince their readers.
◆ mispronounces words without self-correcting	→	◆ have the student reread the sentence and try a different pronunciation using context clues for help; repeat process until he or she comes to a pronunciation that sounds right and makes sense.
◆ cannot tell the difference between cause and effect	→	◆ reteach the lesson Recognize Cause and Effect in Lesson 1.

Lesson at a Glance

Chapter 2, Lesson 1 "Finding New Friends," Part 1

Preview: This lesson presents the first part of a fiction story about a boy in a new school and the friends he makes his first week.

Objectives
- to read a fiction story
- to read words with the initial and final hard and soft *g* sounds
- to read and write words with *er* and *est*
- to recognize causes and effects
- to locate information using an encyclopedia
- to make the subject and verb agree
- to write a descriptive paragraph

Student Worktext Pages 68–75

Story Words
rhythm, planets, astronomy, telescope, observe

Reading and Writing Practice Activities 37–43

Before Reading "Finding New Friends," Part 1

Letters and Sounds

Hard and Soft Sounds of the Letter *g*

Write the words *gasoline, giraffe, bridge, manage,* and *unclog* on the board. Pronounce each word for students. Ask students to tell what letter each of these words has in common. (g) Ask students if they can name the two sounds that the *g* has. (Students should pronounce the hard and soft *g* sounds.) Tell students that the soft *g* sound is the same as the *j* sound. Have a volunteer tell which words have the hard *g* sound. (gasoline, unclog) Circle the letter *g* in these two words. Say each word as you circle the letters and model the blending of the vowel sound with the *g* sound. Then have a volunteer tell which words have the soft *g* sound. (giraffe, bridge, manage) Circle the letter *g* in these words. Say each word as you circle the letters and model the blending of the vowel sound with the *g* sound. Tell students that the hard and soft *g* sounds can occur anywhere in a word. Then have students complete Student Worktext page 68.

Reading and Writing Practice Activity 37: Decoding Words with Hard or Soft *g*.

Story Words

Read aloud these words: *rhythm, planets, astronomy, telescope, observe.* Tell students that these words are important in the next story they will read. Then write the words on the board and point to each one as you say it aloud a second time. Have students follow the ❑ *Read* ❑ *Say* ❑ *Write* sequence by completing **Story Words** on Student Worktext page 69. Remind students to write the story words in the Word Bank at the back of their Student Worktext. To introduce the words in context, write these sentences on the board:

- Listen to the steady rhythm of the music.
- There are nine planets in the solar system.
- Astronomy is the study of the stars.
- A telescope can be used to see long distances.
- We can observe the stars with a telescope.

Have students make a word card for *rhythm*. Ask a volunteer to read the first sentence aloud. Then have students copy the sentence onto the back of the word card. Follow the same procedure for the remaining words. To assess students' abilities to read each new word, listen as individual students read the sentences on the board aloud.

Reading and Writing Practice Activity 38: Reading Story Words.

More Word Work

Have students complete **More Word Work** on Student Worktext page 69.

Reading and Writing Practice Activity 39: Reading and Writing Words with *er* and *est.*

LESSON 1 ▶ Before Reading "Finding New Friends," Part 1

Letters and Sounds

Directions: The letter **g** is a consonant. Read the words. Write them on the lines. Circle each letter **g.**

1. ago ago
2. government government
3. village village
4. gold gold
5. ginger ginger

Directions: The letter **g** has a soft and hard sound. The **g** sound in **gym** is a soft **g.** The **g** sound in **good** is a hard **g.** Circle the words below that begin or end with a soft **g.**

6. gem 7. log 8. edge 9. germ 10. get 11. judge 12. language 13. pig

Directions: Circle the words below that begin or end with a hard **g.**

14. glue 15. good 16. fog 17. fudge 18. go 19. huge 20. gave 21. girl

TIP: Words like **glue** and **good** have the vowel-vowel pattern. Another way to say vowel-vowel is V/V.

Directions: Write the letters on the lines. See how many words you can make.

b f sl h tr c gr

22. b og
23. f og
24. sl og
25. h og
26. c og
27. gr og
28. b udge
29. f udge
30. sl udge
31. tr udge
32. gr udge

Student page 68

Story Words

Directions: Read each word to yourself. Then say the word out loud. Write the word on the line. Check the box after each step.

33. rhythm Read ☑ Say ☑ Write ☑ rhythm
34. planets (plan|ets) Read ☑ Say ☑ Write ☑ planets
35. astronomy (as|tron|o|my) Read ☑ Say ☑ Write ☑ astronomy
36. telescope (tel|e|scope) Read ☑ Say ☑ Write ☑ telescope
37. observe (ob|serve) Read ☑ Say ☑ Write ☑ observe

More Word Work

The ending **er** means "more." The ending **est** means "most." You can add **er** or **est** to many descriptive words.

Example: A baseball is bigger than a golf ball, but a basketball is the biggest of all three.

Directions: Add **er** or **est** to the words below. Write the new word on the line.

38. tall + er = taller
39. kind + est = kindest
40. fast + er = faster
41. loud + er = louder
42. rich + est = richest

TIP: Use an adjective that ends in **er,** also called a **comparative** adjective, when you compare two things. When you compare more than two things, use an adjective that ends in **est,** which is called a **superlative.**

Directions: Circle the correct word for the sentences below.

43. A car is (smaller / smallest) than a truck.
44. The winner of the marathon is the (faster / fastest) runner.
45. A bear is (bigger / biggest) than a dog.
46. A shout is (louder / loudest) than a whisper.
47. The Empire State Building was once the (taller / tallest) building in the world.

Student page 69

Reading "Finding New Friends," Part 1

Preview and Predict

- Tell students that they are going to read a fiction story about a boy named José and the friends he makes during his first week at a new school. Have a volunteer read the title of the selection on Student Worktext page 70 aloud.
- Read aloud the sentences and question under **Use What You Know** at the top of page 70. Invite students to tell about a situation when they didn't know anyone. Students can just name the situation, without describing their feelings or the outcome aloud. Then have students write about what they know on page 70.
- Tell students to preview the selection by reading the first two paragraphs. Invite students to predict what will happen on José's first day.

Have students read Student Worktext pages 70–71 to learn more about José's first week of school.

Strategy Modeling

Make a Prediction Tell students that they can make a prediction, or a guess, about what is going to happen in the story. Sometimes they can use clues that the author gives. Sometimes they can make predictions based only on what they think. Explain to students that by making a prediction they can keep track of story events. Model using information that the author provides in the text. You might say:

In the story, José thinks that his friend Peter might be a little dull. He wonders what it would be like to have a friend who is funny. He wonders what it would be like to have a friend like Fearless. The author then tells about how Fearless and José sit next to each other in science class. I think this is a clue from the author telling us that José and Fearless will become friends.

Have students pause at the top of page 72 to make a prediction before reading on. Then have them finish Part 1 of the story by reading Student Worktext pages 72–73.

Focus on ESL/LEP

Have students who are new to the school tell about their first experiences at the school. Invite them to make comparisons between their new school and their former school—what they thought as they entered the building, whether they knew anyone, and what their first classes were like. Help students talk through their experiences. Invite the other students to ask questions.

Learning Styles

Interpersonal/Group Learning Divide students into small groups. Have them discuss the first part of the story. Ask them to discuss what the most important things to know about their school are. Have them talk about what kinds of qualities they look for in friends.

LESSON 1 ▸ Reading "Finding New Friends" Part 1

Use What You Know

José is starting the year at a new school. We all begin new things at different times in our lives. How does it feel to be in a new place where you don't know anyone? Write what you think on the lines below. Then read on to find out how José feels about being in a new school.

Answers will vary.

FINDING NEW FRIENDS, PART 1

Ding! The bell was loud. In an instant, door after door opened and students flowed into the long hallway. José held his ground the best he could. He turned first this way, then that way, as students whirled past him. He remembered what his mother had said at breakfast that morning. "Today's an exciting day. Just think of all the new friends you're going to make."

José felt **invisible** as he watched the boys and girls, laughing and talking all around him. He wanted to feel excited but he was scared. He said to himself, "They all know where they're going. They already know each other. How will I ever make friends?"

Just then José felt a hand on his shoulder. He looked up into the smiling face of a tall man. "You must be José," the man said. "I'm Principal Wang, welcome to Franklin High School."

"Thank you, sir," said José.

Principal Wang turned to a small boy **hunched over** from the weight of a huge backpack. "This is Peter," said the principal. "He'll be your guide for your first week."

Peter pushed his glasses up on his nose and reached out to shake José's hand. "Hi," he said. "We have most of the same classes, so I'll show you around. I'll make sure you don't get lost or anything."

Ding! The bell rang again. "That's the first period bell. You boys had better get to class. And don't worry about anything, José. You'll soon get into the rhythm of things here." The principal smiled and walked away.

All week Peter showed José how to get around school. He introduced him to his friends. He told him important things like which teachers would allow you to do extra-credit work. He told him which books would be necessary to bring every day. He told him never to order the meatloaf in the cafeteria. Most important of all, he told him never to be late for Mr. Brown's science class.

Student page 70

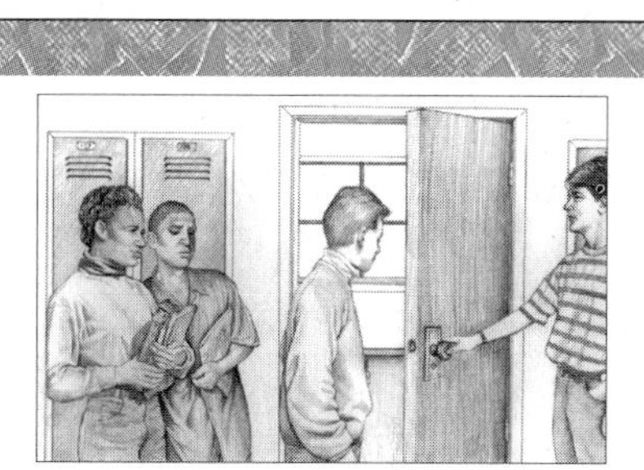

"You see this?" Peter pulled a long metal tube out of his book bag. "Mr. Brown knows I'm interested in the planets and stars. I told him I'm planning to major in astronomy at college, so he loaned me this telescope. He's nice, but he's also strict. His class is one of the hardest in the school. If you get to his class even eight seconds after the late bell rings, he won't let you in. He sends you to the principal's office. Believe me, you don't want to end up there."

José liked Peter. He was a lot like José's friends at his old school. They were the kids who always did their homework. They were the kids whom all the teachers and parents liked. Yes, José liked his new friend, but sometimes he thought maybe Peter was a little dull. He wondered what it would be like to have a friend who was funnier. He wondered what it would be like to have a friend whom his parents and teachers might not like, someone like Fearless.

Everybody in school knew Fearless. The boy's real name was Stan, but the kids called him Fearless. They all thought he was the funniest kid in school. But the teachers didn't always laugh at his jokes. Fearless had a gag in Mr. Brown's class. Every day he would get to class the latest, just as the late bell rang. It drove Mr. Brown crazy the way the kids would laugh. Fearless would high-five his way to the back of the room.

One day in class, Fearless sat at the desk next to José's. José smiled at him, but Fearless just turned away and put his head down on the desk. José sat back to listen to the teacher. Soon he heard a strange sound. He looked over at Fearless. The noise was coming from the boy. Softly, at first, then louder and louder— "Snuchh, shhhhhh. Snuchh, shhhhh."

Student page 71

Ask students the following questions about the selection.

- What did Peter tell José never to order in the cafeteria? (meatloaf)
- Which class did Peter tell José never to be late for? (Mr. Brown's science class)
- Why did Fearless drive Mr. Brown crazy? (He would get to class just as the late bell rang, and he would give his classmates high-fives as if to congratulate himself for pushing the rules to the limits.)
- Why did Fearless know the answer to the question that Mr. Brown asked, even though he was sleeping? (José told him.)
- Why did José avoid looking at Peter when he sat down with Fearless? (Answers may vary. He didn't want to see Peter's look of disapproval. He didn't want Peter to convince him not to stay with Fearless.)
- Why did the lunch monitor tell the boys to calm down? (They were banging on the table and chanting.)
- Why did the boys use the back door to leave the building? (So they wouldn't be seen. Also, it was close to Mr. Brown's science class, so they could get back to class quickly.)
- How were the boys going to get back in through the locked door? (Peter would open it for them.)
- Why did José decide to go for pizza with Fearless? (He thought that if he didn't do it, Fearless would never be his friend.)

What do you think Fearless is doing? Circle your answer.

sneezing   taking notes   sleeping   listening to music

Then keep reading to find out what Fearless is doing.

Fearless was snoring! Every eye in the classroom turned to observe him. The teacher called out, "Stan! There is no sleeping in my class."

Fearless lifted his head from the desk. "I wasn't sleeping. I was just resting. I heard every word you said."

"Oh really," said Mr. Brown. "Then I'm sure you can tell us one part of the scientific process."

Fearless looked at Mr. Brown. Everyone waited for Fearless to speak. José whispered out of the side of his mouth, "Experimentation, experimentation."

"Uh, you know," said Fearless. "Experiments."

Mr. Brown looked surprised but said nothing.

The next day in the lunchroom Fearless called out to José and Peter. "Hey, come here. You're José, right?"

"Yeah," said José.

"That was pretty cool what you did in class yesterday, thanks."

"Oh yeah, well, I just wanted to help," said José.

Fearless nodded to some boys sitting with him. "This is Kenny, Rick, and Chucky."

"Hi," said José.

"Hey," said the boys.

"Hello," said Peter.

Fearless pointed to some empty chairs at the table and said, "Sit down."

José quickly pulled out a chair and sat down. He looked up at Peter. His friend didn't say anything. Then, slowly, Peter sat down, too.

José couldn't believe his luck. He thought Fearless was the coolest kid he had ever known. He was glad to be sitting with him and his friends. However, for some reason, José avoided looking at Peter.

Clang! Fearless dropped his fork on the table. He poked at a soggy fishcake on his plate. "This isn't food," he grumbled. "It's garbage."

The boys laughed loudly. "The meatloaf is even worse," said José. "Why don't they serve hot dogs or pizza?"

"That's a great idea," Fearless smiled. "Let's get pizza!"

"Boy, could I go for a slice," said Kenny.

Rick started to pound the table and Chucky joined in. "Pizza, pizza!" the two boys chanted.

The lunchroom **monitor** walked by, "Calm down boys."

Student page 72

Fearless quieted his friends. He leaned in and whispered, "Who wants to get pizza?"

José whispered back, "What do you mean? Now?"

Fearless nodded, "Let's go to the mall and get some real food."

"You can't leave school," said Peter.

"Why not?" Chucky grinned.

Peter ignored him and turned to José, "Mr. Brown is reviewing for tomorrow's science test. You better not miss class."

"We won't miss class," said Fearless. "We'll be back before the period starts."

"I suppose you think you can just walk in and out the front door without being stopped," said Peter.

"We'll use the back door. The one by the stairs next to Mr. Brown's class," said Fearless.

"That door is always locked," said Peter.

Fearless nodded, "That's why we need you to wait by it at the beginning of the period. When we knock, you open the door."

Peter turned to José, "Don't do this. Don't get in trouble your first week in school."

José looked at Peter. He looked at Fearless. "If I don't do this now," José thought to himself, "Fearless will never be my friend."

José pushed his food tray away. "I'm still hungry," he said.

Fearless smiled and slapped José on the back. "That's the way to do it," he said.

Peter shook his head sadly. "Okay, but if you're not back before the late bell rings, I'm going to class." ▶

Student page 73

Focus on LD

Point out some of the concepts that may be unfamiliar to students:

- astronomy
- telescope
- experiments

After Reading "Finding New Friends," Part 1

Personal Response: You Be the Judge

Read aloud the question under **You Be the Judge** on Student Worktext page 74. Ask students to think about how they deal with peer pressure. Ask them to think about whether they have gotten into trouble for going along with their friends. Then have students answer the questions.

Think About the Story: Reading Comprehension

Have students complete the remaining items on Student Worktext pages 74–75 independently or in pairs. Check their responses to help you assess their story comprehension. If students' responses indicate that they did not understand story events, reread the story aloud, pausing to discuss key events.

Reading Comprehension Skill: Recognize Cause and Effect

Explain to students that knowing the causes of events can help them see the whole story. Tell students that the cause is what makes an event happen. For example, *Because the bus was late* (cause), *I was late for school* (effect). Have students tell the causes and effects in these sentences.

> Lucy was soaking wet when she arrived. She had forgotten to take her umbrella.
>
> My computer doesn't work anymore because I spilled water on the keyboard.
>
> I swam laps all summer to get in shape for the championship swim meet. I placed second.

Have students think about the causes and effects in the story they read. Ask students these questions:

- What happened when Peter told Mr. Brown he wanted to major in astronomy in college? (Mr. Brown loaned Peter his telescope.)
- What will cause a student to get into trouble with Mr. Brown? (being late to class)
- What was the effect when José told Fearless the answer to Mr. Brown's question? (Fearless invited José to sit with him at lunch.)

Look Ahead

Tell students that they will learn more about José in the next story. Ask students to form small groups and use the **Look Ahead** question at the bottom of page 75 to help them predict what will happen next.

LESSON 1 ▸ After Reading "Finding New Friends," Part 1

You Be the Judge

1. José is cutting class to impress a new friend. Is it worth doing something you think is wrong to make a friend? What should he have said when Fearless asked him to go eat pizza? Write what you think on the lines below.
   Answers will vary.

Think About the Story

Use Story Words

Directions: Look at your list of story words on page 69. Write a story word on each line.

2. The class turned to observe Fearless snoring.
3. Astronomy is the study of outer space.
4. A telescope is used to see things from a distance.
5. Peter was interested in the planets and stars.
6. Principal Wang told José he would get into the rhythm of school.

When Did it Happen?

7. Write a number from 1 to 5 in front of each event to show when it happened.
   - 3 José helps Fearless in science class.
   - 5 José decides to cut class.
   - 2 Peter shows José around school.
   - 1 José goes to a new school.
   - 4 Fearless asks José to cut class.

Student page 74

Write Sentences About the Story

Directions: Circle the word that best fits in each sentence. Then write the sentence on the line.

8. Ding! The bell was (louder / (loud)).
   Ding! The bell was loud.
9. José thought Peter was (dull / (duller)) than Fearless.
   José thought Peter was duller than Fearless.
10. Mr. Brown's class was one of the (harder / (hardest)) in school.
    Mr. Brown's class was one of the hardest in school.
11. Peter thought Mr. Brown was a ((nice) / nicer) teacher.
    Peter thought Mr. Brown was a nice teacher.

Words and Meanings

Directions: Think about how the **bold** words are used in the story. Then circle the words that show the meaning of each word or phrase.

12. José feels **invisible** because ____.
    - (a. no one talks to him at school)
    - b. he can't see himself in the mirror
    - c. he can walk through walls
13. A small boy **hunched over** from the weight of a backpack was ____.
    - a. guessing its contents
    - (b. bent over)
    - c. propelled across the room
14. The **monitor** in the lunchroom is ____.
    - a. a computer display
    - b. a large tropical lizard
    - (c. a student assistant)

Look Ahead

15. Who do you think will prove to be a better friend? Should José listen to Peter or to Fearless? Write what you think on the lines below. Then read on to find out what happens.
    Answers will vary.

Student page 75

Reinforce & Extend

STUDY SKILL: Locating Information Using an Encyclopedia

Explain to students that an encyclopedia contains information about many topics. An encyclopedia can be in paper or electronic form. When it is in paper form, it is usually a set of books. In electronic form, an encyclopedia can be on CD-ROM, the Internet, or a computer network.

Tell students that topics in an encyclopedia are arranged alphabetically. Write these words on the board: *computer, Arctic Circle, Saturn, Big Dipper.* Have students write the terms in alphabetical order.

Show students a volume from a set of encyclopedias. Show students an entry and point out and explain the guide words at the top of the page. Explain any abbreviations or special features of the entry. If you have access to an online encyclopedia, show students how to search for a term using key words or the index. Then have students look up the terms on the board in an encyclopedia.

Reading and Writing Practice Activity 40 provides additional practice using an encyclopedia.

LANGUAGE: Subject-Verb Agreement

Write these sentences on the board:

These books are heavy.

This box of books is heavy.

Read the first sentence aloud. Ask a volunteer to tell what the simple subject is. (books) Invite another volunteer to tell what the verb is. (are) Tell students that the subject and verb agree. Explain:

- A verb must "match" or "agree with" its subject.
- A singular subject must have a singular verb. (Michael walks to school.)
- A plural subject must have a plural verb. (Noah and Kerrie walk to school.)

Point out to students what makes a verb singular and plural. Draw a table on the board with three rows and four columns. *Write I, You,* and *He/She/It* in the first column. Write *We, You,* and *They* in the third column. Write *Singular* above the first and second columns and *Plural* above the third and fourth. Conjugate several verbs for students, both regular and irregular, in the second and fourth columns.

Ask students to name the simple subject of the second sentence on the board. (box) Ask them to name the verb. (is) Ask students whether the sentence has subject-verb agreement. (yes)

Write these sentences on the board and have students tell whether the subject and verb agree in each.

They is going to the ball game tonight. (no)

The girls is trying out for the basketball team today. (no)

He do not like spinach. (no)

Reading and Writing Practice Activity 41 provides additional practice with subject-verb agreement.

WRITING: A Descriptive Paragraph

Explain to students that descriptive writing helps the reader to "see" what the writer describes. A good descriptive writer uses details that vividly describe a person, a place, a thing, or an idea. Explain:

- Writers should use words related to the five senses—taste, touch, smell, sound, and sight.
- The readers should feel like they are actually experiencing the same thing as the writer.
- Other sentences add details to support or clarify the idea or viewpoint.
- The last sentence sums up the main idea of the paragraph.

Write the five senses across the top of the board. Ask students to provide words that describe the school on their first day as they first walked into it. Encourage them to use more than just sight descriptions. As students name words or phrases, write them in the appropriate category.

Reading and Writing Practice Duplicate and distribute Activities 42 and 43 on writing a descriptive paragraph. Then have students complete the activities in pairs.

Lesson at a Glance

Chapter 2, Lesson 2 "Finding New Friends, Part 2

Preview: This lesson presents the second part of a fiction story about a boy and the new friends he meets in a new school.

Objectives

- to read a fiction story
- to read words with *ough* and *augh*
- to form words with the suffixes *ly, ful, less, ness, ment,* and *y*
- to recognize the author's purpose in a fiction story
- to organize information using charts and timelines
- to use the correct verb tense
- to recognize the theme in a piece of writing

Student Worktext Pages 76–83

Story Words

army, property, particular, conference, gestured, disappointed

Reading and Writing Practice Activities 44–48

Before Reading "Finding New Friends," Part 2

Letters and Sounds

Reading Words with *augh* and *ough*

Write the words *daughter, wrought, tough, dough,* and *drought* across the board. Pronounce each word. Point out the *augh* in *daughter* and the *ough* in the other words. Ask students to name the word with the same vowel sound as daughter. (wrought) Point out the two different spellings that make the same sound.

Say the words *wrought, tough, dough,* and *drought* aloud again. Explain to students that all of these words have different vowel sounds, even though the letters that make the different sounds (ough) are the same. Tell students that they will have to memorize the pronunciations of these words.

Ask students to name other words that contain *augh* or *ough*. Sort them into categories by pronunciation, writing them on the board underneath the words with a corresponding sound. Then have students complete Student Worktext page 76.

Reading and Writing Practice Activity 44: Reading Words with *augh* and *ough*.

Story Words

Read aloud these words: *army, property, particular, conference, gestured, disappointed.* Tell students that these words are important in the next story they will read. Then write the words on the board and point to each one as you say it aloud a second time. Have students follow the ❑ *Read* ❑ *Say* ❑ *Write* sequence by completing **Story Words** on Student Worktext page 77. Remind students to write the story words in the Word Bank at the back of their Student Worktext. To introduce the words in context, write these sentences on the board:

- The government maintains a national army for defense.
- My uncle owns property on which he plans to build a house.
- His taste in clothes is very particular.
- The teachers attended a conference.
- He gestured for the woman to come forward.
- Tom was disappointed that his team lost.

Have students make a word card for *army*. Ask a volunteer to read the first sentence aloud. Then have students copy the sentence onto the back of the word card. Follow the same procedure for the remaining words. To assess students' abilities to read each new word, listen as individual students read the sentences on the board aloud.

Reading and Writing Practice Activity 45: Reading Story Words.

More Word Work

Have students complete **More Word Work** on Student Worktext page 77.

Reading and Writing Practice Activity 46: Forming Words with Suffixes.

LESSON 2 ▸ Before Reading "Finding New Friends," Part 2

Letters and Sounds

Directions: The letters **ough** and **augh** appear in many words. Read the words below. Write the word on the line. Then circle the letters **ough** or **augh.**

1. through through
2. fought fought
3. caught caught
4. naughty naughty

Directions: The letters **ough** have different sounds in different words. These **ough** words all have the sound like the letter **o** in the word **lost.** Read these words. Write them on the lines.

5. thought thought
6. fought fought
7. sought sought

Directions: These **ough** words all have the sound like the letter **ou** in the word **out.** Read these words. Write them on the lines.

8. bough bough
9. plough plough
10. sough sough

Directions: These **ough** words all sound like the letter **u** in the word **cut.** Read these words. Write them on the lines.

11. enough enough
12. rough rough

Directions: Write the letters on the lines. See how many words you can make.

b f s th thr tr pl en c l t

13. l augh
14. b ought
15. f ought
16. s ought
17. th ought
18. c aught
19. t aught
20. b ough
21. th ough
22. thr ough
23. tr ough
24. pl ough
25. en ough
26. c ough

Directions: These words have three syllables. Write each word on the line. Draw a line between each syllable.

27. general gen|er|al
28. connection con|nec|tion
29. remember re|mem|ber
30. janitor jan|i|tor

Student page 76

Story Words

Directions: Read each word to yourself. Then say the word out loud. Write the word on the line. Check the box after each step.

31. army (ar|my) Read ☑ Say ☑ Write ☑ army
32. property (prop|er|ty) Read ☑ Say ☑ Write ☑ property
33. particular (par|tic|u|lar) Read ☑ Say ☑ Write ☑ particular
34. conference (con|fer|ence) Read ☑ Say ☑ Write ☑ conference
35. gestured (ges|tured) Read ☑ Say ☑ Write ☑ gestured
36. disappointed (dis|ap|point|ed) Read ☑ Say ☑ Write ☑ disappointed

More Word Work

Directions: You can add the letters **ly** to many words. Add **ly** to make a word tell how something was done. Add **ly** to each word.

Example: quick quick + ly = quickly

37. soft softly
38. slow slowly
39. glad gladly
40. bad badly
41. loud loudly

TIP: A suffix is an ending added to a word. The letters **ly** form a suffix. The endings **ful, less, ness, ment,** and **y** are also suffixes.

Directions: Add the suffixes to the words below. Write the word on the line.

Example: harm + less = harmless

42. wish + ful = wishful
43. care + less = careless
44. retire + ment = retirement
45. tall + ness = tallness
46. spook + y = spooky

Student page 77

Reading "Finding New Friends," Part 2

Preview and Predict

- Remind students about Part 1 of the fiction story they read about a boy named José and the friends he made during his first week at a new school. Ask students to summarize what happened in Part 1.
- Tell students that they will finish reading the story in this lesson. Have a volunteer read aloud the title of the selection on Student Worktext page 78.
- Read aloud the sentence and question under **Use What You Know** at the top of page 78. Invite students to think about whether they have broken any school rules and whether they were caught. Then have students write about what they think on page 78.
- Invite students to tell about what they would do if they were the school principal and they caught a student leaving school grounds against school rules.
- Tell students to preview the selection by reading the first few paragraphs. Invite students to predict what will happen when José leaves school.

Have students read Student Worktext pages 78–79 to learn more about José's first week of school.

Strategy Modeling

Summarize Tell students that they can summarize parts of the story as they read to help them understand it. Explain to students that when they summarize, they remember the key events of the story. Summarizing can help students draw conclusions about what they have read. Modeling this process will help develop students' ability to summarize on their own. You might say:

The boys disobeyed school rules by leaving the building for lunch and then lied to the man at the pizza counter. While at the pizza place, they created a scene and didn't clean up after themselves. José apologized and cleaned up before he left. I think José was not having fun because he was nervous about leaving school. I think he was embarrassed about what his new friends were doing.

Have students pause at the top of page 80 to summarize before reading on. Then have them finish the story by reading Student Worktext pages 80–81.

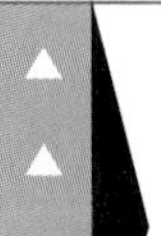

Focus on ESL/LEP

Check that non-native speakers of English know the meanings of idioms and dialogue in the story, such as "We're moving out" and "Then you'll pay."

LESSON 2 Reading "Finding New Friends," Part 2

Use What You Know

To impress his new friend, José has broken school rules. Will he be sorry? Write what you think on the lines below. Then read on to find out what happens.

Answers will vary.

FINDING NEW FRIENDS, PART 2

The boys gathered at the door by the stairwell near Mr. Brown's class. Fearless took a hat out of his pocket and fit it snugly on his head. He spoke as if he were a general in the army. "Listen up boys," he said. "Our **mission** is to get through that door, across the parking lot, and off school property."

Chucky began to chant in a low voice, "Pizza, pizza, pizza!"

Chucky became quiet when Fearless glared at him. "We better watch out for Principal Wang. He keeps an eye on the parking lot at this time of day."

José swallowed hard. Peter touched his arm and said, "Are you sure you want to do this?"

José pretended to feel brave. He shrugged free of Peter's hand. "I said so, didn't I?"

"Yeah, Peter," said Fearless. "Just remember to be here to open the door at the beginning of next period."

"I'll be here," frowned Peter.

"Okay, everybody follow me." Fearless opened the door and poked his head outside. He turned to the boys. "We're moving out. Let's go!"

One by one the boys slipped out the door. Fearless and Rick were in front of José. Chucky and Kenny were behind him. José felt as if he were caught in a strong current. His only choice was to swim along with the others. They kept low, moving from car to car. Suddenly Fearless called out, "Get down!"

All five boys dropped to their knees. José heard a loud banging noise. He raised his head and peeked over the hood of the car. The school janitor was emptying trash into a bin. The janitor finished and went back inside the school. José breathed a sigh of relief. Fearless called out, "Let's move."

Again the boys moved from car to car. With shouts of glee they turned the corner away from school. Once more Chucky began a chant of "Pizza, pizza, pizza!" This time all the boys joined in.

Student page 78

The mall was only a couple of minutes from school. Soon the boys found themselves in front of the pizza shop. They entered and marched straight to the counter. The man behind the counter looked at the clock on the wall. He said, "Aren't you boys supposed to be in school?"

"No," Fearless lied. "It's a half day today."

"Yeah," Kenny added. "Teachers and parents conference."

"In that case, what can I do for you?"

"We want pizza," said Rick.

"Then you boys are in luck, because that's what I sell."

The boys paid for their food and sat down in a booth to eat. The pizza was hot and cheesy. The tomato sauce was spicy. It was very good pizza. José hardly tasted it.

Fearless poked him, "Hey, this was a great idea."

"It's good pizza," said José.

"It's the best," said Fearless. "We're lucky Peter doesn't have the guts to do anything but wait at the door for us."

José felt that he should defend Peter, but he didn't know what to say. He took a bite of pizza instead.

Have you ever wanted to defend a friend? What should José have said to Fearless? Write what you think on the lines below. Then keep reading to find out what takes place.

Answers will vary.

Student page 79

Ask students the following questions about the selection.

- What reason did Fearless give to the man in the pizza shop for the boys being out of school? (It was a half day due to teacher and parent conferences.)
- Why didn't José defend Peter when Fearless made cruel remarks about Peter? (He didn't know what to say. Students may say that he didn't want to offend his new friend.)
- What were the boys doing in the pizza shop that they shouldn't have been? (throwing napkins)
- Why didn't José get to the door in time? (He tripped, which slowed him down.)
- Who caught José outside the door? (Principal Wang)
- Why didn't Peter tell Principal Wang what happened? (He was a good friend. He didn't want to get José into trouble.)
- Why did Peter tell Principal Wang that it was his fault? (He was supposed to be José's guide.)
- Why did Principal Wang decide not to call José's parents? (José was new.)
- What did Peter realize by the story's end? (It's better to have a friend that he can count on, like Peter, than friends like Fearless, whom he couldn't.)

Focus on LD

Point out some of the concepts that may be unfamiliar to students:

- *benefit of the doubt* (When there is a chance that someone could be wrong about his or her ideas about someone else, it is better to not give in to one's feelings of doubt. The person reserves judgment until receiving more information.)
- *can count on* (can depend on)

Just then Chucky wadded up a napkin and threw it at Rick who yelled, "Hey! What are you doing?"

"Sorry," said Chucky, "I was trying to hit Kenny."

"Then you'll pay!" said Kenny. He threw a napkin at Chucky. Soon all the boys were laughing and throwing napkins. All of the boys fought except José. He sat still, not knowing what to do.

The man behind the counter called out, "Boys, you can't do that in here!"

The boys jumped up and ran out of the store laughing. José picked up the napkins his friends had thrown and put them in the garbage can. He looked at the man and said, "Sorry mister."

When the boys got back to school they could see Peter holding open the door. They raced toward him. José tripped, and his feet flew out from under him. He landed on the ground. Looking up, he saw sneakers and blue jeans racing by him. José heard the door slam shut. He leaped up and ran toward the door. He pulled on it. It was locked and wouldn't open. He knocked on the door. He pounded on the door.

Then a hand touched his shoulder. José was fearful as he turned around. "I think you better come with me," said Principal Wang.

José sat in the waiting room outside Principal Wang's office. The door to the office was closed, but José could hear voices coming from inside. It sounded like Principal Wang and a student were talking. José wondered if Fearless or one of the other boys had been caught. He wondered what punishment he would get.

The door opened and Principal Wang gestured for José to come in. He got up and slowly walked into the office. José looked at the other student. "Peter!"

José sat down. Principal Wang looked sternly at the two boys. "José, I'm hoping you can help me understand something. I found you outside banging on the back door to the school. Mr. Brown also found Peter inside hanging around the back door. It seems to me there must be a connection between these two events. However, Peter has chosen not to say anything. Can you tell me what was going on, José?"

"Well," mumbled José.

"Speak up. I can't hear you."

"Sorry, sir. I guess I went to get some pizza at the mall, sir."

"Are you aware that it is against school rules to leave the grounds?"

"Yes sir," said José. "But Peter had nothing to do with it. I just wanted some pizza so I left."

Student page 80

Principal Wang looked at Peter. He looked at José. "I'm very disappointed in you José. Your first week at Franklin High School and you break a very important rule. I'm afraid I'm going to have to call your parents."

Peter sat up in his chair. "Please don't do that! I'm José's guide. I'm supposed to make sure his first week is a good one. It's my fault, sir."

Principal Wang turned to José and asked, "Do you think that's true?"

"No," said José. "Peter tried to stop me, but I wouldn't listen."

Principal Wang was quiet for a long time. Then he said, "I am very **particular** about students following the rules. I know Peter. He is always willing to do the right thing. Since you are new, José, I am willing to give you the benefit of the doubt. Just this one time, I will not call your parents. I will not call either of your parents. But you must both stay after school today. Will you accept these terms?" Both boys nodded.

Out in the hall the two boys looked at each other. José said, "What happened to Fearless and the others?"

"They heard Mr. Brown coming and ran up the stairs. He took me away before I could let you back in. So, did you have fun?"

"Not really," said José. "They were acting like fools when we got the pizza. I think I prefer a friend like you that I can count on."

"Yeah, me too," said Peter.

The two boys smiled and walked back to class.

Student page 81

After Reading "Finding New Friends," Part 2

Personal Response: You Be the Judge

Read aloud the question under **You Be the Judge** on Student Worktext page 82. Ask students to think about the friends they have and what makes them good friends. Then have students answer the question.

Think About the Story: Reading Comprehension

Have students complete the remaining items on Student Worktext pages 82–83 independently or in pairs. Check their responses to help you assess their story comprehension. If students' responses indicate that they did not understand story events, reread the story aloud, pausing to discuss key events.

Reading Comprehension Skill: Recognize the Author's Purpose

Explain to students that everything is written for a reason, or a purpose. Knowing why something was written can give them ideas of what to expect. Have students tell the purpose for each of these writing situations.

- A letter to the principal asking for permission to leave the building for lunch (to persuade or convince)
- A fantasy story about escaping to an underground world with talking animals (to entertain)
- A report about the effects of pollution (to inform, possibly to convince someone to take action)

Invite students to suggest what the author's purpose might be for writing "Finding New Friends." (Answers will vary but may include the idea that the author wanted to write a story about the importance of having friends you can count on.)

LESSON 2 ▸After Reading "Finding New Friends," Part 2

You Be the Judge

1. At first, José thought that Fearless was exciting and that Peter was dull. Who do you think was really the better friend, Peter or Fearless? Write what you think on the lines below.
Answers will vary.

Think About the Story

Use Story Words

Directions: Look at your list of story words on page 77. Write a story word on each line.

2. A conference is a meeting.
3. Students were not allowed to leave school property.
4. Principal Wang gestured for José to come in.
5. Fearless spoke to the boys like an army general.
6. The principal was very particular about students following rules.
7. Principal Wang was disappointed in José.

When Did It Happen?

8. Write a number from 1 to 5 in front of each event to show when it happened.
3 José trips and falls.
1 José, Fearless, and some boys cut class.
5 José and Peter walk back to class.
2 The boys throw napkins in the pizza parlor.
4 The principal catches José.

Write Sentences About the Story

Directions: Use words from the story to answer these questions.

9. What does José do when Peter asks him if he really wants to sneak out for pizza?
José pretends to feel brave and says, "I said so, didn't I?"

Student page 82

10. How do the boys respond when the counter man at the pizza shop says, "Aren't you boys supposed to be in school?"
They lie. Fearless says it's a half day. Kenny says there's a parents and teachers conference.

11. When Principal Wang asks him to explain why he was outside banging on the back door to the school, what does José say?
José says he wanted some pizza so he left and that Peter had nothing to do with it.

Words and Meanings

Directions: Think about how the **bold** words are used in the story. Then circle the words that show the meaning of each word or phrase.

12. Fearless said, "Our **mission** is to get through that door." Here mission means a ____.
a. church
b. goal or aim (circled)
c. business

13. Principal Wang said, "I am very **particular** about students following the rules." Here particular means ____.
a. concerned over details (circled)
b. not interested
c. happy

Why Did It Happen?

Directions: Draw a line from each story event to the reason it happened.

Event	Reason
14. The pizza store owner kicked out the boys from his shop.	Mr. Brown took him away from the door.
15. Peter did not open the door for José.	The boys were throwing napkins.
16. José was taken to the principal's office.	He was caught cutting class.

Student page 83

Reinforce & Extend

STUDY SKILL: Organizing Information Using Charts and Timelines

Explain to students that when they collect information for a topic they will write about, they should organize it in such a way that they can understand it and determine if they are missing any information.

Write these topics on the board: *pollution, air, water, land, fossil fuels, chemical run-off, oil spills, factory pollutants, litter, buried chemicals.* Explain to students that these ideas could be organized better in a chart. Draw a chart on the board. Ask students to name a topic from the list that could be the title for the chart. (pollution) Write *air, water,* and *land* each at the top of a column. Have students tell where to write the rest of the topics in the chart.

air	water	land
fossil fuels factory pollutants	chemical run-off oil spills	litter buried chemicals

Next, explain that a timeline is another way to organize information; however, the information records *when* an event takes place. Draw a long line on the board. Use an example, such as the events of the Civil War, to mark off tick marks on the timeline and label them with dates and events. Tell students that timelines contain information on what, when, where, and who of an event.

Reading and Writing Practice Activity 47 provides additional practice with organizing information using charts and timelines.

LANGUAGE: Past, Present, and Future Verb Tense

Write these sentences on the board.

Last night I couldn't fall asleep.

I can't hear you because I have my headphones on.

Someday Sandra will go to medical school.

Read the first sentence aloud. Ask volunteers to tell whether each sentence already happened, is happening now, or will happen in the future.

Tell students that verb tense tells when an action happens—in the past, present, or future. Explain:

- Use the present tense with repeated actions and actions taking place now. Examples of the present tense are *I usually run early in the morning* and *I am trying to study for this test.*
- Use the past tense to indicate something that already happened.
- Use the future tense to indicate something that has not happened, but will.
- The simple past tense is usually formed by adding *ed* to the end of the verb. Example: *walk, walked.* English has many irregular verbs whose forms must be memorized. Examples: *go, went; eat, ate; am, was; are, were*
- The future tense is formed by adding the words *shall* or *will* to the verb. Example: *I will visit Rome while I'm in Europe.*
- Key words can indicate which tense to use. For example, *yesterday, last night,* and *a long time ago,* tell that an action took place in the past. *Tomorrow, someday,* and *when* tell that an action will happen in the future. *When I go to college, I will study computer science.*

Reading and Writing Practice Activity 48 provides additional practice with verb tenses.

LITERARY APPRECIATION: Theme

Explain to students that the theme is the main idea or message of a story. It is the one central idea of the story. Ask students to name the theme of "Finding New Friends." Ask them to think of the one idea that story is about. (friendship) If students are having trouble identifying the theme, tell them to think about the author's purpose for writing. Students can then whittle down that purpose to one main theme. Invite students to tell the themes of other stories they have read.

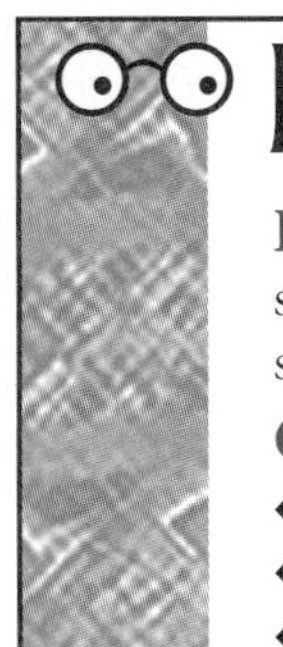

Lesson at a Glance

Chapter 2, Lesson 3 "Second Sight"

Preview: This lesson presents a nonfiction selection about the training of blind people and seeing-eye dogs.

Objectives

- to read a nonfiction selection
- to read and spell words with *ie* and *ei*
- to form compound words
- to make judgments about text
- to form and understand the use of the perfect tenses of verbs
- to write a how-to paragraph that gives directions

Student Worktext Pages 84–91

Story Words

partner, permanent, pedestrian, enduring

Reading and Writing Practice Activities 49–55

Before Reading "Second Sight"

Letters and Sounds

Reading and Writing Words with *ie* and *ei*

Write the words *achieve, deceive, reindeer, height, seize,* and *forfeit* on the board. Tell students that these words contain either *ie* or *ei*. Say the word *achieve* aloud. Explain to students that *ie* is usually pronounced like the *ee* in *need*. Encourage students to name other words with the *ie* spelling.

Then say *deceive, reindeer, height, seize,* and *forfeit* aloud. Circle the *ei* in each word. Tell students that the *ei* spelling has several different sounds. It can sound like the *ee* in *need*, the *a* in *cane*, the *i* in *nice*, or the *i* in *fit*. Tell students that because there are so many sounds for *ei*, there are no rules for pronunciation. Therefore, these words must be memorized.

Go over the "*i* before *e*" rule in the tip box on Student Worktext page 84. Point out that there are exceptions to the rule. Have students look through their Student Worktext for examples of words with the *ie* or *ei* letter combinations. Then have students complete Student Worktext page 84.

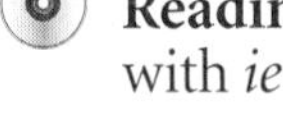

Reading and Writing Practice Activity 49: Reading and Writing Words with *ie* and *ei*.

Story Words

Read aloud these words: *partner, permanent, pedestrian, enduring.* Tell students that these words are important in the next story they will read. Then write the words on the board and point to each one as you say it aloud a second time. Have students follow the ❑ *Read* ❑ *Say* ❑ *Write* sequence by completing **Story Words** on Student Worktext page 85. Remind students to write the story words in the Word Bank at the back of their Student Worktext. To introduce the words in context, write these sentences on the board:

- Doctor Watson was Sherlock Holmes's partner.
- The mark was made with permanent ink.
- A pedestrian was crossing the road in front of her car.
- Survival depends upon enduring life's hardships.

Have students make a word card for *partner*. Ask a volunteer to read the first sentence aloud. Then have students copy the sentence onto the back of the word card. Follow the same procedure for the remaining words. To assess students' abilities to read each new word, listen as individual students read the sentences on the board aloud.

Reading and Writing Practice Activity 50: Reading Story Words.

More Word Work

Have students complete **More Word Work** on Student Worktext page 85.

Reading and Writing Practice Activity 51: Forming Compound Words.

LESSON 3 ▸ *Before Reading "Second Sight"*

Letters and Sounds

Directions: These words have a long **e** vowel sound. They are spelled with an **ie** and sound like the letters **ee** in the word **bleed.** Write the word on the line. Circle the vowels that make the **e** sound in each word.

1. believe believe
2. piece piece
3. brief brief
4. relief relief

Directions: These words have the long **a** vowel sound. They are spelled with **ei** as in the word **neighbor.** Write the word on the line. Circle the vowels that make the long **a** in each word.

5. freight freight
6. vein vein
7. eight eight
8. reign reign

TIP: Here is a rhyme to help you remember an **ei/ie** spelling rule. Use **i** before **e** when sounded as **ee,** except after **c,** or when sounded like **a,** as in **neighbor** and **weigh.**

Directions: As the rhyme reminds us, we use **ei** after the letter **c.** The word **conceit** is an example. Write the word on the line. Circle the vowels **ei** in each word.

9. receive receive
10. deceit deceit
11. perceive perceive
12. ceiling ceiling

Directions: The **ei** after **c** rule does not always work. We use **i** before **e** when **c** has a **sh** sound. The word **glacier** is an example. Write the word on the line. Circle the **ie** in each word.

13. ancient ancient
14. species species
15. conscience conscience

Directions: Below are some words that are missing the letters **ei** or **ie.** Write the correct letters on the line to complete the words.

16. f ie ld
17. rec ei pt
18. sh ie ld
19. w ei ght
20. dec ei ve
21. th ie f
22. sl ei gh
23. w ei gh
24. p ie rce

Student page 84

Story Words

Directions: Read each word to yourself. Then say the word out loud. Write the word on the line. Check the box after each step.

25. partner (part|ner) Read ☑ Say ☑ Write ☑ partner
26. permanent (per|ma|nent) Read ☑ Say ☑ Write ☑ permanent
27. pedestrian (pe|des|tri|an) Read ☑ Say ☑ Write ☑ pedestrian
28. enduring (en|dur|ing) Read ☑ Say ☑ Write ☑ enduring

More Word Work

Directions: Two words can be put together to make a new word called a **compound word.** The compound word usually has a new and different meaning from the words that make it. Use the list to find a match for each word below. Write the matching word on the line. Then write the new compound word.

Example: back + yard = backyard

car book seed cloth pin

29. hand + book = handbook
30. table + cloth = tablecloth
31. bird + seed = birdseed
32. box + car = boxcar
33. hair + pin = hairpin

Directions: Some compound words are joined with a hyphen (-) because the first word modifies the second. Some are not joined at all. Use the list to find a match for each word below. Write the matching word on the line. Then write the new compound word.

Example: saddle + blanket = saddle blanket

eye bus -eater wool

34. school + bus = school bus
35. fire + -eater = fire-eater
36. eagle + eye = eagle eye
37. steel + wool = steel wool

Student page 85

Reading "Second Sight"

Preview and Predict

- Tell students that they are going to read a nonfiction selection about how blind people and guide dogs are trained to work together. Ask students if they have seen a blind person with a guide dog. Ask them if it seemed as though the dog was working.
- Have a volunteer read the title of the selection on Student Worktext page 86 aloud. Have students look at the picture, and invite them to tell what the title means. (A guide dog acts as a blind person's eyes. A blind person's first sight has been lost, so the dog is a person's second chance at sight.)
- Read aloud the sentence and question under **Use What You Know** at the top of page 86. Invite students to tell about a situation when they learned to do something difficult. Then have students write about what they know on page 86.
- Tell students to preview the selection by reading the first two paragraphs. Invite students to predict what the selection will be about.

Have students read Student Worktext pages 86–87 to learn more about the training of guide dogs and their blind masters.

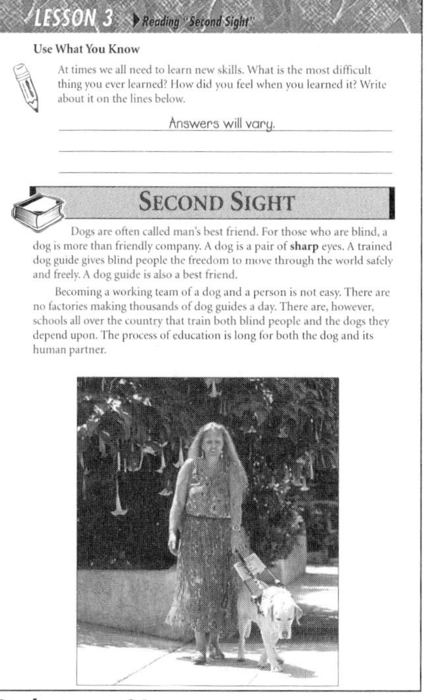

LESSON 3 ▸ Reading "Second Sight"

Use What You Know

At times we all need to learn new skills. What is the most difficult thing you ever learned? How did you feel when you learned it? Write about it on the lines below.

Answers will vary.

SECOND SIGHT

Dogs are often called man's best friend. For those who are blind, a dog is more than friendly company. A dog is a pair of **sharp** eyes. A trained dog guide gives blind people the freedom to move through the world safely and freely. A dog guide is also a best friend.

Becoming a working team of a dog and a person is not easy. There are no factories making thousands of dog guides a day. There are, however, schools all over the country that train both blind people and the dogs they depend upon. The process of education is long for both the dog and its human partner.

Student page 86

A dog begins schooling as a puppy. Around the age of eight weeks, the puppy is placed with a foster family. There it receives training and gets used to being around people. When the dog is about a year old, it goes off to school for a series of tests. These tests help the school decide whether the dog is likely to make a good guide. Dogs that fail the tests are placed in permanent homes. Those that pass the tests go into a training program.

For the next four-to-six months, the dog learns everything it needs to become a dog guide. The dog learns to stay focused. It learns to ignore food, smells, and other animals. It learns to remain undistracted by such noises as shouting or music from a passing car radio. It learns to follow commands like "right," "left," or "forward." The dog learns to stop before every curb and stairway and to avoid moving objects. In short, good dog guides learn to keep their owners safe while they go about the everyday actions of life. A dog that has completed training will be assigned a master.

Before the dog guide and its new master can be united, the owner also has to undergo some training. Not every blind person is able to handle a dog. Just as the school tries to decide which dogs will make a good guide, they must also decide which people will be able to work well with a dog.

To be accepted as a student, each person must first undergo a medical exam. The school must be sure a person is in good shape. The person must also have a good sense of balance and direction. But most important, the school wants to find out if the person is the right kind of person to own a dog. To find this out, the school asks many questions: Do you enjoy a dog following you around your home? Do you enjoy a dog **tongue washing** your face? Have you ever owned a dog before? The school asks these and many other questions to learn if the person will be a good dog owner and student.

Once accepted, the student is still not quite ready to meet the new dog. First the student must attend classes to learn how to care for a dog. The student learns to bathe and brush a dog's hair, to clean a dog's ears, and brush its teeth. It is important to know what to feed a dog and what to do if the animal becomes sick.

Then comes instruction for putting a harness on the dog. The harness is a series of straps attached to a handle. The owner holds onto the harness while walking with the dog. The harness is a sign that the dog is on the job. The dog will know not to be distracted from guiding its partner. This is also the reason why you should never pet or distract a dog guide in harness.

After all these basics are learned, the moment that both dog and owner have been waiting for arrives. They meet each other.

Student page 87

Strategy Modeling

Set a Purpose Explain to students that they should determine ahead of time what information should be gathered from the selection. Students who set a purpose for reading will have definite expectations about the text they are about to read. They will be more engaged in their reading and will notice more in what they read. Model setting a purpose before students read further. You might say:

I want to find out how dogs are trained to be guide dogs and how humans learn to trust guide dogs. I will read the selection to find out.

Have students pause at the top of page 88 to set a purpose for reading before reading on. Then have them finish the selection by reading Student Worktext pages 88–89.

Focus on ESL/LEP

Have students who are from other countries tell about how animals help people there. Encourage students to use culture-specific terms. Invite them to share the names of animals in their native language. Native speakers of English can also think about how animals help people in this country. For example, dogs are also trained to track people and things by learning their smell.

Ask students the following questions about the selection:

- How do the dog and master become a team? (By walking together on the school grounds, through courses, and then off school property around the block and on the streets near the school.)
- What is the hardest part of training for some blind people? (learning to follow the dog or completely trusting the dog)
- What happened when Rod didn't trust Smokie's direction? (He ran into an obstacle and a parking meter.)
- Do you think it's possible for someone to forget his or her blindness, like Rod? (Answers will vary.)
- What does Rod feel for Smokie? (gratitude, love, partnership, friendship)

Focus on LD

If students are having trouble answering the questions above, go back and reread the parts of the story that go along with each question. Interpret each passage as it relates to the question. For example, say "This selection shows Rod's feelings of gratitude and love when he says, 'My gratitude to Smokie is as eternal as my love for him.'"

Learning Styles

Body/Kinesthetic Have students work in pairs to simulate the experience of a blind person. Have one person wear a blindfold and the other person act as the guide. Have the guide lead the blind person around the building. Ask students to see if they can completely trust their guide. Monitor students closely so that no one is harmed.

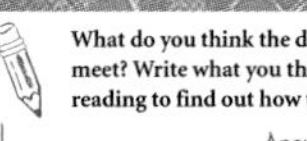

What do you think the dog and owner must learn after they meet? Write what you think on the lines below. Then keep reading to find out how the new partners become a real team.

Answers will vary.

Once dog and master are **matched,** the real work begins. For the next month, the two spend every hour of the day together. They work hard to become a team. At first they practice walking together on the school grounds. They walk the courses set up by their teachers. Then they take their first steps off school property. They take a walk around the block first. Soon they move about all the streets near the school. They walk in streets filled with mailboxes and newsstands, pedestrians, bicycles, and cars. They face all the things that sighted people take for granted.

For some, the hardest part of the training is learning to follow the dog. In his book *Walking with Smokie, Walking with Blindness,* Rod Michalko describes his first experiences learning to follow his dog guide, Smokie. They had trouble on their first trip outside the school building. Rod was told to go to a field behind the school. The route to the field was familiar to him. Rod had been using it since his first days at the school. With Smokie's harness in his hand, Rod left the school. He turned left toward the field. Suddenly, Smokie began moving right. Rod knew that the sidewalk was to the left. He guided Smokie back toward the field. Rod's trainer told him to command Smokie to stay. He asked Rod if the word "guide" meant anything to him. The trainer then explained that Smokie was guiding Rod around a post that had been placed in the middle of the sidewalk.

But this experience was still not enough to teach Rod to follow his dog. Later that week he got into more serious trouble. Rod and Smokie were walking down the street at their usual fast pace. Then Smokie began to veer left. Thinking the dog was making a mistake, Rod did not follow. Just then he bumped into a parking meter. Rod felt the full force of the post in the middle of his chest. It was very painful. **From then on,** Rod always followed Smokie!

Student page 88

When their training is completed, the new dog guide team must get settled at home. Even though their schooling has ended, their learning continues. As long as the two are a team they will continue to learn about each other. They will learn each other's needs, likes, and dislikes. They will learn about the world around them. Rod says that when he and Smokie walk down the street, he forgets his blindness. He focuses on where he is going and the world around him. He also says that Smokie makes him experience his blindness in new ways. His dog helps him to think about what is truly important in life. He says, "Smokie is my guide, my partner, and my friend. My gratitude to Smokie is as eternal as my love for him."

For some, the only bond closer than the one they share with their dog guide is with their husband, wife, or child. They are partners with their dog guide. They know that without the help of their dog, their life would not be as fulfilling. Their partnership is a working one, but it is also an enduring friendship.

◆

Student page 89

After Reading “Second Sight”

Personal Response: You Be the Judge

Read aloud the question under **You Be the Judge** on Student Worktext page 90. Ask students to think about people they know who own dogs. Ask them to think about what would be important to them in life. Then have students answer the question.

Think About the Story: Reading Comprehension

Have students complete the remaining items on Student Worktext pages 90–91 independently or in pairs. Check their responses to help you assess their story comprehension. If students’ responses indicate that they did not understand story events, reread the story aloud, pausing to discuss key events.

Critical Thinking Skill: Make Judgments

Explain to students that they can make judgments about texts to gain a deeper understanding of the meaning. Tell students that judgments are their own decisions about the characters, events, or information in a selection. Ask students to make judgments about “Second Sight.”

- Do you think it’s reasonable to be distrustful of a guide dog at first?
- Do you think a blind person’s sense of what is important is different from a sighted person’s?

Ask students to make judgments about other selections they have read.

LESSON 3 ▸ After Reading “Second Sight”

You Be The Judge

1. Dog-guide schools want to make sure their students are the right kind of person to own a dog guide. What kind of person do you think is best suited to owning a dog? Write what you think on the lines below.
   Answers will vary.
2. Rod Michalko said that his blindness helps him to realize what is important. What do you think he means? What do you think is important?
   Answers will vary.

Think About the Story

Use Story Words

Directions: Look at your list of story words on page 85. Write a story word on each line.

3. A dog guide is trained to be a partner for a sightless person.
4. A pedestrian walked along the sidewalk and then crossed the street.
5. An enduring relationship is one that lasts a long time.
6. Dogs that fail the dog guide test are placed in permanent homes.

The Big Idea

7. Circle the sentence that tells what the whole story is about.
   a. Never pet a dog guide in harness.
   b. People and dogs train a long time to work well as a team. (circled)
   c. Dog guides begin their training when they are still puppies.

Student page 90

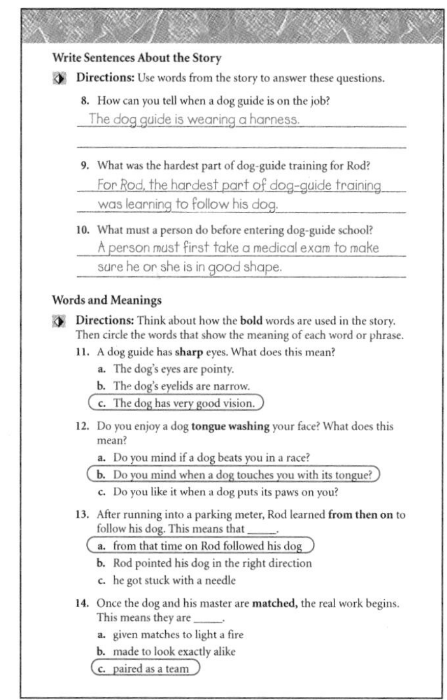

Write Sentences About the Story

Directions: Use words from the story to answer these questions.

8. How can you tell when a dog guide is on the job?
   The dog guide is wearing a harness.
9. What was the hardest part of dog-guide training for Rod?
   For Rod, the hardest part of dog-guide training was learning to follow his dog.
10. What must a person do before entering dog-guide school?
    A person must first take a medical exam to make sure he or she is in good shape.

Words and Meanings

Directions: Think about how the **bold** words are used in the story. Then circle the words that show the meaning of each word or phrase.

11. A dog guide has **sharp** eyes. What does this mean?
    a. The dog’s eyes are pointy.
    b. The dog’s eyelids are narrow.
    c. The dog has very good vision. (circled)
12. Do you enjoy a dog **tongue washing** your face? What does this mean?
    a. Do you mind if a dog beats you in a race?
    b. Do you mind when a dog touches you with its tongue? (circled)
    c. Do you like it when a dog puts its paws on you?
13. After running into a parking meter, Rod learned **from then on** to follow his dog. This means that ____.
    a. from that time on Rod followed his dog (circled)
    b. Rod pointed his dog in the right direction
    c. he got stuck with a needle
14. Once the dog and his master are **matched,** the real work begins. This means they are ____.
    a. given matches to light a fire
    b. made to look exactly alike
    c. paired as a team (circled)

Student page 91

Reinforce & Extend

SPELLING: Words with *ie* and *ei*

1. deceive **2.** counterfeit **3.** believe **4.** ceiling **5.** weight **6.** seize **7.** neither **8.** neighbor **9.** brief **10.** relief

Write the words *chief, perceive, sleigh,* and *either* on the board. Remind students of the rule "*i* before *e* except after *c* or in rhyming with *say*, as in *neighbor* and *weigh*." Point out to students that this is only a general rule and that there are many exceptions. Then have students number a sheet of paper 1–10. Dictate the words above, one at a time, pausing for students to write them. Finally, write the words on the board and have students check each word, making corrections as needed.

Reading and Writing Practice Activity 52 provides more practice spelling words with *ie* and *ei.*

LANGUAGE: Perfect Tenses of Verbs

Write these sentences on the board.

The bus has been on schedule every day this week.

I had been to the museum many times before I got a job there.

Cory will have been at bat 200 times after today's game.

Read the sentences aloud. Ask volunteers to circle the verb in each sentence. (*has been, had been, will have been*). Ask students to tell what each verb has in common. (They all contain the word *been* and a form of the helping verb *have*.) Tell students that all of these sentences have perfect tense verbs. Remind students that tense tells the time of the verb. Explain:

- The perfect tense is used when an event happens presently or at a time when spoken of.
- The perfect tense is formed from the verb *have* and the past participle of the main verb.
- The present perfect states an action that is still going on. Add *has* or *have* before the past participle. The verb in the first sentence is in the present perfect tense. The week is still happening, so the perfect tense (not the simple past) is used.
- The past perfect tense states an action that began and was completed in the past. It is often used to relate *two* events that happened in the past. Add *had* before the past participle to form the past perfect tense. The verb in the second sentence is in the past perfect tense because it tells about two actions, both of which are completed. The past perfect tense shows which one happened first (had been to the museum many times).
- The future perfect states an action that will begin in the future and will end at a specific time. Add *will have* before the past participle. The third sentence is in the future perfect tense. The action has not happened yet.

Reading and Writing Practice Activity 53 provides additional practice with the perfect tenses.

WRITING: A How-to Paragraph

Tell students that to give directions or explain things, they have to know the details. They must either gather the details or think carefully about what they know. Explain to students that they should follow these steps when writing a how-to paragraph.

- Take notes about the subject. Either research it or write down the information that you know.
- Explain your topic clearly. Begin with a topic sentence or title that names the subject.
- Explain the topic from start to finish using steps.
- Read your paragraph to test whether you were clear enough or left anything out. For example, in writing directions to a place, imagine you are actually going there. This will make your how-to paragraph more visual.

Reading and Writing Practice Duplicate and distribute Activities 54 and 55 on writing a how-to paragraph giving directions. Then have students complete the activities in pairs.

Lesson at a Glance

Chapter 2, Lesson 4 "Student Volunteer"

Preview: This lesson presents a nonfiction selection about the different ways students volunteer their time to help other people or groups.

Objectives

- to read a nonfiction selection
- to read and spell words with the schwa sound
- to form contractions
- to compare and contrast ideas
- to use the correct pronoun
- to write a business letter

Student Worktext Pages 92–99

Story Words

southern, bonus, boredom, yellow

Reading and Writing Practice Activities 56–62

Before Reading "Student Volunteer"

Letters and Sounds

Reading and Writing Words with the Schwa Sound

Write the words *furnace, lunches, spirit, carrot,* and *submit* on the board. Tell students that these words contain the five vowels and that each of these vowels can make the schwa sound. Pronounce the schwa sound for students. It sounds like a short *u* sound but only occurs in unstressed syllables. Pronounce the words, emphasizing the stressed syllable. Invite volunteers to come to the board and circle the letter that makes the schwa sound in each word. (*a, e,* second *i, o, u*) Write the schwa symbol ə on the board and tell students that this symbol is used in the dictionary to represent the schwa sound.

Explain to students that combinations of letters (digraphs) can also have the schwa sound. For example, jeal<u>ou</u>s and cert<u>ai</u>n. Words with certain endings often have the schwa sound. These include *al, el, le, er, or, ar, es, is, en, on, ion, ed, id, sion, tion.* Write the words *squirrel, movable, doctor,* and *fashion* on the board. Invite students to circle the letters that make the schwa sound in each word. (*e, e, o, io*)

Have students complete Student Worktext page 92.

Reading and Writing Practice Activity 56: Reading and Writing Words with the Schwa Sound.

LESSON 4 ▸ Before Reading "Student Volunteer"

Letters and Sounds

TIP: The sound of the **i** in the word **easily** is called the **schwa** sound. The vowels **a, e, i, o, u** can all make the **schwa** sound. The **schwa** sound is usually in the unstressed part of the word.

Directions: Write the words on the lines. Then circle the letters that make the **schwa** sound.

1. recommend recommend
2. divide divide
3. license license
4. suppose suppose
5. compass compass

TIP: The letter patterns **al, el, le, er, or, ar, es, is, ed, id, en, on,** and **ion** can all stand for the **schwa** sound.

Directions: Write the words on the lines. Then circle the letters that make the schwa sound.

6. table table
7. technical technical
8. maple maple
9. material material
10. humor humor
11. flower flower
12. added added
13. candid candid
14. particular particular
15. counter counter
16. piston piston
17. companion companion
18. person person
19. listen listen
20. question question
21. collision collision
22. decision decision
23. fasten fasten

Directions: The suffixes **sion** and **tion** are found at the end of many words. Circle the suffix that correctly completes the words below. Write the new word on the line.

24. posi (sion / tion) position
25. inva (sion / tion) invasion
26. preci (sion / tion) precision
27. addi (sion / tion) addition
28. crea (sion / tion) creation
29. colli (sion / tion) collision
30. tradi (sion / tion) tradition

Student page 92

Story Words

Read aloud these words: *southern, bonus, boredom, yellow.* Tell students that these words are important in the next story they will read. Then write the words on the board and point to each one as you say it aloud a second time. Have students follow the ❏ *Read* ❏ *Say* ❏ *Write* sequence by completing **Story Words** on Student Worktext page 93. Remind students to write the story words in the Word Bank at the back of their Student Worktext. To introduce the words in context, write these sentences on the board:

- The sun rises in the east and moves across the <u>southern</u> sky before setting in the west.
- At the end of the year, I got a <u>bonus</u> with my paycheck.
- When I do the house cleaning, I listen to music to help to lessen my <u>boredom</u>.
- My little brother always colors the sun <u>yellow</u> in his pictures.

Have students make a word card for *southern.* Ask a volunteer to read the first sentence aloud. Then have students copy the sentence onto the back of the word card. Follow the same procedure for the remaining words. To assess students' abilities to read each new word, listen as individual students read the sentences on the board aloud.

Reading and Writing Practice Activity 57: Reading Story Words.

More Word Work

Have students complete **More Word Work** on Student Worktext page 93.

Reading and Writing Practice Activity 58: Forming Contractions.

Story Words

Directions: Read each word to yourself. Then say the word out loud. Write the word on the line. Check the box after each step.

31. southern (south|ern) Read ☑ Say ☑ Write ☑ southern
32. bonus (bo|nus) Read ☑ Say ☑ Write ☑ bonus
33. boredom (bore|dom) Read ☑ Say ☑ Write ☑ boredom
34. yellow (yel|low) Read ☑ Say ☑ Write ☑ yellow

More Word Work

Directions: You can make a **contraction** by joining two words together. **I'm** is a contraction of the words **I** and **am.** Match the contractions with the two words that make them. Write the words on the line.

35. we'll we will — a. it is
36. can't can not — b. could have
37. it's it is — c. we would
38. we'd we would — d. we will
39. could've could have — e. can not

TIP: When two words are joined to make one new word, letters are left out to shorten them. An apostrophe (') marks the place where letters are left out.

Student page 93

Reading "Student Volunteer"

Preview and Predict

- Tell students that they are going to read a nonfiction selection about how students volunteer their time and effort to help other people and organizations. Ask students if they know anyone who volunteers and invite them to describe what the volunteers do.
- Invite a student to read the title of the selection on Student Worktext page 94 aloud. Have students look at the picture, and ask them to tell what they know about volunteer building projects. (Students will probably have heard of Habitat for Humanity.)
- Read aloud the sentences and questions under **Use What You Know** at the top of page 94. Invite students to think about times when they have helped people. They need not have built houses or run a food drive. Then have students write about what they know on page 94.
- Challenge students to think of other ways they could help in their school and community by volunteering. For example, tutoring other students, coordinating a study group, or helping pick up trash on the school grounds.
- Tell students to preview the selection by reading the first paragraph. Have students tell about rewards that they might get from volunteering. Ask students to predict what kinds of volunteer work will be discussed in the selection.

Have students read Student Worktext pages 94–95 to learn more about how students volunteer.

Strategy Modeling

Clarify Explain to students that if they are unclear or confused about an idea from the text, they can read ahead for specific information in order to clarify the idea. Model clarifying by reading ahead before students read further. After reading the paragraph about Priya and Habitat for Humanity, you might say:

I do not completely understand what real benefits there are from volunteering. I know that it makes people feel good and it builds up physical skills, such as carpentry, but what can volunteering actually do for me? If I read on, I see that volunteering may help build a résumé that may be useful in getting a job.

Have students pause at the top of page 96 to clarify anything before reading on. Then have them finish the selection by reading Student Worktext pages 96–97.

Learning Styles

Interpersonal/Group Learning Invite students who have done volunteer work to prepare a short presentation to the class. If you have several volunteers, you may want to make this a group activity. Have the students describe their daily activities, any preparation they must do, and the rewards that they receive for volunteering. Encourage the other students to ask questions and sense the person's motives for volunteering.

LESSON 4 ▸ Reading "Student Volunteer"

Use What You Know

This is a story about students who help other people. At times we all help others. How have you helped people around you? Did you work alone or with others? Write your answers on the lines below.

Answers will vary.

STUDENT VOLUNTEER

Every year, over half of all students in the United States volunteer their time and **services.** While some simply collect money once a year for a favorite charity, others work hours each week for a group. Volunteers tutor other students and work in hospitals and homeless shelters. They help at daycare centers and senior citizen homes. They answer the phones at crisis centers. Though their level of help varies, volunteers all help society. Some even charge full-speed ahead and create volunteer groups of their own. Student volunteers give freely and, in the process, they gain many rewards.

Our country has a long tradition of volunteer service to others. In colonial times it was common for people to help each other. People would care for sick neighbors or bring food and clothing to families in need. By the middle of the 1800s, people who had formerly worked on their own

Student page 94

began to form groups to help others. Volunteer groups such as the Red Cross, Boys Clubs, Goodwill Industries, and the American Cancer Society were all formed during this period. These groups and many others like them continue their good work to this day.

Student volunteers come from many backgrounds, both rich and poor. They live in the cities and rural areas of the southern and northern states. They can also be found from east to west. They're male and female students with excellent and average grades. They represent every ethnic group, race, and religion. Though different in every possible way, volunteers share the belief that they can bring about change.

Jessica, a student at the University of Missouri in Columbia, explains why she volunteers. "I've been taught about the importance of giving back to the community all my life. I've assisted in holiday **drives** at school, and at church for families in need. As a high school student, I began to realize that volunteering was not just an activity that benefited nameless people in faraway places, but rather something that helped real families, just like mine, to get by during hard times. This motivated me to increase my own volunteering, as well as to talk my peers into such activities."

Like Jessica, many students volunteer because of a strong desire to make changes in the world. When they see a problem, such as homelessness, they want to help. That was why Priya, a student volunteer living in Atlanta, got involved in Habitat for Humanity. Habitat is a group that fights homelessness by building houses. Volunteers do everything from nailing down shingles to painting walls. Priya said, "I loved building for Habitat. It was hard but very gratifying." Priya doesn't feel helpless in the face of life's challenges. As a volunteer for Habitat, she helped many people. Learning new skills was a bonus.

Some students find volunteer work may help to build a résumé. This can be useful when applying to colleges or for a job. Jack had volunteered his services at many nonprofit theaters in Oklahoma City where he lives. He is a talented actor. Volunteering to work at theaters was something he loved to do. Jack also found that his volunteer work helped him to get a job he wanted. His theater credentials was a deciding factor in landing a part-time job with a film company. It's important to know that many employers, including federal and state governments, accept volunteer experiences as work history.

Besides being a good way to build a résumé, Jack also thinks that volunteering is fun. He describes a good volunteer experience he had. "As president of my high school's chapter of the National Honor Society, I volunteered our club to ring the Salvation Army bell at a local mall over Christmas break. Not enough of our members signed up for **shifts.** A few

Student page 95

Ask students the following questions about the selection:

- What should you ask yourself before volunteering? (what you would like to get from the experience)
- What are the benefits of volunteering? (learning new skills, gaining work experience, sharing a hobby, meeting new people, making friends)
- How can you learn more about volunteer opportunities? (go to the library to view listings of volunteer groups, contact the National Volunteer Center)
- How can students form volunteer groups? (develop a group at school with an adviser)
- What are some of the volunteer activities mentioned in the selection? (holiday drives at school, helping needy families through religious groups, building houses, acting in a community theater, collecting money by ringing a bell, conducting a children's story hour, bringing live music to senior citizens, educating the public about recycling, printing stories for literacy groups, loading trucks with food for the needy)

Learning Styles

Interpersonal/Group Learning Have students work in pairs or groups to discuss ways that they, as students, could get other students involved in volunteer activities. For example, they might suggest making posters or sending out flyers showing pictures of people or organizations that have benefited from volunteer service. They might try to emphasize the benefits of volunteering—making friends, having fun, feeling good about yourself.

Focus on ESL/LEP

Have students who are from other countries tell about how people help each other in those countries. Encourage students to explain culture-specific ideas. For example, a student from Asia might tell about how the elderly are revered in society and how people show respect to the elderly by helping to care for them or providing them with companionship. Students might also tell about how volunteers have helped them learn the English language or become familiar with American customs.

of us had to split up about twenty hours of leftover time. I was not too eager to ring the Salvation Army bell in the cold in five-hour shifts for two days in a row, but it turned out to be a great experience. After a couple of hours, our boredom overcame our embarrassment, and we started singing Christmas carols. It was a lot of goofy fun, and people seemed to be much more generous once we started singing."

Would you like to be a volunteer? Explain why or why not on the lines below.

Answers will vary.

Before volunteering, ask yourself what you'd like to get from it. Do you have a certain concern, such as pollution or the environment? Are you interested in learning a new skill or gaining things to put on your résumé? Do you have an interest or hobby, such as music or art that you want to share with others? Are you simply interested in meeting new people and making new friends? Once you've answered these questions, you're ready to seek out volunteer groups.

A good place to start your search is at your school library. The librarian can **direct** you to listings of volunteer groups. Another resource is the National Volunteer Center. There are offices located in states all across the country. They are ready and able to direct you to groups in your region.

If you see an unmet need in your area, you can start your own group. Maybe you would like to create a weekly story hour for neighborhood children. Maybe you could bring live music to senior citizen centers. Perhaps you see a need to teach the public about proper ways to recycle.

Whatever your goal, you'll need to get organized. A great place to form your group is at school. A teacher who is willing to advise you can help your group become an official student group. Schools can often provide space for meetings. Sometimes, they can even provide funding.

Student volunteers have done wonderful things to help their areas. They have painted kitchen walls yellow for Habitat for Humanity. They have sung Christmas carols and played the triangle for the Salvation Army. Students have printed collections of stories for literacy groups. They have

Student page 96

loaded trucks to deliver food to the hungry. They have done all this and much more. It seems like the only thing students are unwilling to do is not try to make the world a better place.

Whether you start your own group or join an existing one, you'll find that the rewards of volunteering are great. You will make new friends, learn new skills, and learn things to help you get a job. And, perhaps most important, you will enjoy the feeling of helping others.

◆

Student page 97

After Reading "Student Volunteer"

Personal Response: You Be the Judge

Read aloud the question under **You Be the Judge** on Student Worktext page 98. Ask students to think about whether there are any negatives to volunteering. Then have students answer the question.

Think About the Story: Reading Comprehension

Have students complete the remaining items on Student Worktext pages 98–99 independently or in pairs. Check their responses to help you assess their story comprehension. If students' responses indicate that they did not understand story events, reread the story aloud, pausing to discuss key events.

Reading Comprehension Skill: Compare and Contrast

Explain to students that comparing is exploring the similarities of two things and contrasting is exploring the differences. For example, to compare and contrast two restaurants, you might talk about how the food, prices, environment, and service were alike and different. Tell students that they can compare and contrast ideas in the text to help them understand it better. Have students compare and contrast volunteer work with paid work.

LESSON 4 ▸ After Reading "Student Volunteer"

You Be the Judge

1. There are many different reasons to volunteer. Do you think students should volunteer? Why or why not? Write what you think on the lines below.

   Answers will vary.

Think About the Story

Use Story Words

Directions: Look at your list of story words on page 93. Write a story word on each line.

2. Volunteers paint walls yellow.
3. Student volunteers come from the northern, eastern, western, and southern parts of our country.
4. When people complain of boredom they are usually to blame.
5. The good feeling volunteers gain is a bonus for their hard work.

Who Did What?

Directions: Match the person or group with the correct sentence.

6. Priya b
7. Goodwill Industries d
8. Jack a
9. Student volunteers e
10. Jessica c

a. got a job with a film company.
b. built houses for Habitat for Humanity.
c. is a student at the University of Missouri.
d. was founded in the middle of the 1800s.
e. come from all over the country.

Student page 98

Write Sentences About the Story

Directions: Use words from the story to answer the questions.

11. Do many students in the United States care about helping other people?

    Every year over half of all students volunteer. They collect money for charities, tutor, and work for volunteer groups.

12. Why do students volunteer to help other people?

    Some want to make changes in the world. Some find that volunteer work may help apply to colleges or get jobs.

13. What questions must you ask yourself if you want to do volunteer work?

    What would you like to get from the experience? Do you want to join a group or start you own?

Words and Meanings

Directions: Think about how the **bold** words are used in the story. Then circle the words that show the meaning of each word or phrase.

14. Volunteers believe in **services** to others. Here services means ____.
    a. the army
    b. giving help (circled)
    c. going to church
15. The librarian can **direct** you to books about volunteer groups. Here direct means ____.
    a. the librarian can help you put on a show
    b. the librarian will be right with you
    c. the librarian can show you books (circled)
16. Jessica has assisted in holiday **drives** at school. Here drives means ____.
    a. an effort to raise money (circled)
    b. a car pool
    c. a trip
17. Jack said, "Not enough of our members signed up for **shifts**." He means ____.
    a. moving around
    b. work periods (circled)
    c. dresses

Student page 99

Reinforce & Extend

SPELLING: Words with the Schwa Sound

1. bountiful
2. hesitate
3. esteem
4. holiday
5. original
6. anticipation
7. astronomy
8. lesson
9. signal
10. actor

Remind students that the schwa sound can be spelled by any vowel and many combinations of vowels. The schwa sound is heard in unstressed syllables in words with two syllables or more. Tell students that they will not be able to tell how to spell words with the schwa sound just from the pronunciation. Then have students number a sheet of paper 1–10. Dictate the words above, one at a time, pausing for students to write them. Finally, write the words on the board and have students check each word, making corrections as needed.

Reading and Writing Practice Activity 59 provides additional practice spelling words with the schwa sound.

LANGUAGE: Pronouns

Write these sentences on the board:

She and I have the same class.

Give the books back to us when you are finished.

We gave them a new computer.

Invite students to the board to circle all the pronouns in the sentences. (first sentence: She, I; second sentence: us, you; third sentence: We, them) Remind students that a pronoun stands for a noun. Explain:

- There are two cases of personal pronouns: subjective and objective.
- Subjective pronouns are the subject of a sentence or clause. *I, you, he, she, it, we,* and *they* are subjective pronouns.
- Objective pronouns are the object of a phrase, sentence, or clause. *Me, you, him, her, it, us,* and *them* are objective pronouns.

Reading and Writing Practice Activity 60 provides additional practice with pronouns.

WRITING: A Business Letter

Tell students that people still write business letters, even though e-mail is very popular. Explain to students that they can write a business letter to request information, make a complaint, or persuade someone. Bring in several business letters to show students. Explain the following steps to writing a business letter.

- Write the heading, which gives the writer's complete address and the date.
- Write the inside address, which gives the name, title, and address of the person to whom you are writing.
- Write the salutation, or the greeting. Use a colon after the salutation. For example, *Dear Mr. Walker:*
- Write the body of the letter. You should open with your reason for writing. Then present all the important facts that your reader needs to know. Use short, clear paragraphs. Then explain what action you want the reader to take.
- Follow with the closing and your signature. The first word of the closing should be capitalized. A comma should follow the last word. For example, *Yours truly,* is often used. In a typed letter leave several spaces after the closing before typing your name. Sign your letter in the space after you print it.
- When you have finished the letter, proofread it for mistakes. Errors make a bad impression. Make sure the reader will be able to follow what you say. Make sure you did not say too much or too little.

Discuss the formatting of a business letter with students. There should be blank lines between the different sections.

Reading and Writing Practice Duplicate and distribute Activities 61 and 62 on writing a business letter. Then have students complete the activities in pairs.

Lesson at a Glance

Chapter 2, Lesson 5 "Blood Brothers," Part 1

Preview: This lesson presents a fiction story about a rivalry between two brothers.

Objectives
- to read a fiction story
- to read words with the schwa sound
- to use the suffixes *able* and *ible*
- to distinguish fact from opinion
- to use diagrams and maps as graphic aids
- to use possessive pronouns
- to understand the use of narrative voice

Student Worktext Pages 100–109

Story Words

column, molecules, repeated, western, Paris

Reading and Writing Practice Activities 63–67

Before Reading "Blood Brothers," Part 1

Letters and Sounds

Reading and Writing Words with the Schwa Sound

Write the words *woman, absent, cousin, balcony,* and *subtract* on the board. Tell students that these words each contain one of the five vowels that have the schwa sound. Remind students what the schwa sound and symbol are. Remind students that the schwa sound only occurs in unstressed syllables. Pronounce the words, emphasizing the stressed syllable, so that students can clearly hear the syllable that is unstressed. Invite volunteers to come to the board and circle the letter that makes the schwa sound in each word. (a, e, i, o, u) Then have students complete Student Worktext page 100.

Reading and Writing Practice Activity 63: Reading and Writing Words with the Schwa Sound.

Story Words

Read aloud these words: *column, molecules, repeated, western, Paris.* Tell students that these words are important in the next story they will read. Then write the words on the board and point to each one as you say it aloud a second time. Have students follow the ❑ *Read* ❑ *Say* ❑ *Write* sequence by completing **Story Words** on Student Worktext page 101. Remind students to write the story words in the Word Bank at the back of their Student Worktext. To introduce the words in context, write these sentences on the board:

- They have asked me to write a column for the school newspaper.
- All of the elements can be broken down into molecules.
- My mother repeated herself when I didn't answer her question.
- California is in the western United States.
- The Eiffel Tower is located in Paris.

Have students make a word card for *column.* Ask a volunteer to read the first sentence aloud. Then have students copy the sentence onto the back of the word card. Follow the same procedure for the remaining words. To assess students' abilities to read each new word, listen as individual students read the sentences on the board aloud.

Reading and Writing Practice Activity 64: Reading Story Words.

More Word Work

Have students complete **More Word Work** on Student Worktext page 101.

Reading and Writing Practice Activity 65: Using the Suffixes *able* and *ible.*

LESSON 5 ▸ Before Reading "Blood Brothers," Part 1

Letters and Sounds

TIP: The **a** vowel sound in **ago** is called the **schwa** sound. The letters **a, e, i, o, u, io,** and **le** can all stand for the **schwa** sound.

Directions: Write the words on the lines. Then circle the **schwa** sounds.

1. person ___person___
2. listen ___listen___
3. tragedy ___tragedy___
4. direction ___direction___
5. position ___position___
6. castle ___castle___
7. wrestle ___wrestle___
8. fasten ___fasten___
9. companion ___companion___
10. collision ___collision___
11. comedy ___comedy___
12. question ___question___
13. thimble ___thimble___
14. decision ___decision___

TIP: A **schwa** sound is usually in the unstressed part of the word.

Directions: Write each word where it belongs in the chart.

sleepily, noisily, whistle, castle, enlighten, whiten, soften, nestle

happily	frighten	thistle
15. sleepily	17. enlighten	20. whistle
16. noisily	18. whiten	21. castle
	19. soften	22. nestle

Student page 100

Story Words

Directions: Read each word to yourself. Then say the word out loud. Write the word on the line. Check the box after each step.

23. column (col | umn) Read ☑ Say ☑ Write ☑ ___column___
24. molecules (mol | e | cules) Read ☑ Say ☑ Write ☑ ___molecules___
25. repeated (re | peat | ed) Read ☑ Say ☑ Write ☑ ___repeated___
26. western (west | ern) Read ☑ Say ☑ Write ☑ ___western___
27. Paris (Par | is) Read ☑ Say ☑ Write ☑ ___Paris___

More Word Work

Directions: The letters **able** put together two **schwa** sounds at the end of many words such as **teachable.** The suffix **able** means "likely to" or "able to." Read the words. Write them on the lines.

28. capable ___capable___
29. durable ___durable___
30. portable ___portable___
31. peaceable ___peaceable___

Directions: The letters **ible** put together two **schwa** sounds at the end of many words such as **eligible.** Read the words. Write them on the lines.

32. horrible ___horrible___
33. visible ___visible___
34. credible ___credible___
35. terrible ___terrible___

Student page 101

Reading "Blood Brothers," Part 1

◆ *Preview and Predict*

- Tell students that they are about to read a story about the relationship between two brothers. Ask students whether they have any siblings. Ask them to describe their relationships. For example, competitive, friendly, and so on.
- Invite a student to read the title of the selection on Student Worktext page 102 aloud. Ask students to tell what they think the title means. (The meaning will be revealed in Part 2 of the story.)
- Have students look at the illustration on Student Worktext page 102. Ask students to predict what the characteristics of the two brothers in the story will be.
- Read aloud the sentence and question under **Use What You Know** at the top of page 102. Invite students to share information about conflicts they have with their own siblings or between siblings that they know about. Then have students answer the question.
- Have students preview the story by reading the first paragraph on page 102. Invite students to tell what they think the relationship between the two brothers is like.
- Have students read Student Worktext pages 102–103 to learn more about the brothers' relationship.

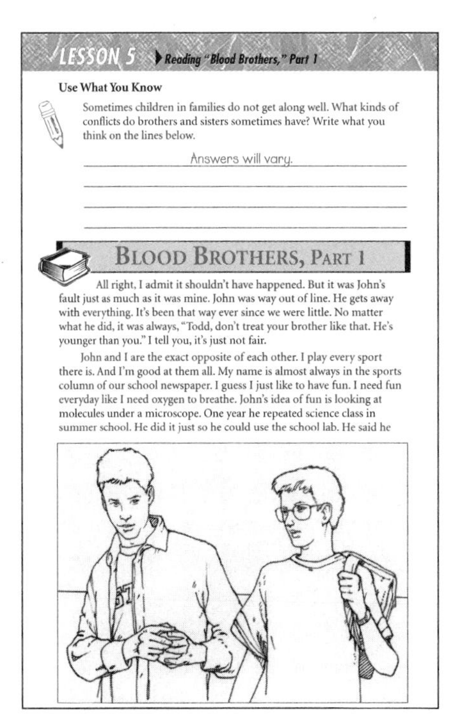

LESSON 5 ▸ Reading "Blood Brothers," Part 1

Use What You Know

Sometimes children in families do not get along well. What kinds of conflicts do brothers and sisters sometimes have? Write what you think on the lines below.

Answers will vary.

BLOOD BROTHERS, PART 1

All right, I admit it shouldn't have happened. But it was John's fault just as much as it was mine. John was way out of line. He gets away with everything. It's been that way ever since we were little. No matter what he did, it was always, "Todd, don't treat your brother like that. He's younger than you." I tell you, it's just not fair.

John and I are the exact opposite of each other. I play every sport there is. And I'm good at them all. My name is almost always in the sports column of our school newspaper. I guess I just like to have fun. I need fun everyday like I need oxygen to breathe. John's idea of fun is looking at molecules under a microscope. One year he repeated science class in summer school. He did it just so he could use the school lab. He said he

Student page 102

had some projects that couldn't wait until the fall. Do you have any idea how embarrassing it is to have a brother who talks like that? The fact that he talks like that is just one of the reasons I like to call him "nerds." Notice I said "nerds" not "nerd." He is such a nerd I have to use the plural form of the word. Calling him a nerd isn't enough. John is definitely "nerds."

Anyway, I guess the fight started the night Karen told everyone that she was getting married. Karen's our sister. She was a senior in college then, but she was home for the weekend. So she and the whole family came to my basketball game, and it was great. We were playing our biggest rivals, and the score was close right up to the end. I had a great game. I was the highest scorer that night. In the last ten seconds I shot a three-point basket to win the game. The crowd **went wild.** Everyone was cheering so loudly I thought the roof of the gym would blow off. You'd think that my family would be proud. But no, it was just the usual pat on the head. My dad said, "Congratulations, kid."

Mom said, "You did a good job, Todd." And of course, John had to say something stupid. He said something about how terrible the gym smelled. But I knew I could count on Karen. And sure enough, she suggested we get ice cream.

I remember we passed the award case in the school's main hall. I've got quite a few awards in there. My latest one was for track and field. Karen hadn't seen it yet, so I pointed it out to her. She didn't even get a chance to say anything before Dad **butted in.** He said, "Karen, did you know John made the honor roll this term?"

My mom put her arms around John like she was going to hug him to death. She said, "We're so proud he's taking advanced science and western studies courses this year."

Hello everybody, do you remember me? I'm your other son. Are you unable to see me? I know everybody thinks that I'm an idiot. I know they think that John is a genius, but do they have to rub it in so much? Do they have to remind me of it every two seconds?

Well, everybody finally stopped gushing over John. Then we made our way out to the parking lot. As we got closer to the car, I noticed John was walking kind of fast. I figured he was trying to get to the car first and get a window seat. And I knew my parents would make me let Karen have the other window. That would mean I'd be **stuck** in the middle. No way, I thought. I'm not being crushed to death all the way to the ice cream parlor. So I started walking faster, too. John sped up. He was just about to reach the car door when I sped up and brushed past him. I guess it had rained during the game because the ground was wet and slippery. I swear I didn't touch John. But just as I got ahead of him, I heard a loud thump. I turned around and there was John on the ground. He was hollering like a baby. Everybody made a huge fuss over him. Mom said, "Todd, give your brother a hand."

Student page 103

Focus on ESL/LEP

Divide students into small groups to discuss the story. Draw ESL/LEP students into small group discussions to ensure that their ideas are expressed. Encourage students to give each other their full attention.

Learning Styles

Auditory/Verbal Because the story is written in the first-person point of view, students could turn the text into a monologue. Have students take turns reading passages from the text and dramatizing them for the class. Encourage students to make the reading realistic by using the appropriate tone, voice, and body language.

Strategy Modeling

Reread/Read Ahead Ask students to name some of the things they can do if they come to something that confuses them while they are reading. Point out that often a reader can clear up confusion by reading something again. A reader can also read ahead to see if something later on in the story clears up the confusion. To model rereading, you might say:

I am confused about the characters in this story. Who is writing this story? How many people are in this family? I know there are two boys, but I'm confused about who is who. I will reread the first four paragraphs to see if these details are revealed. Okay, I see that Todd is writing this story. John is his younger brother. Karen is their sister. They have a mom and a dad.

If students have trouble grasping other details while reading the story, have students pause. Suggest applicable parts of the story for students to reread. Before rereading, have students pinpoint specific details that are confusing to them. Then have them figure out those details by rereading. If students are still confused, have them read ahead to see if details are made clearer later in the story.

Have students read Student Worktext pages 104–105.

Focus on ESL/LEP

The story contains several instances of literary language and idioms. Explain and discuss the following lines used in the first part of the story.

- I need fun everyday like I need oxygen to breathe.
- Everyone was cheering so loudly I thought the roof of the gym would blow off.
- My mom put her arms around John like she was going to hug him to death.
- I know they think that John is a genius, but do they have to rub it in so much?
- To tell you the truth, my throat felt a little tight and my eyes were stinging.
- John thinks he can cheat me out of Karen's bedroom.
- Well, John can think again.
- He was playing it cool.
- This is war, brother, war.

I reached out to help John up, and he **scooted** into the car. Before I could say anything, he slid over to the window. Karen was standing behind me. So I had no choice but to get in the car and sit in the middle.

We finally got to the ice cream parlor and Karen told us her news. She said that she was engaged to a boy she met at college. They were going to be married after they graduated in June. Everybody started talking at once—about a church wedding and a honeymoon in Paris, France. I couldn't believe how quickly Karen and my parents had agreed on everything. All I could think was that Karen was leaving us for good. I guess my parents realized it, too, because Mom started crying. Dad looked like he wanted to cry, too. To tell you the truth, my throat felt a little tight and my eyes were stinging. I watched John calmly slurping down his milkshake. I said to myself, "Why can't he be the one to get married and leave the house?"

Karen looked at me and said, "What did you say, Todd?"

"Oh, nothing," I said. "Just that I'll miss you after you leave." Karen smiled and patted my arm. Mom suddenly got all businesslike.

"Well," she said. "I am not looking forward to cleaning out Karen's room."

It got quieter because John stopped hosing up his milkshake for two seconds. He said, "Don't worry Mom, I'll help you."

I looked over at John. What was he up to? Then Karen said, "I guess my room will be up for grabs after the wedding."

"That's it!" I thought to myself. "John thinks he can cheat me out of Karen's bedroom." It's bigger than ours and closer to the bathroom. "Well, John can think again. That bedroom is mine. I'm the oldest, and it's only fair that I should get it. For the last fifteen years of my life John has gotten everything I wanted. But he is not getting Karen's bedroom." Then I said to

Student page 104

my mom, "I'll help you clean it out, too." John looked me straight in the eye and slurped up his milkshake. He was playing it cool. But I was just as capable to play it cool. I smiled at him and thought, "This is war, brother, war."

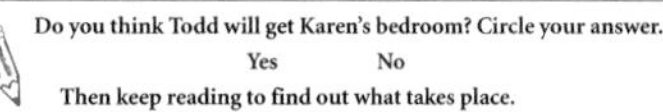

Do you think Todd will get Karen's bedroom? Circle your answer.

Yes No

Then keep reading to find out what takes place.

For the rest of the year I did everything I could think of to get Karen's bedroom. The first thing I did was tell my parents I wanted it. I told them it was only fair, since I was the oldest and deserved it. But all they would say was, "We haven't decided what is going to happen to Karen's room. We'll just have to wait and see."

That's when it hit me. If I was going to get Karen's bedroom I had to do more than try to make myself look good. I had to make John look bad. I know that sounds pretty rotten, but this was war. Soon I came across the perfect chance to get John in trouble.

Our parents are very strict about when to be home. If they say you have to be home by nine o'clock, you better be home by nine o'clock. Like my dad always says, "Nine o'clock doesn't mean nine-thirty. It doesn't mean a quarter past nine, either. It means nine o'clock."

It used to make me groan just thinking about my dad saying that. But now it brought a smile to my face. I actually rubbed my hands together like a movie bad guy as I pictured my dad yelling at John. I could see my mother in the background. She had her hand on her forehead and she was saying, "How could you do this to us John?"

It was a Saturday, and my parents were going to have dinner at Brian's house that night. That's Karen's boyfriend. Our parents were meeting Brian's parents for the first time. The next week they were coming to our house for dinner. Mom and Dad were upstairs getting ready to leave when the phone rang. I answered, and it was John. He was calling from his science club, the "Astronuts." That's not the real name of the club. But that's what I call it. It's a bunch of kids from school who have nothing better to do than look up at the sky, point at stars, and say "Oh! Ah!" Boring!

Anyway, John told me to tell our parents that the club was going to let out two hours later than usual. They were expecting two planets to run into each other or something. I told him I'd pass the message on. He was so happy to get back to his fellow "Astronuts" that he just said "thanks" and hung up. Mom and Dad came downstairs. They were both so nervous and

Student page 105

Have students finish the selection by reading Student Worktext pages 106–107.

Ask students the following questions about the selection.

- What did Todd do to encourage his parents to let him move into Karen's room? (He did all his chores before he was reminded. He tried to get John into trouble.)
- Why did John look good when he let Todd do the dishes when it was his turn? (for not wanting to fight)
- How did the rivalry with the chores continue? (John invented a new recycling system after Todd offered to take out the garbage. Todd offered to mow the lawn for their father after John took over their mother's garden. John fixed the lawnmower after it broke when Todd was using it.)
- Why did Todd look in Karen's room on the day of the wedding? (He noticed one of John's experiments was missing.)
- Who dropped the plant in Karen's room? (Todd. He grabbed it and John tried to stop him. When Todd pulled it away, the plant slipped.)
- Who started the physical fight between the two boys? (John. He jumped on Todd.)
- Who found the boys fighting? (Karen)

Focus on ESL/LEP

Explain and discuss the following sentences from the second half of the selection.

- No matter what I did, I just couldn't seem to catch a break.
- I noticed that some of the plants for one of his precious experiments were missing. (Point out the sarcasm.)
- We were grunting and rolling around like we were trying out for the school wrestling team. The way it was going, John seemed like he had a good chance of making first string.

Learning Styles

Body/Kinesthetic Have students work with a partner to role play a situation between the two brothers, such as their rivalry over the chores. The situation can either be from the story or imagined. Students may want to write text and perform it as a mini-dramatization rather than improvising.

excited about meeting Brian's family. Even if I had given them John's message, I don't think they would have heard me. They said they'd be home at eleven. "Good," I thought. "That's a whole half hour before John will get home."

I was eating snacks and watching TV. Then, around nine o'clock, John comes home. "What are you doing here? You're supposed to be looking for aliens!" I said.

"I'm supposed to be watching a meteor shower," said John in a snooty voice. "And even you should know you can't do that in the rain."

He was right. It was pouring rain outside. I guess I'd been so caught up in the movie that I didn't even notice. Great! Even the weather was on John's side. But I wasn't ready to give up. Not yet.

The next Friday morning I got up for school and went down for breakfast as usual. But the house was very quiet. Then I noticed a note in the kitchen:

Boys–I had to go out to the store. There has been a change of plans. Brian's family is coming for dinner tonight at six o'clock. I want you both to come home right after school. Remember, this is a very important night for Karen. Your lunches are in the refrigerator. I'll see you later.

Love,

Mom

I thought, "Boy would John get in trouble if he didn't get home in time." I knew that he was planning to go to the river after school with another club of his. He'd be filthy when he came home. I could just see the look on Mom's face when John came in around six o'clock covered in mud. There was no way John would get Karen's room after ruining this dinner!

I wrote out a new note from Mom saying only that she was at the store, and that our lunches were in the refrigerator. Then I heard John coming downstairs, so I hid in the laundry room. I heard him open the refrigerator and get his lunch. Soon I heard him leave. I grabbed the note I had written, then put Mom's note back. Everything was falling into place.

The only problem was that I kept thinking about my mom's note. All day at school it was as if I could hear her saying, "Remember, this is a very important night for Karen." By the end of the day I was a total wreck. When the final bell rang, I ran to John's classroom and told him we had to get home right away. It was a great plan, but I just couldn't do it.

Student page 106

I was pretty discouraged, but I wasn't about to give up. I did all my chores without any complaining. I even did them before my parents could remind me, but so did John. We actually got into a terrible fight about whose turn it was to do the dishes. In the past, the fight had always gone, "It's your turn, not mine." This time I knew it was really John's turn. But I was arguing that it was my turn to do the dishes! The sneak actually let me win! And wouldn't you know, he still got to look good for not wanting to fight.

That's how things kept going. When I offered to take out the garbage, John invented a new recycling system. When John took over my mom's garden, I offered to mow the lawn for my dad. It wasn't my fault the lawn mower broke. Of course, John fixed the lawn mower and finished mowing the lawn. No matter what I did, I just couldn't seem to catch a break.

Finally, it was the day of the wedding. In between crying and hugging, Mom and Karen were getting ready. Dad was running around looking for the camera and blowing his nose. I was alone in the bedroom I shared with John. I was glad that John wasn't there. I could practice knotting my tie without him laughing at me. All of a sudden I noticed that some of the plants for one of his precious experiments were missing. I thought, "What's going on?" Then I began to wonder where he was. I decided to look for him. I stepped out into the hall and heard a noise coming from Karen's room. The door was slightly open and I stepped inside.

I couldn't believe what I saw. There was John setting up his plants in Karen's room. "You little sneak!" I yelled.

"What's your problem?" said John.

"My problem is that you're trying to steal Karen's room."

"I'm just putting some plants in here."

"Oh, no you're not," I said. I walked over to the plants. John tried to block me, but I stepped around him. Then I picked up one of his plants to take back to our room. John told me to stop and tried to grab the plant out of my hand. I pulled away from him. The plant slipped to the floor and its container broke. Dirt and the plant spilled all over the floor. John went crazy. I had never seen him so angry. He jumped on me and knocked me to the floor. We were grunting and rolling around like we were trying out for the school wrestling team. The way it was going, John seemed like he had a good chance of making first string.

Suddenly the bedroom door opened. "What is going on in here?"

John and I rolled apart. I rubbed the dirt out of my eyes and looked up into my sister's face. Karen was wearing her wedding dress and looked beautiful. She also looked mad. ▶

Student page 107

After Reading "Blood Brothers," Part 1

Personal Response: You Be the Judge

Read aloud the questions under **You Be the Judge** on Student Worktext page 108. Ask students to think about what is fair. Then have students answer the questions.

Think About the Story: Reading Comprehension

Have students complete the remaining items on Student Worktext pages 108–109 independently or in pairs. Check their responses to help you assess their story comprehension. If students' responses indicate that they did not understand story events, reread the story aloud, pausing to discuss key events.

Critical Thinking Skill: Distinguish Fact from Opinion

Explain to students that they need to be able to tell fact from opinion when they read. This means that they need to realize what is true versus what someone thinks. An opinion may be supported, or backed up, with facts, but it is still only one person's or group's thoughts.

Ask students whether the following statements from the story are facts or opinions of the narrator. Tell them to ask themselves whether the statements are true, or only what someone thinks is true. Remind students that true statements can be proven.

- One year he repeated chemistry class in summer school. (fact)
- And of course, John had to say something stupid. (opinion)
- I know everyone thinks I'm an idiot. (opinion)
- Karen is engaged to a boy she met at college. (fact)
- John thinks he can cheat me out of Karen's bedroom. (opinion)
- Karen was wearing her wedding dress and she looked beautiful. (The first part is fact; the second is opinion)

Have students look through other writing (for example, a book review) for facts and opinions.

LESSON 5 ▶ After Reading "Blood Brothers," Part 1

You Be The Judge

1. Do you think Todd should get the bedroom? Why or why not? Write what you think on the lines below.
Answers will vary.

2. What would be a fair way to decide who gets the room? Write what you think on the lines below.
Answers will vary.

Think About the Story

Use Story Words

Directions: Look at your list of story words on page 101. Write a story word on each line.

3. John's idea of fun is looking at molecules under a microscope.
4. Karen will honeymoon in Paris.
5. Todd's name is always in the sports column of the school newspaper.
6. John repeated a science class in summer school.
7. Todd's brother is taking a class in western studies.

Write Sentences About the Story

Directions: Use words from the story to answer these questions.

8. What are John and Todd's different ideas of fun?
John likes science activities like looking at molecules under a microscope. Todd plays all kinds of sports like basketball and track and field.

9. Why did John repeat a science class in summer school?
John said he had some projects to do and wanted to use the school lab.

Student page 108

10. Why does Todd want Karen's bedroom?
Todd wants Karen's bedroom because it is both closer to the bathroom and bigger than the bedroom he shares with John.

The Big Idea

11. Which sentence tells what the whole story is about? Circle it.
a. Todd calls his brother "nerds."
(b. Todd and John both want Karen's bedroom.)
c. Karen is getting married.

Words and Meanings

Directions: Think about how the **bold** words are used in the story. Then circle the words that show the meaning of each word or phrase.

12. The crowd **went wild.** What does this mean?
a. The crowd turned into animals.
b. The crowd went to a place called Wild.
(c. The crowd got very excited.)

13. Dad **butted in.** What does this mean?
a. Dad said, "But."
(b. Dad interrupted the conversation.)
c. Dad bumped into Todd and Karen.

14. Todd did not want to be **stuck** in the middle of the backseat. What does this mean?
a. Todd did not want to be glued to the seat.
b. Todd did not want to be pushed into the car.
(c. Todd did not want to have to sit in the middle of the backseat.)

15. John **scooted** into the car. What does this mean?
(a. John moved quickly into the car.)
b. John was riding a scooter.
c. John looked into the car.

Look Ahead

16. What will Karen say to her brothers? Write what you think on the lines below. Then read on to find out if you are right.
Answers will vary.

Student page 109

Reinforce & Extend

STUDY SKILL: Using Diagrams and Maps as Graphic Aids

Read the following text to students:

A fossil fuel, such as oil, is taken to a furnace where it is burned. The heat from the burning fuel heats water that flows through pipes. When this water boils, it produces steam. The steam is sent to a turbine, which is a wheel with blades. The steam pushes against the blades and causes it to spin. A shaft is connected to the turbine. It rotates when the blades of the turbine are moved. The shaft is connected to a generator. When the shaft rotates, it causes a magnet inside the generator to spin. When the magnet spins, it produces electricity in nearby coils. The electricity is sent from the generator to homes and businesses over wires.

After reading the text once, ask students if a diagram might be easier to understand. Draw a diagram on the board from the text. Then read the text again slowly and point out the parts of the diagram as you read the corresponding text.

Repeat the procedure for a map. Begin your reading with something like this: *To get to the art museum from the school, turn right onto High Street. . . . and so on.* Then read the directions more slowly or write them down and have students draw a map to go with the text. Encourage students to draw visuals for the selection in this lesson, such as one showing how the characters are related.

Reading and Writing Practice Activity 66 provides additional practice with diagrams and maps as graphic aids.

LANGUAGE: Possessive Pronouns

Write these sentences on the board.

Jenna's book is due at the library.

I am painting Rose and Jerry's house.

Invite students to the board to circle the possessive nouns in the sentences. (Jenna's, Jerry's) Tell students that possessive pronouns can be used to replace possessive nouns. Explain:

- Possessive pronouns show ownership. They come before nouns.
- The possessive pronouns *my, your, his, her, its, our,* and *their* come before nouns. Note that *its* as a possessive pronoun does not have an apostrophe.
- Some possessive pronouns can stand alone instead of coming before nouns. They are *mine, yours, his, hers, ours,* and *theirs.*

Have students replace each possessive noun in the sentences on the board with a possessive pronoun.

Write the following sentences on the board. Have students replace the underlined words with the correct possessive pronoun.

That blue guitar is <u>Ginny's</u>. (hers)

The dinosaur bones are <u>Kwan and Kyle's</u>. (theirs)

The critics panned <u>Roger's and my</u> play. (our)

Reading and Writing Practice Activity 67 provides additional practice using possessive nouns.

LITERARY APPRECIATION: Narrative Voice

Tell students that voice is the way that a writer expresses his or her ideas. In good writing, you can "hear" a writer's voice. That is, the writer's voice comes through in his or her writing. Voice gives writing personality. Ask students to think about "Blood Brothers." Have them reread the first paragraph. Invite them to tell whether they can hear the writer's (the narrator's) voice. (Students should be able to recognize voice. This story is an excellent example of strong voice.) Have students tell why this story exemplifies voice. (Answers may include: The writer wrote the way people actually talk. That makes him seem real. He used expressions and idioms that people really use. He was excited to tell the story. He had definite opinions. His feelings really showed in his writing.) Invite students to cite actual lines from the text that show voice. For example: *I tell you, it's just not fair.*

Lesson at a Glance

Chapter 2, Lesson 6 "Blood Brothers," Part 2

Preview: This lesson presents the same fiction story as Lesson 5 about a rivalry between two brothers, but this story is told from the other brother's point of view.

Objectives

- to read a fiction story
- to read and spell vowel diphthongs in longer words
- to write words with the suffixes *ous, eous,* and *ious*
- to recognize point of view and bias
- to use adjectives and adverbs
- to write a personal narrative with dialogue

Student Worktext Pages 110–119

Story Words

chemistry, trophy, celebrate, cultivate

Reading and Writing Practice Activities 68–74

Before Reading "Blood Brothers," Part 2

Letters and Sounds

Reading and Writing Vowel Diphthongs in Longer Words

Write the words *daily, wayward, devoid, deployed,* and *pronounce* on the board. Say the words aloud. Ask students to circle the vowel combination in each word. (ai, ay, oi, oy, ou) Explain to students that the sounds these vowel combinations make are called diphthongs. Explain that a diphthong is the sound made when two vowels glide together in the same syllable to sound like one sound. Say each word aloud again, emphasizing the diphthong and the blending of the initial consonant with the diphthong. Invite volunteers to say the diphthong sound in each word.

Write the diphthongs *ai, ay, oi, oy,* and *ou* across the board. Have students give other examples of words with diphthongs and write them under the corresponding letter combination.

Have students complete Student Worktext page 110.

Reading and Writing Practice Activity 68: Decoding Words with Diphthongs.

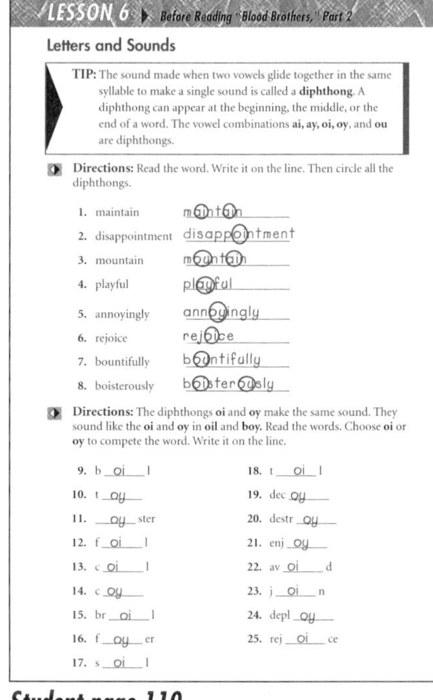

LESSON 6 ▸ Before Reading "Blood Brothers," Part 2

Letters and Sounds

TIP: The sound made when two vowels glide together in the same syllable to make a single sound is called a **diphthong**. A diphthong can appear at the beginning, the middle, or the end of a word. The vowel combinations **ai, ay, oi, oy,** and **ou** are diphthongs.

Directions: Read the word. Write it on the line. Then circle all the diphthongs.

1. maintain maintain
2. disappointment disappointment
3. mountain mountain
4. playful playful
5. annoyingly annoyingly
6. rejoice rejoice
7. bountifully bountifully
8. boisterously boisterously

Directions: The diphthongs **oi** and **oy** make the same sound. They sound like the **oi** and **oy** in **oil** and **boy**. Read the words. Choose **oi** or **oy** to compete the word. Write it on the line.

9. b oi l
10. t oy
11. oy ster
12. f oi l
13. c oi l
14. c oy
15. br oi l
16. f oy er
17. s oi l
18. t oi l
19. dec oy
20. destr oy
21. enj oy
22. av oi d
23. j oi n
24. depl oy
25. rej oi ce

Student page 110

Story Words

Read aloud these words: *chemistry, trophy, celebrate, cultivate.* Tell students that these words are important in the next story they will read. Then write the words on the board and point to each one as you say it aloud a second time. Have students follow the ❑ *Read* ❑ *Say* ❑ *Write* sequence by completing **Story Words** on Student Worktext page 111. Remind students to write the story words in the Word Bank at the back of their Student Worktext. To introduce the words in context, write these sentences on the board:

- I studied about atoms, molecules, and elements in chemistry class.
- Jace won a trophy for finishing first in the science fair.
- I like to celebrate my birthday.
- My parents cultivate roses in their greenhouse.

Have students make a word card for *chemistry*. Ask a volunteer to read the first sentence aloud. Then have students copy the sentence onto the back of the word card. Follow the same procedure for the remaining words. To assess students' abilities to read each new word, listen as individual students read the sentences on the board aloud.

Reading and Writing Practice Activity 69: Reading Story Words.

More Word Work

Have students work in pairs to complete **More Word Work** on Student Worktext page 111.

Reading and Writing Practice Activity 70: Using the Suffixes *ous, eous,* and *ious.*

Story Words

Directions: Read each word to yourself. Then say the word out loud. Write the word on the line. Check the box after each step.

26. chemistry (chem|is|try) Read ☑ Say ☑ Write ☑ chemistry
27. trophy (tro|phy) Read ☑ Say ☑ Write ☑ trophy
28. celebrate (cel|e|brate) Read ☑ Say ☑ Write ☑ celebrate
29. cultivate (cul|ti|vate) Read ☑ Say ☑ Write ☑ cultivate

More Word Work

Directions: The suffixes **ous, eous,** and **ious** are found at the end of many words. Read the words. Write them on the lines. Circle the suffixes.

30. humorous humorous
31. beauteous beauteous
32. gracious gracious
33. dangerous dangerous
34. spacious spacious
35. marvelous marvelous
36. mountainous mountainous
37. perilous perilous
38. horrendous horrendous
39. hideous hideous
40. envious envious

Student page 111

Reading “Blood Brothers,” Part 2

Preview and Predict

- Tell students that they are going to continue the story about the relationship between two brothers. Invite a volunteer to summarize what happened in Part 1 of the story.
- Ask students to look at the illustration on page 112. Have students tell whether the illustration reflects the incident at the trophy case that Todd related in Part 1. (No. John, the younger brother, was receiving the attention.)
- Have students preview the story by reading the first two paragraphs on page 112. Ask students what they notice about the story. (It is written by John, the younger brother.) Ask students to predict what this story will be about. (It will tell about the same events as in Part 1, but from a different perspective.)

Have students read Student Worktext pages 112–113 to learn more about John’s side of the story.

LESSON 6 Reading “Blood Brothers,” Part 2

Use What You Know

Part 1 of this story was told through Todd. Part 2 is John’s story. How do you think the boys will differ in their views? Write what you think on the lines below.

Answers will vary.

BLOOD BROTHERS, PART 2

Maybe you think what I did was wrong. After all, it was my own brother I was fighting. I can understand if you think I was wrong. Believe me, I’m prepared to accept that. But, as the old saying goes, there are two sides to every story. Here’s my side of the story.

Ever since I can remember, Todd has always **made a big deal** of the fact that he is older than I am. I would point out that he is only older by a year. He would always say, “Yeah John, but I’m still older than you are. And I’m bigger. I’m also faster and stronger than you are.”

Student page 112

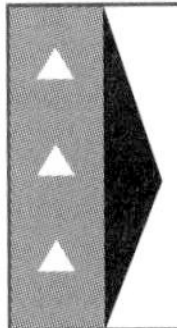

Focus on ESL/LEP

Discuss with students how you can tell immediately that this part of the story was written from a different viewpoint from the first.

Learning Styles

Auditory/Verbal Have students read John’s version of the story aloud. Students should take turns reading passages from the text and dramatizing them for the class. Encourage students to make the reading realistic by using the appropriate tone, voice, and body language. Students should have a different perspective now that they know the other side of the story.

I have to admit everything he said was true. He was great at everything. I am hopeless at every sport ever invented. I finally got tired of losing every race we ran together. I got tired of looking like a fool when I struck out at baseball. I got tired of tripping over my own feet when we played basketball. So I stopped playing sports and got interested in nature and science instead. Even so, I still couldn’t get away from the fact that Todd was the family star.

My parents would never admit that they like Todd better, but it’s true. Actually, I don’t blame them. It’s pretty hard not to like Todd better than me. He’s more exciting than I am. He hits a home run or scores a basket, and everybody cheers. Nobody cheers because you’ve memorized the names of all the elements for chemistry. They don’t cheer because you’re good at grammar. They don’t care if you know the difference between a suffix and a prefix, either. It wouldn’t have been so bad if I wasn’t reminded all the time how great my brother was, but everything was about Todd. Mom was always putting out a new trophy Todd had just won. Dad was always talking about a race where Todd had just finished first. Sometimes I would complain about having to spend every second of my life at games where Todd was competing. Whenever I objected my mother would say, “Don’t be fresh,” and my dad would say, “Where’s your family spirit?”

I was there the time Todd won the big school basketball game. Our whole family was there. Even our sister Karen had come home from college. Todd won the game almost all by himself. The whole school was cheering for him. Karen and my parents couldn’t stop telling him how great he was. I never know what to say at those times. I just stand around. I hang my head and look at my shoes. I’m not jealous. I just feel like such a phony slapping Todd on the back and saying, “Great job, kid.” Usually I would try and make some kind of a joke. I said, “The better the game is the worse the gym smells.” Todd just looked at me like I was from Mars.

Todd didn’t want us to forget how wonderful he is, so he dragged all of us over to the school’s award case. He’s won almost every trophy in there. Everybody gushed over him for about an hour. I guess my parents started to feel bad for me. My mom put a fake smile on her face and said, “John, tell everybody about your science classes.” Then Dad jumped in saying how proud he is of all his kids.

I hate when they do that. It only makes me feel worse. I know they’re all thinking, “Poor John, he’s such a disappointment compared to his brother.” I was feeling pretty down that night. I just wanted to go home, but I still had to watch the family celebrate at the ice cream shop. How was I supposed to eat and listen to Todd bragging at the same time? It would be a miracle if I didn’t get sick.

We left the school and headed out to the car. I wanted to be by myself for a minute. I was walking a little faster than everybody else. Before I

Student page 113

Strategy Modeling

Access Prior Knowledge Explain to students that they can think about what they already know to help them understand what they are currently reading. They now know two sides of the story. Have them think about how their knowledge of Todd's side of the story affects their reading of John's story. Model this process for students. You might say:

John thinks that his parents like Todd better. He says that his parents are always talking about Todd's achievements because he is more exciting. From reading Part 1, I know that Todd feels exactly the opposite. Todd thinks that John receives all the attention. They cannot both be right. Each brother just sees the situation differently.

Have students finish reading Student Worktext pages 114–115 to find out more about John's side of the sibling rivalry. Have students pause at the top of page 115 to apply prior knowledge before reading on.

Focus on ESL/LEP

The story contains several instances of literary language and idioms.

Explain and discuss the following lines used in the first half of Part 2.

- Sometimes I would complain about having to spend every second of my life at games where Todd was competing.
- Todd just looked at me like I was from Mars.
- Everybody gushed over him for about an hour.
- I knew I'd be standing in Todd's shadow for the rest of my hideous life.

knew what was happening, Todd ran up and pushed me to the ground. I couldn't believe it. He's always doing things like that. Everybody acts like it's just fun and games. Well, it may be a game to them, but it's not fun for me. Then, Todd reached down to help me up. He was acting like he was coming to my rescue, like he was a big hero or something. I was so mad I just pulled away from him and got in the car.

All the way to the ice cream shop I thought about my life. My future looked pretty bleak. I knew I'd be standing in Todd's shadow for the rest of my hideous life. I felt like I couldn't take it anymore.

That night, my older sister Karen said something that gave me hope. She told us she was going to get married and leave home. Suddenly I realized I had the solution to my problems. I could move into Karen's old room and finally have a place to myself. Karen's room was the perfect place to grow some plants I wanted to cultivate. Her room faced south and got more sunlight than ours did. I could make a small greenhouse in there. Maybe I could even build a small lab. I could do some serious work. I could find the cure for the common cold. I could find the cure for cancer! I just knew I could do it. Then everything would be different. I wouldn't just be Todd's kid brother anymore. I'd be on television and in the newspapers. I'd be famous. Finally I'd be the one everyone cheered for.

I was so excited I almost asked my parents for the room right then and there. But I knew that would be a mistake. The minute I said I wanted it, Todd would want it, too. So when my mom said Karen's room would need cleaning out, I told her I'd help. Then Todd said he'd help also. He never volunteers to do anything. My **heart sank**. I knew he wanted the room. No, he didn't really want the room. He just didn't want me to get it. He was grinning at me. I knew he was thinking, "Too bad little brother."

I was madder than I've ever been in my life. I decided right then and there that Todd was not going to get Karen's bedroom. That room was mine. No matter what I had to do I was going to get it. It wasn't just for me. It was important for the world. Just think of all the people I would cure with my work. For once in his life, Todd would not win.

Do you think John will get the bedroom? Circle your answer.

Yes **No**

Then keep reading to find out what takes place.

The more I thought about it, the more I realized that it wasn't Todd who stood between Karen's bedroom and me. It was my parents. Todd was a big pain all right, but he wasn't the problem. The problem was getting my parents to think that I should be the one to get the bedroom.

Student page 114

I decided to look at the problem like a scientist. I remembered stories about how companies used to get people to buy hot dogs and soda while they were watching a movie. The stories told how a picture of popcorn or somebody drinking a cold soda would be put right into the movie. But the picture of the food went by so quickly—it didn't even last a second—that the people didn't even know they had seen it. Only somewhere deep inside their mind did they know it. After the food was shown in the movie, people would get up to buy food.

I thought about taking a video and putting pictures into it. I'd put in my report card with straight A's. I'd put in the note from Todd's teacher saying she was sorry to hear my mother's father had died—Grandpa isn't dead. Todd just said that to get out of taking a test. Boy did he get in trouble! I'd also put in pictures of me taking out the garbage and washing my dad's car. Then I'd have pictures of Todd. There would be a picture of him standing at the open refrigerator, drinking milk right out of the carton. Mom hates when he does that. Another picture would show Todd fooling around with my father's golf clubs. He's not supposed to do that. And the last picture would show Todd's side of the bedroom. All you would be able to see was Todd's unmade bed and a huge pile of dirty clothes.

I could just imagine the whole family watching the movie together. After the places where I put in pictures of Todd, my parents would get mad. They'd start to yell at him. Todd wouldn't know what was going on. Then the really quick pictures of me being a perfect son would go by. My parents would turn to me, they'd say, "John, you are such a great kid. We think you should get Karen's bedroom." Yeah, that would be how I could get what I want.

But let's face it, there's no way I could put pictures into a video. Even if I could, I didn't know how to get pictures of myself doing those things. I couldn't exactly say, "Todd, take a picture of me washing Dad's car." Still, I wasn't ready to give up on the whole idea yet. I began to think that if you could change people with pictures, maybe you could also change people with sound.

I had also heard stories about how in wartime people have used loud music to harm an enemy. Any music will do, but if you play something your enemy hates, it's even better. So I set up a little project. I told my family I was doing an experiment to see how different kinds of music would affect plants. I put the plants in the dining room next to my CD player. I stacked up a whole bunch of CDs to play to the plants.

I started to hang out with my parents in the dining room. Sometimes I would just be with my mom. Sometimes I would just be with my dad. Sometimes all three of us would be together. At those times I would play music I know my parents love. You could just look at them and see them

Student page 115

Have students finish the selection by reading Student Worktext pages 116–117. Ask students the following questions about the selection.

- Why didn't John tell Todd how great he was in the game? (He felt phony.)
- Why didn't John like his parents to praise him in front of Todd? (It made him feel worse because he felt like they were doing it because he was a disappointment to them.)
- Why did John want to move into Karen's room? (to cultivate his plants)
- Why did John want to solve the world's problems, like finding a cure for cancer? (He wanted to be recognized for his achievements like Todd. He wanted to be out of Todd's shadow.)
- Why did John jump on Todd and start the fight? (Todd dropped his plant. It looked like he just threw it on the floor.)
- Why did Karen think the boys were lucky? (They had each other. She had always wanted a sister.)
- What are blood brothers? (Friends who forge a bond of loyalty.)
- Why did John and Todd want to be blood brothers when they were younger? (They saw it in a movie.)
- What did John remember as the nice things Todd had done for him in the past? (stood up for him at school, picked him first to play on his team)
- Did the brothers make up? (yes)
- Which brother got Karen's room? (neither)

relax. They'd smile and sway a little to the music. Whenever Todd would come in I'd make an excuse about having to leave. But first I would change the music. I'd put on something loud and very screechy. My parents would start to cover their ears; they'd twist in their seats and soon get up and leave. Even Todd didn't look too happy. I'm not so sure the music had any effect on the plants but it sure had an effect on my family!

The idea was that my parents would have good feelings around me and bad feelings around Todd. They would start to dislike him and wouldn't want to do anything nice for him. Then naturally they'd want me to get Karen's room. Well, it was a great idea, but it didn't work out the way I had hoped. My parents just told me to move my experiment to the basement. So just like Todd, I was back to begging them and trying to please them.

The day of Karen's wedding, I was feeling pretty low. I was alone in our bedroom. I was thinking about all the months since Karen told us she was getting married. I had done everything I could think of to get on my parent's good side. I'm always helpful. But lately I had been especially helpful. But so had Todd. And I knew that they were more impressed by him. He never used to do anything around the house, so of course they noticed it more when he started helping. It didn't matter that I worked much harder than Todd. It was like I wasn't there.

Later, I sat on my bed and looked around the room. I looked at Todd's trophies and medals all over the place. I looked at my plants crowded together under the window. They weren't doing well. They needed more space and light. That was when I decided to move them. I wasn't trying to be sneaky. I just wanted to give my plants a chance to grow.

Student page 116

I had just moved a few of the plants into Karen's room when Todd burst in the door. He started yelling at me and calling me names. Then he did something that really made me mad. He said it was an accident. To me it looked like he just grabbed one of my plants and threw it on the floor. The pot broke. I got so mad I really did see red. I jumped on Todd. We fell to the floor. We began rolling around in the dirt and broken pottery pieces.

Suddenly Karen was in the room. She pulled us apart. Todd yelled out, "John was trying to steal your room."

"That's not true."

"Quiet!" said Karen. "I don't want to hear another word. Look at the two of you. You're filthy and you're bleeding!"

"Yeah, well, Todd—"

"Just be quiet," she said.

"Yeah, John—"

"You too, Todd. I don't want to hear a word from either of you. You don't know how lucky you are. All my life I wished I had a sister. When you were little you two were so close. You were always together. You were always laughing. Now look at you, covered in dirt and bleeding. The last time you were both bleeding was when you decided to become blood brothers. Do you remember that? You'd seen some movie where two friends cut themselves and mixed their blood together. Mom was mad. She said you were already blood brothers. But you said you just wanted to make sure. What happened to those two brothers? What happened to those two friends?"

I started to remember all the times Todd stood up for me at school. I remembered how he let me teach him the names of all the planets and stars. I remembered how he always picked me first to play on his team, even though I was the worst player in the world. I remembered all the fun we used to have, and I felt pretty bad. I guess Todd did too, because he wiped some blood off my arm. He wiped some of his own blood from under his nose. Then he mixed our blood together. He said, "I guess we're still blood brothers."

We didn't get mushy or anything. There was no time for that anyway. We had to hurry and get cleaned up and changed for Karen's wedding. We got there just in time, and it was great. All the grownups said it was a beautiful wedding, which is what they always say. But I think Karen's really was. We laughed almost the entire day. The whole family had a great time.

By the way, neither Todd nor I got Karen's old bedroom. Our parents decided to turn it into a family room. We still share a bedroom, but we don't mind it so much anymore.

◆

Student page 117

Learning Styles

Visual/Spatial Work with students to develop a chart that compares and contrasts the two brothers' views of the same situation. Write "Todd" in one column and "John" in the other. At the left, write an event from the story, such as *the reason John moved his plants to Karen's room.* Under "Todd", you might write *thought John was taking over Karen's room in a sneaky way.* Under "John" you might write *moved the plants because they weren't doing well.* Other events or ideas that you might compare and contrast are *the walk to the car after the game, the scene outside the trophy case,* and *the reasons for wanting Karen's room.*

After Reading "Blood Brothers," Part 2

Personal Response: You Be the Judge

Read aloud the question under **You Be the Judge** on Student Worktext page 118. Ask students to think about how they have changed as they have gotten older. Then have students answer the question.

Think About the Story: Reading Comprehension

Have students complete the remaining items on Student Worktext pages 118–119 independently or in pairs. Check their responses to help you assess their story comprehension. If students' responses indicate that they did not understand story events, reread the story aloud, pausing to discuss key events.

Critical Thinking Skill: Recognize Point of View and Bias

Explain to students that point of view is the position or angle from which the story is told. Remind them that Part 1 and Part 2 of the story were told from different points of view. Ask students how they were able to recognize that Part 2 of the story was told from a different point of view from Part 1. (The narrator says that this is the other side of the story. The "I" in the story is a different person.)

Explain to students that stories (narratives) are written in either first- or third-person point of view. First-person point of view means that one of the characters is telling the story. The character is probably biased, or tends to tell one side of the story, just as in "Blood Brothers." Third-person point of view means that someone from outside the story is telling it.

Ask students to tell whether these sentences are told in first- or third-person point of view.

I have been told many times that I am smart. (first)

Kiana had always been told that she was smart. (third)

Discuss how point of view affects the reader's feelings about the characters and events. Have students tell how their view of each brother has changed by reading the same story from John's perspective. For example, they might have felt sorry for Todd in Part 1; now they have both sides and they feel sorry for John. Ask students to tell whether they think each brother's story was biased.

Have students look through other fiction stories to identify the point of view of the narrator.

- Ask them to identify other characters who might have a different version of the story.
- Tell students to think about whether a first-person narrator they identify is biased and how another character might tell more, or a different side, of the story.

LESSON 6 ▸ *After Reading "Blood Brothers," Part 2*

You Be the Judge

1. Karen said that John and Todd used to be close friends. She wants to know why they are always fighting now. Why do you think they fight more now? Write what you think on the lines below.

Answers will vary.

Think About the Story

Use Story Words

Directions: Look at your list of story words on page 111. Write a story word on each line.

2. A birthday party is held to celebrate someone's birth.
3. A greenhouse is a perfect place to cultivate plants.
4. The winner of a race may win a trophy or a medal.
5. John did a lot of memorization for his chemistry class.

When Did It Happen?

6. Write a number from 1 to 4 in front of each event to show when it happened.

4 Karen told the boys to stop fighting.
3 John put his plants in Karen's bedroom.
1 The family went to Todd's basketball game.
2 John decides he wants Karen's bedroom.

What Are the Facts?

7. Why did John think his parents liked Todd better than him? Circle the reasons.

a. They told him they did.
b. John thinks Todd is more exciting than he is.
c. John thinks his parents are always praising Todd.
d. His parents gave Todd Karen's bedroom.
e. His mother displays Todd's many trophies.

Student page 118

Write Sentences About the Story

Directions: Use words from the story to answer these questions.

8. Why does John like nature and science instead of sports?

John feels hopeless and is tired of losing.

9. Why does John want to move into Karen's room?

John would finally have some privacy. He could build a lab or a greenhouse and do some serious work.

10. Why does Todd say, "I guess we're still blood brothers"?

When Todd and John were little, they decided to become blood brothers, like two friends in a movie. After the fight Todd mixed their blood together for a second time.

Words and Meanings

Directions: Think about how the **bold** words are used in the story. Then circle the words that show the meaning of each word or phrase.

11. Todd has always **made a big deal** about being older than John. What does this mean?

a. Todd has always played cards with John.
b. Todd has always stressed that he is older.
c. Todd is always buying and selling things.

12. John said, "My **heart sank.**" He means he ______.

a. is having a heart attack
b. has heartburn
c. felt sad

Why Did It Happen?

Directions: Draw a line from each story event to the reason it happened.

What Happened	Why
13. John moved his plants to Karen's room	because Todd dropped John's plant.
14. John offered to help his mom clean Karen's room	because they would grow better.
15. John pushed Todd down	in order to convince his parents to give him the room.

Student page 119

Reinforce & Extend

SPELLING: Diphthongs

1. employed
2. nourish
3. portrait
4. plaintive
5. disarrayed
6. moistened
7. resourceful
8. rejoice
9. voiceless
10. bargain

Remind students that diphthongs are spelled in different ways. For example, *oi* and *oy* usually sound the same, as do *ai* and *ay*. Then have students number a sheet of paper 1–10. Dictate the words, pausing for students to write them. Next, write the words on the board and have students check each word.

Reading and Writing Practice Activity 71 provides additional practice with diphthongs.

LANGUAGE: Adjectives and Adverbs

Write these sentences on the board.

The wild jaguar swiftly hunted its prey.

The tigers at the zoo are tame.

Ask students to name the words that describe things in the sentences. (*wild, swiftly, tame*) Tell students that these words are adjectives and adverbs. Explain:

- Adjectives describe nouns. Adverbs describe (or modify) verbs, adjectives, and other adverbs.
- Adjectives can come before or after the noun they describe.
- Adverbs usually come after the verbs that they modify. Adverbs come before adjectives and other adverbs that they modify.
- An adjective describes "what kind," "which one," or "how many."
- Many adverbs end in *ly*. An adverb describes "how," "when," "where," or "why."

Reading and Writing Practice Activity 72 provides additional practice with adjectives and adverbs.

WRITING: A Personal Narrative with Dialogue

Tell students that "Blood Brothers" is a personal narrative. Explain that a personal narrative is a true story about yourself. It is about experiences in your life. Explain to students how to write one:

- Select a subject. Think about something memorable that happened to you.
- Organize your thoughts by writing them down. Answer the five W's: who, what, when, where, and why.
- Start writing at the beginning of your story. You will write in first-person point of view. Make your opening interesting so that your reader will want to continue.
- Share your thoughts and feelings. Write interesting details. Use words that are specific.
- End your personal narrative by giving your reader something to think about.

Remind students that they can use dialogue to make their writing seem more real. Look back again at "Blood Brothers" to see how the writing came alive with the use of dialogue. Dialogue draws the reader into the action.

Reading and Writing Practice Duplicate and distribute Activities 73 and 74 on writing a narrative with dialogue.

Application

At Home Have students look in the newspaper for anecdotal columns written in the first person. Ask them to analyze the column for the features discussed in class. Encourage students to write their own personal narrative modeled on the personal narrative style.

Lesson at a Glance

Objectives

- to complete a trade book successfully
- to practice the word study and phonics skills learned in Chapter 2
- to practice reading the high-frequency and content words learned in Chapter 2
- to build reading fluency

Recommended Books

Dogsong by Gary Paulsen
Scorpions by Walter Dean Myers
Tangerine by Edward Bloor
Do Bananas Chew Gum? by Jamie Gilson
The Ear, the Eye, and the Arm by Nancy Farmer
Bud, Not Buddy by Christopher Paul Curtis
Four Perfect Pebbles by Lila Perl and Blumenthal Lazan
Joey Pigza Swallowed the Key by Jack Gantos
Racing the Sun by Paul Pitts
Sing Down the Moon by Scott O'Dell
Song of the Trees by Mildred D. Taylor
Stonewords, A Ghost Story by Pam Conrad
Summer Soldiers by Susan Hart Lindquist

Before Reading

Introduce the Book

Display some of the books from the recommended trade book list. (Or, if the whole class will read the same book, display just that book.) Tell students that they will read a chapter book. Explain that these books use words that are the same as or similar to the words in Chapter 2, and that they will read the book for fun; they will not be expected to learn new skills.

Set a Purpose

Review the Access Prior Knowledge process students used for the Chapter 1 Independent Reading lesson on pages 46 and 47 of this book. Then have students finish this statement:

The topic in this book is similar to ________, which I already know about.

Summarize

Tell students that at the end of each chapter they should stop to write one or two sentences explaining what happened in the chapter. Remind students that summarizing helps to keep the details straight while reading. Also, this chapter-by-chapter summarizing will result in a complete summary of the book when they are finished.

Reading

Compare and Contrast

Explain to students that comparing is finding the similarities between two things and contrasting is exploring the differences. For example, to compare and contrast two cities, you might talk about the climate, language, architecture, transportation, and size. Have students compare and contrast the personality, appearance, and actions of characters in a book by completing a chart like the one below.

	Character	Character	Character
Personality			
Appearance			
Actions			

Identify Cause and Effect

Explain to students that knowing the causes of events can help them both see and understand the whole story. Tell students that the cause is what makes an event happen. For example, *Maryanne did not study for her social studies test* (cause), *so she received a bad grade* (effect). Ask students to write three examples of cause and effect sentences of their own on a piece of paper and then discuss their sentences with the class.

After Reading

Evaluate/Make Judgments

Tell students to choose an action by a character in the story. Ask them to tell if they think the character made the right choice and to explain why or why not.

In nonfiction, tell students to choose a topic in the story and give their evaluation of some aspect of the topic.

Author's Purpose

Ask students to try to put themselves in the author's shoes and to think why the author wrote the story. (For example: To entertain? To inform? To surprise? To prove a point? To scare?)

Extension Activities

Reading

For their own personal interests, suggest that students read other books from the recommended list.

Writing

Suggest that students complete one of these activities:

- Write a ten-sentence summary of the book. Use at least 20 words with the letter patterns studied in the chapter. Circle the targeted words.
- Write a personal letter to a friend or family member describing the book and what you liked and disliked about it.

Research

Suggest that students research the book's author. Students can find out other books that the author has written and facts about the author's life.

Chapter 2 Review

The Chapter Review on Student Worktext pages 120–128 will help students review and practice the skills presented in Chapter 2. The review is divided into four parts, A–D.

Suggestions to help students complete the Chapter Review:

- Make sure the students understand that the Chapter Review is not a test. You may have students work in pairs and then compare responses, or you may work through the review as a class.
- Read the instructions for each part aloud.
- Have students complete one part of the review at a time. Pause to go over the answers and have students mark corrections using a second color.

Chapter Test

Reproducible blackline masters of the Chapter 2 Test can be found on pages 132–134 of this book. Use the test to assess students' comprehension of the skills taught in the chapter.

Additional Practice

Reading and Writing Practice Activities 37–74 can be used to reinforce the skills taught in Chapter 2.

Part A

Part A reviews the phonics skills taught in the chapter. Read aloud the summaries presented in the tip boxes before each exercise. Then have the students complete the items. If students show difficulty understanding and using the new letters and sounds, review individual lessons or assign the corresponding Reading and Writing Practice Activities: 37, 44, 49, 56, 63, and 68.

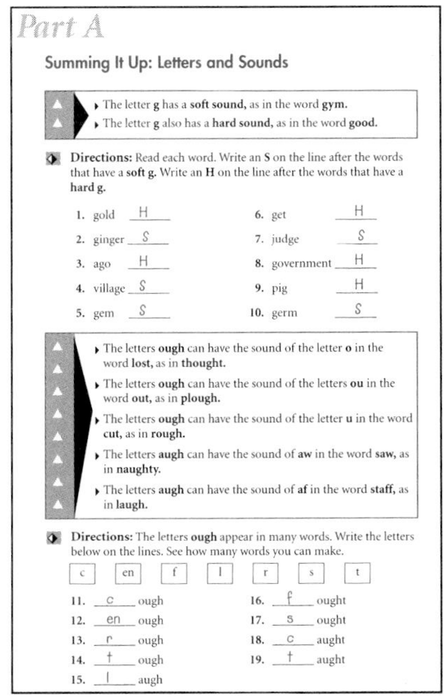

Part A

Summing It Up: Letters and Sounds

- The letter **g** has a **soft sound,** as in the word **gym.**
- The letter **g** also has a **hard sound,** as in the word **good.**

Directions: Read each word. Write an **S** on the line after the words that have a **soft g.** Write an **H** on the line after the words that have a **hard g.**

1. gold H
2. ginger S
3. ago H
4. village S
5. gem S
6. get H
7. judge S
8. government H
9. pig H
10. germ S

- The letters **ough** can have the sound of the letter **o** in the word **lost,** as in **thought.**
- The letters **ough** can have the sound of the letters **ou** in the word **out,** as in **plough.**
- The letters **ough** can have the sound of the letter **u** in the word **cut,** as in **rough.**
- The letters **augh** can have the sound of **aw** in the word **saw,** as in **naughty.**
- The letters **augh** can have the sound of **af** in the word **staff,** as in **laugh.**

Directions: The letters **ough** appear in many words. Write the letters below on the lines. See how many words you can make.

c en f l r s t

11. c ough
12. en ough
13. r ough
14. t ough
15. l augh
16. f ought
17. s ought
18. c aught
19. t aught

Student page 121

- The letter pair **ie** makes the long **e** vowel sound.
- The letter pair **ei** follows the letter **c** and makes the long **a** vowel sound.
- The letter pair **ei** can stand for the long **e** sound, but only if the letter **c** sounds like **s,** as in **glacier.**
- A rhyme that helps you remember is: Use **i** before **e** when sounded like **ee,** except after **c,** or when sounded like **a,** as in **neighbor** and **weigh.**

Directions: Read the words. They are missing the letters **ei** or **ie.** Write the correct letter pair to complete the words. Write the complete word on the line.

20. c ei ling ceiling
21. y ie ld yield
22. th ie f thief
23. rec ei pt receipt
24. rel ie ve relieve
25. v ei n vein

- The sound of the letter **a** in **ago** is called the **schwa** sound.
- The vowels **a, e, i, o,** and **u** can all stand for the **schwa** sound.
- The letter patterns **el, al, le, er, or, ar, en, on, ed, id,** or **ion** can all stand for the **schwa** sound.
- The **schwa** is usually in an unstressed part of the word.

Directions: Write the word on the line. Circle the schwa sounds in the words.

26. company company
27. suppose suppose
28. horrible horrible
29. position position
30. hasten hasten
31. spectacular spectacular
32. person person
33. terrible terrible
34. able able
35. mechanical mechanical
36. shower shower
37. inspection inspection
38. capable capable
39. cereal cereal
40. portable portable
41. creation creation

Student page 122

- The sound made when two vowels glide together in the same syllable to make a single sound is called a **diphthong.** Examples are the **oi** sound in **foil** or the **ou** sound in **horrendous.**
- A diphthong can appear at the beginning, the middle, or the end of a word.
- The vowel combinations **ai, ay, oi, oy,** and **ou** are diphthongs.

Directions: Read the word. Write it on the line. Then circle all the diphthongs.

42. rainstorm rainstorm
43. horseplay horseplay
44. appointment appointment
45. enjoyment enjoyment
46. resounding resounding
47. voiceover voiceover

Directions: Complete the words below with either **oi** or **oy.** Write the word on the line.

48. j oy joy
49. br oi ler broiler
50. f oy er foyer
51. t oi ling toiling
52. c oy coy

Student page 123

Part B

Part B reviews the word study and structural analysis skills taught in the chapter. Read aloud the summaries presented in the tip boxes before each exercise. Then have the students complete the items. You may want to review the skills by looking back at individual lessons, presenting examples on the board, or assigning the corresponding Reading and Writing Practice Activities: 39, 46, 51, 58, 65, and 70.

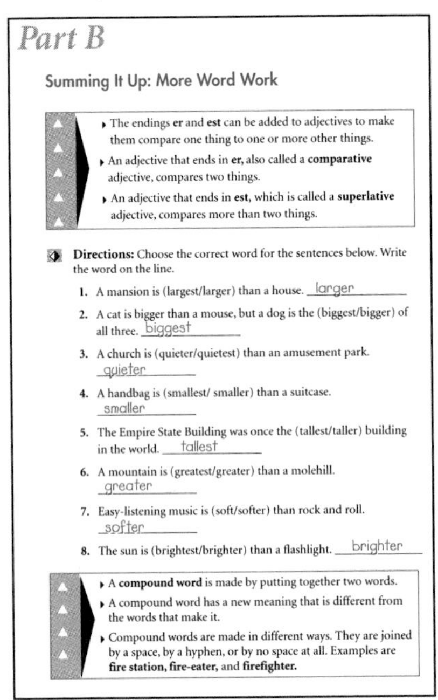

Part B

Summing It Up: More Word Work

- The endings **er** and **est** can be added to adjectives to make them compare one thing to one or more other things.
- An adjective that ends in **er**, also called a **comparative** adjective, compares two things.
- An adjective that ends in **est**, which is called a **superlative** adjective, compares more than two things.

Directions: Choose the correct word for the sentences below. Write the word on the line.

1. A mansion is (largest/larger) than a house. larger
2. A cat is bigger than a mouse, but a dog is the (biggest/bigger) of all three. biggest
3. A church is (quieter/quietest) than an amusement park. quieter
4. A handbag is (smallest/ smaller) than a suitcase. smaller
5. The Empire State Building was once the (tallest/taller) building in the world. tallest
6. A mountain is (greatest/greater) than a molehill. greater
7. Easy-listening music is (soft/softer) than rock and roll. softer
8. The sun is (brightest/brighter) than a flashlight. brighter

- A **compound word** is made by putting together two words.
- A compound word has a new meaning that is different from the words that make it.
- Compound words are made in different ways. They are joined by a space, by a hyphen, or by no space at all. Examples are **fire station, fire-eater,** and **firefighter.**

Student page 124

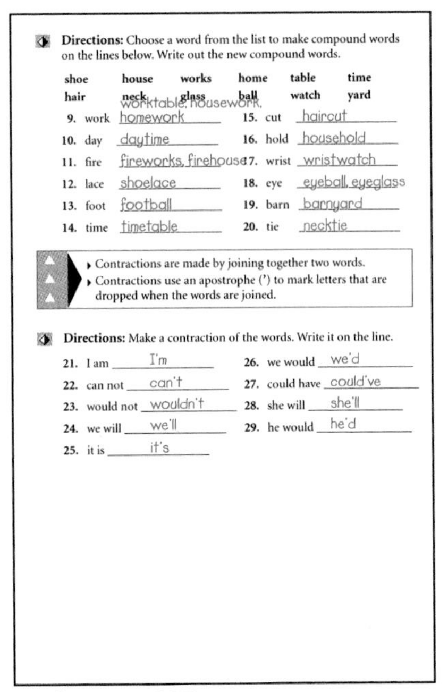

Directions: Choose a word from the list to make compound words on the lines below. Write out the new compound words.

shoe	house	works	home	table	time
hair	neck	glass	ball	watch	yard

9. work homework, worktable, housework
10. day daytime
11. fire fireworks, firehouse
12. lace shoelace
13. foot football
14. time timetable
15. cut haircut
16. hold household
17. wrist wristwatch
18. eye eyeball, eyeglass
19. barn barnyard
20. tie necktie

- Contractions are made by joining together two words.
- Contractions use an apostrophe (') to mark letters that are dropped when the words are joined.

Directions: Make a contraction of the words. Write it on the line.

21. I am I'm
22. can not can't
23. would not wouldn't
24. we will we'll
25. it is it's
26. we would we'd
27. could have could've
28. she will she'll
29. he would he'd

Student page 125

Part C

Part C reviews the story words from each story in the chapter. Students are asked to recognize story words and their meanings, and to place them in sentences. Have students review the story words in the Word Bank at the back of their Student Worktext or refer to the stories in the chapter to help them complete the review. For additional practice and word recognition, assign the corresponding Reading and Writing Practice Activities: 38, 45, 50, 57, 64, and 69.

Part C

Story Words

Directions: On the lines below, write the word from the list that matches each clue.

army	**observe**	**astronomy**	**rhythm**
column	**particular**	**telescope**	

1. a branch of the military ___army___
2. to watch closely ___observe___
3. the study of outer space ___astronomy___
4. a row ___column___
5. a steady sound or movement ___rhythm___
6. a device for seeing things far away ___telescope___
7. something specific ___particular___

Directions: Select a word from the list to finish the sentence. Write the word on the line.

repeated conference gestured Paris planets disappointed

8. Mars is one of the ___planets___ in our solar system.
9. She ___gestured___ for Bill to sit down.
10. The Eiffel Tower is in ___Paris___.
11. Because they couldn't hear her, she ___repeated___ the directions.
12. The teacher and Ann's parents had a ___conference___.
13. The coach was ___disappointed___ with the loss.

Directions: Read each word. On the lines below, write a number to tell how many syllables it has.

14. molecules ___3___
15. southern ___2___
16. boredom ___2___
17. cultivate ___3___
18. particular ___4___

Student page 126

Part D

Part D reviews the content of the stories in the chapter. Students are asked to identify fiction and nonfiction, story characters, details, and cause and effect. If students are having difficulty remembering story details, have them reread stories they have trouble recalling and work in pairs or as a class to complete Part D again.

Directions: On the lines below, write the word from the list that matches each clue.

trophy	**yellow**	**partner**	**pedestrian**	**permanent**
property	**bonus**	**chemistry**	**western**	

19. the color of a banana ___yellow___
20. the science dealing with chemicals ___chemistry___
21. lasting forever ___permanent___
22. an award or prize ___trophy___
23. the opposite of eastern ___western___
24. an added benefit ___bonus___
25. a helper or friend ___partner___
26. land ___property___
27. someone who is walking ___pedestrian___

Part D

Think About the Stories

Fiction or Nonfiction?

Directions: Write **fiction** next to the stories that were made up by the writer. Write **nonfiction** next to the stories that tell about real life.

1. "Finding New Friends" ___fiction___
2. "Second Sight" ___nonfiction___
3. "Student Volunteer" ___nonfiction___
4. "Blood Brothers" ___fiction___

Student page 127

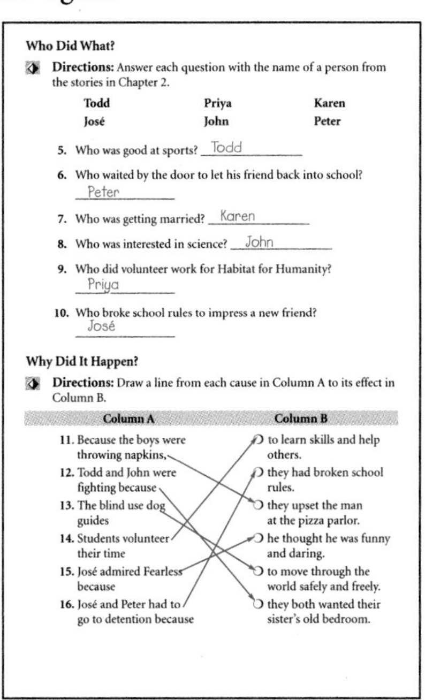

Who Did What?

Directions: Answer each question with the name of a person from the stories in Chapter 2.

Todd	**Priya**	**Karen**
José	**John**	**Peter**

5. Who was good at sports? ___Todd___
6. Who waited by the door to let his friend back into school? ___Peter___
7. Who was getting married? ___Karen___
8. Who was interested in science? ___John___
9. Who did volunteer work for Habitat for Humanity? ___Priya___
10. Who broke school rules to impress a new friend? ___José___

Why Did It Happen?

Directions: Draw a line from each cause in Column A to its effect in Column B.

Column A	Column B
11. Because the boys were throwing napkins,	to learn skills and help others.
12. Todd and John were fighting because	they had broken school rules.
13. The blind use dog guides	they upset the man at the pizza parlor.
14. Students volunteer their time	he thought he was funny and daring.
15. José admired Fearless because	to move through the world safely and freely.
16. José and Peter had to go to detention because	they both wanted their sister's old bedroom.

Student page 128

Chapter 3 Planning Guide

Skills and Learning Objectives

	Student Pages	Phonics and Phonograms	Word Study	Reading Strategy
Lesson 1 Lava Spill	130–139	Vowel variants in longer words	Prefixes *mid-, mis-*	Clarify
Lesson 2 Foster Child	140–150	*r*-controlled vowels in longer words	Prefixes *sub-, trans-*	Set a Purpose
Lesson 3 Our Nation's Capital	151–161	Homophones with *r*-controlled vowels	Decoding multisyllabic words with affixes	Access Prior Knowledge
Lesson 4 Sally Ride	162–173	Decoding multisyllabic words with unusual spellings	Adverbs	Summarize

Independent Reading

Independent Reading Lesson:
Teacher's Guide pages 120–121
List of Recommended Books to Read:
- *Shipwreck at the Bottom of the World*
- *The Pinballs*
- *Freedom Crossing*
- *Missing May*
- *Sarah Bishop*
- *What Do You Mean I Have Attention Deficit Disorder?*
- *Virtual War*
- *Waiting for the Rain*
- *The Watsons Go to Birmingham*
- *Within Reach, My Everest Story*
- *The Cay*
- *All-of-a-Kind Family*
- *Homecoming*
- *I'm Deaf and It's Okay*

Assessment and Review

Chapter 3 Summary of Skills and Strategies:
Student Worktext page 174

Chapter 3 Review:
Student Worktext pages 175–182
Teacher's Guide pages 122–125

Chapter 3 Test:
Teacher's Guide pages 135–137

Level E Test:
Teacher's Guide pages 138–140

Reading Comprehension/ Critical Thinking	Spelling	Study Skill	Language	Writing	Literary Appreciation	Learning Styles	Focus on LEP/ESL or LD	Application	Reading and Writing Practice Activities
Recognize the Main Idea and Supporting Details		99	99	99		95, 97	95, 96		75–81
Draw Conclusions	105		105	105		102	101, 104		82–88
Categorize	112		112	112		107,109	107, 108, 110		89–95
Note Sequence	119		119	119		115, 116	114, 117, 118	117	96–102

Common Reading Errors

If the Student . . .		Then . . .
◆ holds reading material unnaturally close to eyes	→	◆ arrange for a vision screening.
◆ fails to construct overall meaning from text because he/she does not ask the basic question, "Does this make sense?"	→	◆ reteach the lessons on Clarify and Main Idea in Lesson 1; discuss story ideas frequently while reading; encourage the student to construct oral summaries of passages or stories; model constructing oral summaries of passages or stories.
◆ confuses the sequence of events in written text	→	◆ reteach Note Sequence in Lesson 4; suggest that the student read more slowly and note signal words such as *first* and *next.*
◆ is unable to increase the rate of reading with fewer errors	→	◆ encourage the student to practice reading and rereading familiar text to build fluency.
◆ has difficulty making syllable breaks in multisyllabic words	→	◆ reteach decoding multisyllabic words in Lesson 4; have students make syllable breaks in multisyllabic words.

Lesson at a Glance

Chapter 3, Lesson 1 "Lava Spill"

Preview: This lesson presents a nonfiction selection about volcanoes—how they are formed, their destructive nature, and their benefits to society.

Objectives

- to read a nonfiction selection
- to read longer words with vowel variants
- to form words with the prefixes *mid* and *mis*
- to note main idea and supporting details
- to identify test-taking strategies
- to identify prepositions and prepositional phrases
- to write a summary

Student Worktext Pages 130–139

Story Words

volcano, destruction, ancient, benefit, electricity

Reading and Writing Practice Activities 75–81

Before Reading "Lava Spill"

Letters and Sounds

Vowel Variants in Longer Words; Phonograms *aught, ought*

Write the words *fought, because,* and *drawing* on the board. Read each word aloud and have students repeat each word after you say it. Ask students to say the vowel sound that is the same in all three words.

Ask a volunteer to circle the *aw* sound in *fought.* (ou) Tell students that the *gh* has become silent in the English language over time and is not actually part of the vowel sound spelling. Explain to students that knowing how to read *fought* can help them to read other words that end in *ought.* Have students tell other words with the *aw* sound that are spelled the same way. (bought, sought, thought) Write these words on the board and model blending with the *aw* sound.

Repeat this procedure for *because* and *drawing.* Sum up by having the class read aloud the three words on the board. Have them repeat the *aw* sound. Then have students complete Student Worktext page 130.

Reading and Writing Practice Activity 75: Vowel Variants in Longer Words.

Story Words

Read aloud these words: *volcano, destruction, ancient, benefit, electricity.* Tell students that these words are important in the next story they will read. Then write the words on the board and point to each one as you say it aloud a second time. Have students follow the ❑ *Read* ❑ *Say* ❑ *Write* sequence by completing **Story Words** on Student Worktext page 131. Remind students to write the story words in the Word Bank at the back of their Student Worktext. To introduce the words in context, write these sentences on the board:

- The volcano erupted.
- The hurricane caused a lot of destruction.
- People in ancient times built the pyramids.
- We can all benefit from recycling.
- To save electricity, turn off the lights when you leave the room.

Have students make a word card for *volcano.* Ask a volunteer to read the first sentence aloud. Then have students copy the sentence onto the back of the word card. Follow the same procedure for the remaining words. To assess students' abilities to read each new word, listen as individual students read the sentences on the board aloud.

Reading and Writing Practice Activity 76: Reading Story Words.

More Word Work

Have students work in pairs to complete **More Word Work** on Student Worktext page 131. Explain the difference in meaning between *mid* and *mis.*

Reading and Writing Practice Activity 77: Reading and Writing Prefixes *mid* and *mis.*

LESSON 1 ▶ Before Reading "Lava Spill"

Letters and Sounds

Directions: The letters **ou, au,** and **aw** can all stand for the **broad o** sound in **wrong.** Read each word. Write the word on the line.

1. thoughtlessness thoughtlessness
2. automatic automatic
3. awkwardly awkwardly

Directions: Write the word on the line, then circle the letters that make the **broad o** sound.

4. daughter-in-law daughter-in-law
5. thoughtfulness thoughtfulness
6. Pawnee Pawnee
7. launchpad launchpad
8. wrought wrought
9. awesomely awesomely
10. automobile automobile
11. sought sought
12. trauma trauma
13. pawnbroker pawnbroker
14. thought thought
15. automatic automatic

Directions: Write the letters on the lines. How many words can you make?

b c cl fl h th tr d

16. b ough
17. c ough
18. d ough
19. th ough
20. tr ough
21. h awk
22. b ought
23. th ought
24. c ause
25. cl ause
26. c aw
27. cl aw
28. fl aw
29. th aw
30. h aughty
31. fl aunt

Student page 130

Story Words

Directions: Read each word to yourself. Then say the word out loud. Write the word on the line. Check the box after each step.

32. volcano (vol|ca|no) Read ☑ Say ☑ Write ☑ volcano
33. destruction (de|struc|tion) Read ☑ Say ☑ Write ☑ destruction
34. ancient (an|cient) Read ☑ Say ☑ Write ☑ ancient
35. benefit (ben|e|fit) Read ☑ Say ☑ Write ☑ benefit
36. electricity (e|lec|tric|i|ty) Read ☑ Say ☑ Write ☑ electricity

More Word Work

Directions: The prefixes **mid** and **mis** are found at the beginning of many words. The prefix **mid** means **"at"** or **"near the middle."** The prefix **mis** means **"wrong."** Read the word. Write the word on the line.

37. midweek midweek
38. misspell misspell
39. midpoint midpoint
40. mistake mistake

Directions: Choose the correct prefix, **mis** or **mid,** for each word. Write the word on the line.

41. night midnight
42. ship midship
43. behave misbehave
44. lands midlands
45. judge misjudge
46. deed misdeed
47. stream midstream
48. fortune misfortune

Student page 131

Reading "Lava Spill"

Preview and Predict

- Tell students that they are going to read a nonfiction selection about volcanoes. They will learn how volcanoes form and about certain volcanic eruptions. Have a volunteer read the title of the story on Student Worktext page 132 aloud.
- Point out the illustration of an erupting volcano on page 132. Ask students to tell whether they have heard about any volcanoes that have erupted. Ask them if they know what makes a volcano erupt.
- Read aloud the sentence and question under **Use What You Know** at the top of page 132. Ask students to think about different forces of nature, such as thunderstorms, tornadoes, hurricanes, and earthquakes. Invite students to tell about their experiences with a powerful force of nature. Then have them write about their experiences on page 132.
- Ask students whether they think volcanic eruptions are always harmful. Discover whether students can name any benefits.
- Ask students to preview the story by reading the first paragraph, which is anecdotal. Ask students to tell what they would do if scientists predicted a volcanic eruption near their home. Have students consider the desire to see the eruption, safety, and not wanting to leave the area for an important reason.

Have students finish reading Student Worktext pages 132–133 to find out more about volcanoes.

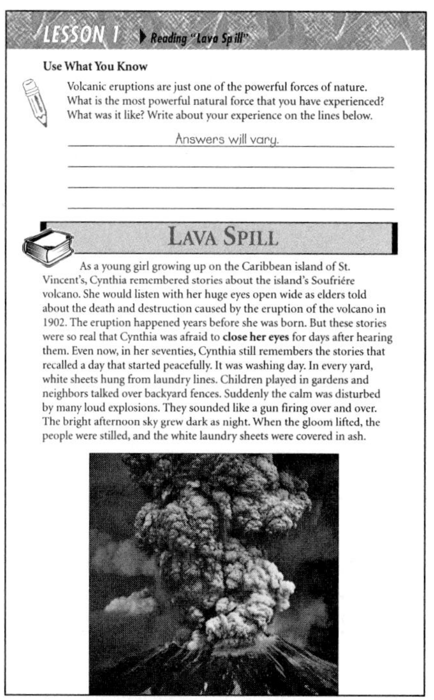
LESSON 1 ▸ Reading "Lava Spill"

Use What You Know

Volcanic eruptions are just one of the powerful forces of nature. What is the most powerful natural force that you have experienced? What was it like? Write about your experience on the lines below.

Answers will vary.

LAVA SPILL

As a young girl growing up on the Caribbean island of St. Vincent's, Cynthia remembered stories about the island's Soufriére volcano. She would listen with her huge eyes open wide as elders told about the death and destruction caused by the eruption of the volcano in 1902. The eruption happened years before she was born. But these stories were so real that Cynthia was afraid to **close her eyes** for days after hearing them. Even now, in her seventies, Cynthia still remembers the stories that recalled a day that started peacefully. It was washing day. In every yard, white sheets hung from laundry lines. Children played in gardens and neighbors talked over backyard fences. Suddenly the calm was disturbed by many loud explosions. They sounded like a gun firing over and over. The bright afternoon sky grew dark as night. When the gloom lifted, the people were stilled, and the white laundry sheets were covered in ash.

Student page 132

On the island of Martinique, Mount Pelée erupted in the same year with even more tragic results. At the time of the eruption, an election was in progress. The candidates competed with loud rumblings from the island's volcano as they made their speeches. These rumblings were so distressing that some people left the island. Others wishing to vote in the election remained. When Mount Pelée erupted, the number of dead reached almost 30,000. It was one of the most destructive volcanic eruptions of the 1900s.

Though both Soufriére and Mount Pelée are in the Caribbean, volcanoes are found in many places in the world. In the United States, Mount St. Helen's erupted in the state of Washington. The results were disastrous. The volcano had been showing signs of increased activity for months. People came from all over the world to witness the event. A party mood prevailed as t-shirts, mugs, and other things were sold to the crowd. Though the police attempted to set up "safe zones," many people ignored them and moved forward to get a closer look at the volcano. They misjudged its power.

On the morning of May 18, 1980, these onlookers got more than they bargained for. Mount St. Helen's erupted. A huge, black cloud rose from the volcano. The cloud moved rapidly. It trapped many people in its intense heat and covered the area with ash. Many people suffered burns. A number of people died from these burns or from the poisonous gases released by the volcano. The impact of this one eruption even changed our weather patterns for years afterward.

In ancient times, people created myths, or stories, to explain the power of volcanoes. The Greeks claimed that a god named Zeus wished to **even a score** between himself and a monster named Typhon. Zeus set Typhon on fire and buried him under Mount Aetna. According to the legend, the monster's powerful screams caused the mountain to burst. The Romans told of the god Vulcan setting up a blacksmith shop on the Greek Isle of Lemnos. There he violently fanned his fire and carelessly threw hot rocks into the air. "Volcano" was the name they gave to Vulcan's workshop. It is the word we use today to name the force of nature.

Even in modern times, there have been people who thought the power of volcanoes is due to magical forces. In Hawaii some people believe in a volcanic character named Madam Pele. There are people who claim to have seen her when she takes the form of an old or young woman and walks the earth. Stories tell of drivers stopping their cars to give a ride to a strange woman. The woman sometimes speaks to the driver, and sometimes she is silent. At some point during the ride the driver looks away from the passenger. When the driver turns back to speak to her, the strange woman has left.

Student page 133

Focus on ESL/LEP

In the story, Cynthia listened to the island elders' stories of the eruption of the volcano. Explain to students that many cultures pass on their heritage through stories in this way. Ask students to think of stories that have been passed down in their own families. Divide students into small groups to allow them to talk about their experiences. Encourage non-native speakers of English to include culture-specific terms in their account.

Learning Styles

Auditory/Verbal Pronounce some of the difficult proper nouns in this selection for students so they know how to say them:

- Soufriére (sue-free-ER)
- Martinique (mar-tuh-NEEK)
- Peleé (puh-LAY)
- Kilauea (key-lah-WAY-uh)
- Mauna Loa (mau-nuh-LOW-uh)

◆ *Strategy Modeling*

Clarify Tell students that they can reread a passage to help them understand its meaning better. When rereading a difficult passage, students should look for key points that they missed. You might say:

> *The story tells about a Greek legend in which a character named Zeus set a monster named Typhon on fire and buried him beneath a mountain. Typhon caused a volcano to erupt. The story also tells about a character named Vulcan who lived on a Greek island and caused eruptions. I don't understand why there are two myths. If I reread the paragraph that tells about the myths, I see that Vulcan was Roman. The Romans must have had different myths from the Greeks.*

Have students finish reading Student Worktext pages 134–135 to find out more about volcanoes. Tell students to pause to clarify if anything confuses them.

Focus on ESL/LEP

Geologic and scientific terms may be difficult for non-native speakers of English to understand, since they are not commonly used. Explain terms like *core, mantle, crust,* and *currents* to the class. Draw diagrams to illustrate the terms.

Focus on LD

Proceed slowly through the technical information about how volcanoes form and the different varieties of volcanoes. You might want to have students pause to think about each sentence before they read further.

There are also those who believe that Madam Pele rewards those who are good to others. She appears to them and warns of upcoming volcanic eruptions. Some have even said that her warning allowed them to flee a volcanic eruption. Others claim that Madam Pele has changed the lava flow from an active volcano. This allowed them to spare their home and property.

There are other stories about Madam Pele's terrible anger when she feels wronged. The volcanic eruption in Hawaii in December of 1935 is one such story. The story describes how after the eruption of Mauna Loa, lava flowed down its mountainside toward the town of Hilo. As you will learn later, scientists sometimes bomb a lava flow to change its course or to stop its flow. Officials decided to attempt a bombing of the eruption's lava flow in hopes of saving the town. Some Hawaiians feared that such a step would anger Madam Pele and they warned against doing it. Despite their warnings, the army provided planes to drop bombs on the lava flow. On December 27, the planes dropped their bombs. A few days later the lava flow stopped, sparing the town of Hilo. Though many were happy, others warned that Madam Pele would soon take her revenge.

A month later over Luke Field in Oahu, two army planes ran into each other. There were a total of eight men on board the planes at the time of the crash. Of the eight men, six of them had been involved in bombing the lava flow a month earlier. The only survivors of the accident were two men who had not been involved in bombing Madam Pele's volcano. Those who understand science and the laws of nature think the crash was just an accident. But those who believe in the volcano goddess are sure that this was an act of Madam Pele's revenge.

Today scientists study the natural causes of volcanoes. To understand this powerful force, it is necessary to know the structure of the earth. Earth is made up of three layers. The center is called the core; it is made up of nickel and iron. The middle layer, or mantle, is made of a semi-solid rocky material. The outermost layer is known as the crust and is made up of brittle rock. The earth's core is very hot. Currents of heat rise through the mantle, cooling off as they near the crust. These cooler currents then sink back down to the core. Once again they heat up and rise to the surface. This rising and falling pattern continues again and again. Over the course of time, this process shapes the surface of the earth. It causes the brittle crust to stretch and contract until it breaks up into pieces like a jigsaw puzzle. The pieces of this puzzle are called plates.

With all this activity going on inside the earth, these plates are in constant movement. The edges of the plates bump up against each other. One plate may be pushed under the edge of the other. Scientists believe

Student page 134

that the part of the plate that is pushed underneath becomes so hot that it melts. The melted substance, known as magma, rises up through the edges of two plates to form a volcano. Not all volcanoes occur at the edges of two plates. The volcanoes that form the Hawaiian Islands are in the middle of a plate. Scientists say that these volcanoes rise over hot spots. These areas of heat rise up through the mantle and burst through the crust.

Because they are formed differently, volcanoes look different. For example, the slopes of Mount St. Helen's are made up of many layers of rock and lava to form a composite volcano. Composite volcanoes are the result of many eruptions that rise up in the shape of a cone and often reach great heights.

Dome volcanoes are sometimes found on the slopes, or within the craters, of composite volcanoes. Dome volcanoes are made from lava and are usually small and round in shape.

A caldera is a crater volcano. Calderas are formed when heat causes a great explosion. It creates a large bowl-like hole as it breaks through the crust. Its name comes from the Spanish word for cauldron. Looking into one is like looking into a hot bubbling pot or cauldron.

The Hawaiian Islands have formed from shield volcanoes, which are broad and have low slopes. At the time of eruption the lava is very fluid and **moves like lightning.** It flows long distances. This makes the broad, gentle slopes that cause them to look like an overturned shield.

There are also many different kinds of volcanic eruptions. Eruptions may be made up of gas, rocks, and lava. As big as a fireworks display, these eruptions are often deadly to human and animal life. Some volcanic eruptions come without warning, like the one on Mount Pinatubo. This volcano in the Philippines hadn't erupted for over 400 years. It took everyone by surprise. It was one of the biggest eruptions of the 1900s. Most volcanoes give plenty of warning. Volcanoes like Mount St. Helen's can rumble and spew rocks for months and years before actually erupting.

How do you think it would be possible to stop or slow the flow of lava from a volcanic eruption? Write what you think on the lines below. Then keep reading to find out what scientists have tried.

Answers will vary.

Student page 135

Have students read Student Worktext pages 136–137 to finish the selection about volcanoes.

You might ask students the following questions about the selection:

- Have people been able to stop the flow of lava after a volcano has erupted? (Sometimes. Natural and human-made barriers have been used.)
- How does water help to slow or stop the movement of lava? (Water cools the lava, making it heavier and therefore, slower. Sometimes lava will stop completely if a crust has formed.)
- Why is fighting lava with water difficult? (A huge amount of water is required.)
- How did some Hawaiians think they could stop the lava flow? (by making offerings to the volcano) Does this method work? (Answers may vary.)
- How have volcanic eruptions helped people? (Solidified lava has been used to make buildings, walls, streets, and barriers to the sea. Volcanic soil is good for crops. Springs heated by volcanoes are used for healthful purposes. Volcanoes produce precious metals and minerals such as gold, silver, zinc, lead, and diamonds. Volcanoes also create beautiful landscapes.)

Because of the great dangers of volcanic eruptions, people have tried to create ways to stop the flow of lava. One way is using natural and human-made barriers. Sometimes hills, gullies, walls, and ditches have stopped lava flow. But there have also been times when the lava simply piled higher and higher, flowed over a barrier, and continued in the same direction. Experts who have experience using barriers against lava flow explain that the barriers must have a very wide base. They must also be made of thick and heavy material if the lava is not to break through.

Another way of fighting hot lava is to cool it with water. Pouring on water can help slow the lava as the cooling lava becomes heavy. Sometimes water can make the lava form a solid crust and stop it completely. The first time water was used against lava was in 1960 when the Hawaiian volcano Kilauea erupted. Lava flowed through the town of Kapoho, destroying many homes and offices. The fire department slowed the lava by spraying it with water. This gave people enough time to gather their belongings and flee their homes. The major problem of fighting lava this way is that it requires huge amounts of water.

Sometimes the outer part of a flowing river of lava will form a crust. This creates a tube that keeps the lava hot inside. It allows the lava to stay liquid for longer periods. The lava then flows much farther than it would otherwise. To stop it midstream, the roof of the lava tube is bombed. This makes a vent in the tube that cools the lava and slows its flow. This was first tried in Hawaii when Mauna Loa erupted in 1935. Some Hawaiians were upset that scientists were trying to stop the lava flow with bombs.

Student page 136

They believed that the way to stop lava flows was to make offerings to the volcano. The argument was never truly settled, because the eruption of Mauna Loa stopped for unknown reasons.

Volcanoes can be deadly, but they also benefit people and the planet itself. In Europe, ancient hardened lava has been used to make buildings, walls, and streets. The Dutch have used volcanic rubble to build barriers against the North Sea. All over the world, volcanic soil is some of the best for growing crops. Many people are grateful for the benefits of hot springs and for electricity created by the heat of volcanoes. Volcanic action also forms gold, silver, copper, zinc, lead, and diamonds. Lastly, volcanoes create some of the most beautiful landscapes in the world. For all these reasons, people continue to risk living near volcanoes.

From the ancient Greeks to the modern-day tourists who travel the world to view them, volcanoes have long **captured people's imagination.** Though sometimes destructive, their benefits are great and their beauty and power are awe-inspiring. Those who witness a volcanic eruption are often at a loss to describe the event. They remember the experience all their lives, however. The stories of what they have seen are eventually passed on from person to person.

Student page 137

Learning Styles

Visual/Spatial Some science classes use models of volcanoes to show volcanic eruptions. Check with a science teacher to see whether you can borrow a model of a volcano, or create your own model for students. Demonstrate how volcanoes erupt and how to stop lava flows. If you have access to a science kit, you may want to bring in a piece of hardened lava.

Learning Styles

Interpersonal/Group Learning Divide students into groups. Have each group learn more about a specific volcanic eruption. Have students give group presentations on the information they find. Have each group divide the tasks necessary to make a presentation. Group members should work on the research together.

After Reading "Lava Spill"

Personal Response: You Be the Judge

Read aloud the question under **You Be the Judge** on Student Worktext page 138. Ask students to name some benefits and risks of living near a volcano. Then have students answer the question.

Think About the Story: Reading Comprehension

Have students complete the remaining items on Student Worktext pages 138–139 independently or in pairs. Check their responses to help you assess their story comprehension. If students' responses indicate that they did not understand story events, reread the story aloud, pausing to discuss key events.

Reading Comprehension Skill: Recognize the Main Idea and Supporting Details

Invite a volunteer to answer the question from **The Big Idea** on Student Worktext page 139. Tell students that the main idea is the main topic for the entire selection. Explain to students that in works of nonfiction, a main idea must have supporting details—facts, examples, or reasons that provide evidence for the main idea.

Write the main idea on the board. (*Volcanoes are a natural force that is both destructive and beneficial.*) Underneath the sentence write 1. *destructive* on one side of the board. On the other side, write 2. *beneficial.* Explain:

- The story contains details to explain, or support, the main idea.
- The story therefore explains both the destructive nature and benefits of volcanoes.
- Most of the time, a paragraph contains one supporting idea.

Ask students to skim the story for examples of destruction caused by volcanic eruptions and the benefits of volcanoes. Write their examples under the appropriate heading on the board. You may want to use lowercase letters (a., b., etc.) to list examples in outline form.

Provide students with a short (one page or less) article from a magazine, newspaper, or book. Ask students to work with a partner to identify the main idea and supporting details. Have them create an outline like the one you made on the board.

LESSON 1 ▸ After Reading "Lava Spill"

You Be the Judge

1. Because of the many benefits, people continue to live and work near volcanoes. Do you believe the benefits outweigh the risks? Why or why not? Write what you think on the lines below.
Answers will vary.

Think About the Story

Use Story Words

Directions: Look at your list of story words on page 131. Write a story word on each line.

2. Ancient people made up stories to explain the causes of volcanoes.
3. People have found ways to produce electricity from volcanic heat.
4. A volcano is a powerful force of nature.
5. The destruction caused by the eruption of Mount St. Helen's was tragic.
6. Though volcanoes are destructive, they are also a benefit to people.

Write Sentences About the Story

Directions: Circle the word that best fits in each sentence.

7. It is a (mistake/disbelief) to think we know everything about volcanoes.
8. Mount St. Helen's (erupting/erupted) in 1980.
9. Our word volcano (be/comes) from a Roman myth.
10. The mantle is the (middle/midriff) layer of the earth.

Student page 138

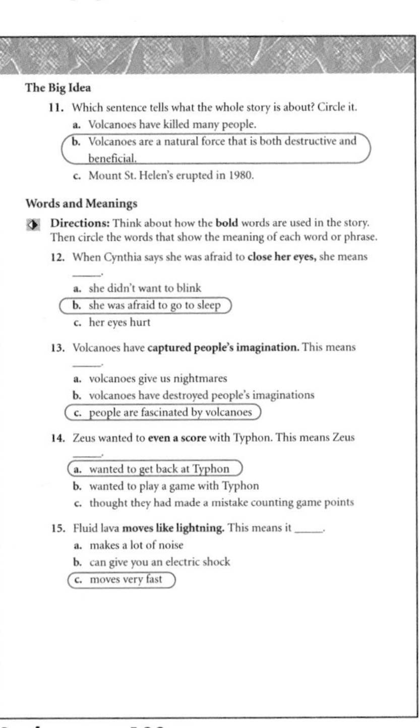
The Big Idea

11. Which sentence tells what the whole story is about? Circle it.
    a. Volcanoes have killed many people.
    b. Volcanoes are a natural force that is both destructive and beneficial.
    c. Mount St. Helen's erupted in 1980.

Words and Meanings

Directions: Think about how the **bold** words are used in the story. Then circle the words that show the meaning of each word or phrase.

12. When Cynthia says she was afraid to **close her eyes,** she means ____.
    a. she didn't want to blink
    b. she was afraid to go to sleep
    c. her eyes hurt
13. Volcanoes have **captured people's imagination.** This means ____.
    a. volcanoes give us nightmares
    b. volcanoes have destroyed people's imaginations
    c. people are fascinated by volcanoes
14. Zeus wanted to **even a score** with Typhon. This means Zeus ____.
    a. wanted to get back at Typhon
    b. wanted to play a game with Typhon
    c. thought they had made a mistake counting game points
15. Fluid lava **moves like lightning.** This means it ____.
    a. makes a lot of noise
    b. can give you an electric shock
    c. moves very fast

Student page 139

Reinforce & Extend

STUDY SKILL: Test-Taking Strategies

Explain the following test-taking strategies to students:

- Listen carefully to the instructions that your teacher gives you.
- Read the directions carefully. Make sure you have read all the words. Ask your teacher if you have any questions.
- Don't spend too much time on one question. If the test is multiple choice, cross out the answers that you know are not right. Then decide the correct answer from the remaining choices.
- Check to make sure that you have answered all the questions.
- Turn in your test when you are sure you have finished and you feel good about your answers.

Ask students questions about the steps above to help them remember the strategies.

Reading and Writing Practice Activity 78 provides additional practice with test-taking strategies.

LANGUAGE: Prepositions and Prepositional Phrases

Write these sentences on the board:

The tree frog sat on the log.

The song says that we go over the river and through the woods to Grandmother's house.

We read "The Midnight Ride of Paul Revere."

Then write a list of the following commonly used prepositions on the board: *above, at, before, below, beside, between, by, during, for, from, into, of, to, next to, on, over, through, under, with.*

In each sentence, have students identify the preposition. Circle the preposition when students name it. Explain:

- Prepositions are words that show the relationship of a noun to another word in the sentence.
- A prepositional phrase is a group of words that begins with a preposition and ends with a noun or pronoun.

Ask students to find the grouping of words that starts with the preposition and ends with a noun. Ask students which word shows a relationship. Underline the prepositional phrase when they name it. Repeat this procedure for each prepositional phrase in the sentences.

Reading and Writing Practice Activity 79 provides additional practice with prepositions and prepositional phrases.

WRITING: A Summary

Ask students whether they have ever told a friend about a movie they have seen. Then ask a volunteer to tell you about a movie. Tell the student to just say what happened and to leave out the details.

Explain that the student has just given you a summary of the plot of a movie. Tell students that a summary contains the most important ideas without all the details. Explain that they can summarize things they have read in order to remember them.

To write a summary, students should:

- State the main idea.
- Write the key points. Each point should be a separate sentence.
- Arrange the points logically. The ideas should not jump around.
- Use their own words.

Have student write a summary of "Lava Spill" or another selection they have read. Tell students that they can usually follow the order that was presented in the original. Have them trade papers with a classmate to make sure they covered all the key points and wrote a summary that was easy to follow.

Reading and Writing Practice Duplicate and distribute Activities 80 and 81 on writing a summary. Then have students complete the activities in pairs.

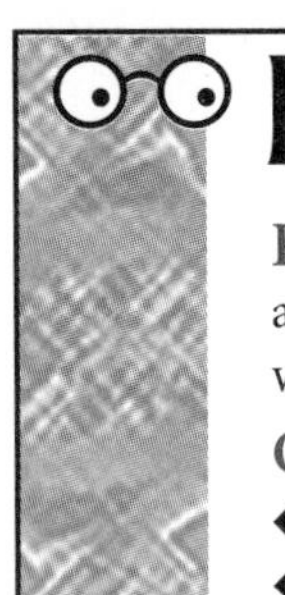

Lesson at a Glance

Chapter 3, Lesson 2 "Foster Child"

Preview: This lesson presents a fiction story about a girl from the city who goes to the country to live with a foster family.

Objectives

- to read a fiction story
- to read and spell *r*-controlled vowels in longer words
- to understand and write words with the prefixes *sub* and *trans*
- to draw conclusions about what happens in a story
- to write job-related words that are frequently misspelled
- to identify and write compound sentences
- to write a persuasive paragraph

Student Worktext Pages 140–150

Story Words

caseworker, peered, routine, necessary, allowance, accusing

Reading and Writing Practice Activities 82–88

Before Reading "Foster Child"

Letters and Sounds

Longer Words with *r*-Controlled Vowels

Write the words *tornado, harmless, married, merely,* and *refurbish* across the top of the board. Read each word aloud and have students repeat each word after you say it. Explain that there is a vowel followed by the *r* sound in each word. Ask volunteers to say the vowel + *r* sound in each word, after you model with tornado. Circle the letters that make the vowel + *r* sound after the student says the sound.

Next have students say words that have the same vowel + *r* sound as each word on the board. Write the words they give underneath the word with the corresponding sound. Point out the different spellings for the same vowel + *r* sounds and circle them. Then have students complete Student Worktext page 140.

Reading and Writing Practice Activity 82: Longer Words with *r*-Controlled Vowels.

Story Words

Read aloud these words: *caseworker, peered, routine, necessary, allowance, accusing.* Tell students that these words are important in the next story they will read. Then write the words on the board and point to each one as you say it aloud a second time. Have students follow the ❑ *Read* ❑ *Say* ❑ *Write* sequence by completing **Story Words** on Student Worktext page 141. Remind students to write the story words in the Word Bank at the back of their Student Worktext. To introduce the words in context, write these sentences on the board:

- The caseworker found a new home for the boy.
- The groundhog peered cautiously out of its hole.
- Every day is the same routine.
- It is necessary to eat foods from the four food groups every day.
- I am paid an allowance to do chores.
- The police officer was accusing the truck driver of speeding.

Have students make a word card for *caseworker*. Ask a volunteer to read the first sentence aloud. Then have students copy the sentence onto the back of the word card. Follow the same procedure for the remaining words. To assess students' abilities to read each new word, listen as individual students read aloud the sentences on the board.

Reading and Writing Practice Activity 83: Reading Story Words.

More Word Work

Have students work in pairs to complete **More Word Work** on Student Worktext page 141. Write the prefixes *sub* and *trans* on the board and explain their meanings.

Reading and Writing Practice Activity 84: Reading and Writing Prefixes *sub* and *trans.*

LESSON 2 ▶ Before Reading "Foster Child"

Letters and Sounds

Directions: These words have the sound of the **or** in **fort.** Circle the letters that make this **or** sound.

1. fortunately
2. boardinghouse
3. fourteen
4. fluorescent

Directions: These words have the sound of the **ar** in **barn.** The letters **ear, or,** and **ar** can all have this sound. Circle the letters that make this **ar** sound.

5. artfully
6. carnival
7. heartless
8. sorry

Directions: These words have the sound of the **ar** in **share** in them. The letters **ear, ere, ar,** and **air** can all have this sound. Circle the letters that make this **ar** sound.

9. therefore
10. warily
11. unfairness
12. bearable

Directions: These words have the sound of **ir** in **irritate.** The letters **ear, eer, ere, ir,** and **ier** can all have this sound. Circle the letters that make this **ir** sound.

13. tearfully
14. hemisphere
15. buccaneer
16. cavalier

Directions: These words have the sound of **ur** in **fur.** The letters **ear, or, ir, er,** and **ur** can all have this sound. Circle the letters that make this **ur** sound.

17. earnestly
18. turbine
19. certainly
20. birdhouse
21. worthless

Directions: Write each word below under the word that has the same vowel sound.

sorrowful, afford, wearable, aboard, atmosphere, pouring, farmhouse, hearing, fairly, barely

fortunately	artfully	therefore	tearfully
22. afford	25. sorrowful	27. wearable	30. atmosphere
23. aboard	26. farmhouse	28. fairly	31. hearing
24. pouring		29. barely	

Student page 140

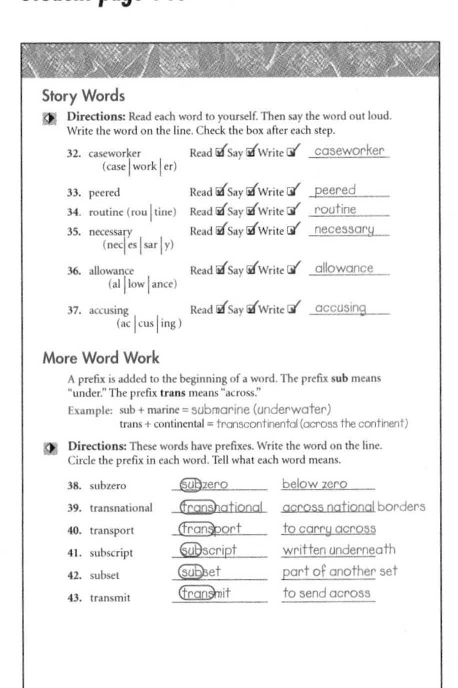

Story Words

Directions: Read each word to yourself. Then say the word out loud. Write the word on the line. Check the box after each step.

32. caseworker (case | work | er) Read ☑ Say ☑ Write ☑ caseworker
33. peered Read ☑ Say ☑ Write ☑ peered
34. routine (rou | tine) Read ☑ Say ☑ Write ☑ routine
35. necessary (nec | es | sar | y) Read ☑ Say ☑ Write ☑ necessary
36. allowance (al | low | ance) Read ☑ Say ☑ Write ☑ allowance
37. accusing (ac | cus | ing) Read ☑ Say ☑ Write ☑ accusing

More Word Work

A prefix is added to the beginning of a word. The prefix **sub** means "under." The prefix **trans** means "across."

Example: sub + marine = submarine (underwater)
trans + continental = transcontinental (across the continent)

Directions: These words have prefixes. Write the word on the line. Circle the prefix in each word. Tell what each word means.

38. subzero — subzero — below zero
39. transnational — transnational — across national borders
40. transport — transport — to carry across
41. subscript — subscript — written underneath
42. subset — subset — part of another set
43. transmit — transmit — to send across

Student page 141

Reading "Foster Child"

Preview and Predict

- Tell students that they are going to read a story about a girl from the city who moves to the country to live with foster parents. They will learn about her life in the country and about how the family overcomes stereotypes of city and country life. Have a volunteer read the title of the story on Student Worktext page 142 aloud.
- Ask students whether they know what foster care is. Explain that it is often temporary care for children whose families cannot take care of them properly. Ask students if they know any reasons that children are taken into foster care. (Answers may include that the parents are having problems, that the family cannot afford to support the children, or that the family doesn't have the money or time to care for the children.)
- Ask students whether they think living in foster care would be difficult. Have them consider that many children in foster care are well looked after and that families are hand-selected.
- Read aloud the sentence and questions under **Use What You Know** at the top of page 142. Ask students whether they have been to the country. Invite students to tell about their experiences. Then have them write about their thoughts or experiences on page 142.
- Ask students to preview the story by reading the first three paragraphs. Have students tell whether they think Sandra already has ideas about what life in the country will be like. Then ask students to tell whether they think Sandra will eventually like life in the country.

Have students finish reading Student Worktext pages 142–143 to find out about Sandra's experience in the country.

Focus on ESL/LEP

For some students who are new to the United States, life in the country may be a common experience. Invite students who have lived in the country to talk about their experiences. Encourage them to talk about details, such as daily activities, people, plants, animals, and formal education. Invite students to use words from their own language. Help them translate certain words or concepts into English.

LESSON 2 ▸ Reading "Foster Child"

Use What You Know

Sandra leaves from the city to live with a foster family in the country. What do you know about life in the country? Is it different from life in the city? How? Write what you think on the lines below.

Answers will vary.

FOSTER CHILD

Sandra stared out the window. The flat land and the road seemed to go on endlessly. She wasn't too happy about this trip. She was on her way to a foster home. It was a two-hour car ride from the city to her new home. Her new home was on a farm in the country. Her caseworker, Susan, was driving her there. Susan was always asking Sandra questions about her life. Sometimes Sandra just wanted to be left alone.

Sandra wanted to live with her own family. Her mother and father had problems and neither one could care for her. She was taken away for foster care. She missed her friends from her old neighborhood. They still lived with their families. Sandra and her friends used to hang around together. Sometimes they would stay out really late into the night. Her parents didn't notice that she wasn't at home.

The car pulled off the main road and onto a long, dirt and gravel driveway. As they rode up to the house, Sandra peered out the window again. This didn't look like the farms she had seen in books and on TV. There were no rows of corn growing in the fields. There were three large glass buildings instead of a barn with chickens and cows. The sign out front said "Groves Greenhouse." The Groves were her new "family."

The Groves came outside when the car pulled up. As they walked over, a large, brown barking dog came bounding down the steps. Mr. Grove whistled sharply. The dog stopped barking, then ran right up to Sandra and put his front paws on her shirt. She smiled and patted its head.

"Hello, Sandra," said Mr. Grove. "This is Jasper. We rescued him from the animal shelter about two years ago. We think he is part collie and part mutt! He is very friendly, as you can see."

Sandra didn't say anything. She continued to pet Jasper.

"I am Charlie and this is Amy Jo. We are happy to have you with us."

Sandra just stared at them. She didn't know what to say to country people. She was nervous and was glad that Jasper was there. She wished she were back at home. She was never at a loss for words there.

Student page 142

"Right. So, come on in and we'll show you around," said Amy Jo.

Susan had been to the farm before. She had to check it out to make sure Sandra could live there. She had said, "Nice to see you again," when they arrived. She told Sandra that she had met the Groves. She had to learn about them and to judge whether they would be good foster parents. Susan had given her approval.

Charlie told Sandra that the house was really an old farmhouse that they had restored. It was run-down when they bought it. However, it was attached to land that would be good for their business.

They walked up a curving, wooden staircase. Sandra's room was at the end of the hallway. It had a window that looked out on a yard with trees and flowers. The room had simple furniture and a small rug on the hardwood floor. Sandra didn't like that all three adults seemed to be looking at her, expecting something from her.

Charlie and Susan went down to get Sandra's things from the car. Amy Jo said, "I want to give you a tour of the farm. Why don't you relax here for a little while first? The car ride was long."

Sandra said, "Yeah." She never went on long car rides. She grew up in the city. Her family didn't go on vacations.

Charlie and Susan brought up her bag and her backpack. When Charlie left the room, Susan said that she would be leaving to go back to the city. She reminded Sandra that she had her phone number and to call if she wanted to talk. Susan said, "I think you'll like living on the farm. Give it a chance."

Amy Jo came back and led Sandra outside. "Do you go by Sandra or Sandy?" Amy Jo asked.

"Sandra," she replied. She only let her parents and friends call her Sandy.

"Okay, Sandra. Welcome to Groves Greenhouse. What we do is grow flowers and plants to sell to people and small businesses. We deliver large orders to our customers. They may also take their purchases home with them. We grow many kinds of flowers and other plants. Some of them are grown in the greenhouses,"—she pointed to the glass buildings—"and some are grown in the fields. All of our plants receive proper care, including watering and weeding."

Sandra had never seen so many kinds of plants in one place. She wondered how the Groves could keep track of all of them.

Amy Jo led Sandra into one of the greenhouses. It was warm inside. "The glass helps to keep in the warm air. It also lets the sun's rays get in easily and then traps the warmth inside." She pointed to one of the glass panes. It was open, like a window. "We have vents that allow the air to move around. We don't want it to get too hot in here. The plants need warmth, but not too much, because we don't grow many tropical plants."

Student page 143

Strategy Modeling

Set a Purpose Explain to students that they should determine ahead of time what information should be gathered from the story. Students who set a purpose for reading will have definite expectations about the text they are about to read, will be more engaged in their reading, and will notice more in what they read. Model setting a purpose before students read further. You might say:

I know that Sandra is moving from the city to the country to live with her new foster family. I know that she has certain ideas about what the country will be like. I think life in the country is a lot different from life in the city. Because I know some things about life in the city, I will read for information about life in the country.

Or you might say:

I know that Sandra is a foster child who is not too happy to be going to foster care. I think the new way of life will be good for Sandra. I am going to read to find proof that Sandra is being helped in her new environment.

Have students finish reading Student Worktext pages 144–145 to find out more about Sandra's experiences with her new family and environment. Point out that they will pause at the top of page 145 to set a new purpose for continuing to read.

Learning Styles

Auditory/Verbal Have those students who read and understood the story well retell the story to auditory learners in pairs or small groups. Have the students retelling the story make notes about what details to include, or follow along in the text to not miss any important details as the story is told. Have students listening to the story answer comprehension questions when the story is finished.

Learning Styles

Body/Kinesthetic Have students role play a foster care situation in which a foster child is being introduced to his or her new family. Divide the students into groups with one student playing the foster child and the other students playing the caseworker and foster family. Have them use gestures and body movements, as appropriate.

Sandra decided that she wouldn't melt in the greenhouse, although **the air seemed sticky**. She looked around at the flowers and other plants. She decided that she wasn't interested in this business of the Groves. It was nothing like the people who sold flowers in the city.

Amy Jo continued to lead Sandra into each of the three greenhouses. Amy Jo pointed out plants that Sandra had never heard of before. The flowers were brightly colored, mixed in with the green of the leaves and stems. The air smelled good. Sandra could smell the flowers without getting close. The Groves also grew vegetables and many kinds of plants that Amy Jo called shrubs.

When they left the greenhouses, Amy Jo told Sandra about the plants in the fields. They had a system that watered the plants. The water was set on a timer so that the Groves didn't have to turn it on and off. When the plants grew larger, they would be transplanted.

After the tour, the Groves and Sandra ate dinner. They had homegrown vegetables with the meal. Sandra had to admit that they tasted good. She didn't usually have meals like this. When Amy Jo asked her if she enjoyed the meal, Sandra replied with "Yes!"

Sandra's first day drew to a close. She still went to bed feeling lonely, but the day had passed quickly. She lay in bed listening to the crickets. It was so quiet out here in the country. Sometimes she heard Jasper bark at some unknown creature. She missed the sounds of the people, cars, and sirens that she was used to hearing in the city.

The next morning Sandra was up early, at least for her. She found Charlie and Amy Jo already hard at work in the greenhouses. Amy Jo was cutting back some of the plants and removing dead flowers. Charlie was spraying something on the leaves of some of the plants. He said it was a

Student page 144

mix to help the plants grow. He said it would also keep some of the insects away. He handed Sandra a watering can. He pointed out the hose to her. She must have stared blankly at him because he told her to fill the watering can. After she filled it, she came back, and he told her which plants to water. Sandra did as she was told.

This became the morning routine. Each day she would spend the morning watering the plants. Sometimes she used a hose and sometimes she used the watering can. Sandra didn't realize that she would have to work for her foster parents. She wasn't happy about this at all. During summers at home, she hung around with her friends all day. In the city she didn't have to work.

Sometimes the Groves were visited by customers in search of plants for their garden. Charlie and Amy Jo would let them wander around, offering help when necessary. When someone wanted to buy something, they went to the cash register that was in the corner of one of the greenhouses. Charlie told Sandra that he would teach her how to use the cash register someday soon.

"Great," she thought. "More work."

One day, Jasper's barking marked the arrival of the Groves' accountant, Ray. The Groves had told Ray about Sandra, so he was not surprised to see her. He tried to **strike up a conversation** with her. "Are you enjoying yourself on the farm?" he asked.

Sandra shrugged her shoulders.

Ray seemed interested in Sandra's work. He asked her more questions about her life in the city. She gave him short answers and continued with her work. Ray and Charlie went into the house to discuss the **books.** Amy Jo was helping a customer on another part of the farm. Some workers were loading shrubs into a delivery truck that another customer had brought. Sandra decided that she needed a break.

She went for a walk around the farm, careful to avoid Amy Jo's eyes. She hid herself among the shrubs and sat down to think. She still missed the city and her friends. She thought country life was boring. There was no excitement. There were hardly any people around. There were no subways. "How do they have any fun?" she thought.

Do you think Sandra will grow to like the country? Why or why not? Write what you think on the lines below. Then keep reading to find out the answer.

Answers will vary.

Student page 145

Have students read Student Worktext pages 146–148 to finish the selection.

You might ask students the following questions about the selection.

- ◆ Why was Sandra worried about her friends' visit? (She thought they would laugh at her new life on the farm. She also didn't want to know that she had been left out of too many things at home.)
- ◆ When does Sandra finally admit to enjoying working in the greenhouse? (when her friends come to visit and she shows them what she does there)
- ◆ Why does Sandra decide that she is glad she came to live with the Groves? (They seem to care about her and they trust her.)
- ◆ Why does Charlie immediately suspect Sandra's friends when he finds that the money is missing? (They are from the city. He is stereotyping the way people from the city behave.)
- ◆ Why did Sandra think Charlie was being unfair? (Because he was blaming her friends because they were from the city. He hadn't seen them take the money.)
- ◆ Why do you think Amy Jo didn't want Sandra to pay them back using her allowance? (They didn't think that she stole the money. Also, it would take a long time to pay them back.)
- ◆ What really happened to the money? (The Groves' accountant, Ray, stole it from the cash register.)
- ◆ Why did Charlie apologize to Sandra? (for accusing her friends of stealing and being quick to judge them)

After a while, she returned to the greenhouse. Ray was leaving and Jasper was barking. "See you next time, old boy," Ray said to the dog.

That night, while they were eating dinner, Charlie told Sandra that she was doing a great job on the farm. Sandra was pleased. Amy Jo said that they really liked her work. She told Sandra to tell her if the work was too much for her. Sandra said that she would.

The next day, Amy Jo told Sandra that she had some news for her. Susan, her caseworker, had arranged for three of Sandra's friends to come visit. Amy Jo was going to pick them up from the bus station.

Sandra was excited, but also worried. She wondered what her friends would think of her new life. She hoped they wouldn't laugh at her for working on a farm. She hadn't seen them in a while. She hoped she hadn't been left out of too many things back home.

Sandra went with Amy Jo to pick up her friends, Cara, Jago, and Yolanda. Sandra and her friends hugged each other when they were reunited. As they drove back to the farm, Amy Jo told Sandra's friends about the business. She said it had been a good summer for the business. She was happy with the way things were going. She also praised Sandra for helping out in the greenhouses. Sandra felt good about her work.

When they returned, Sandra gave the girls a tour of the farm. She showed them how she watered the plants. She named a few of the plants for her friends. She tried to impress them. Yolanda asked her about what she did for fun on the farm. Sandra told her that it was pretty quiet. She said that she and Jasper went for long walks.

"Don't you get bored?" said Yolanda.

"Why do they make you work?" said Cara.

Sandra became defensive. "Well, there isn't that much time to be bored," replied Sandra. "Charlie and Amy Jo wanted to help me enjoy

Student page 146

nature and some of the food we eat. Besides, they give me an allowance for helping out. I don't have to help. I like it." Sandra had admitted it. She enjoyed working in the greenhouse. She liked the routine of caring for the plants. It made her feel good to think that she was responsible for them.

The girls stayed in the greenhouse a while. In the afternoon, Ray came by and the girls went to play with Jasper. Sandra enjoyed showing him off as well. He and Sandra had both learned how to adjust to farm life.

It was time to drive the girls back to the bus station. Sandra was sorry to see them go, but she wasn't as sad as she once was. She told her friends to come back to visit. She hoped they would stay longer next time and learn more about the farm.

When Amy Jo and Sandra returned to the house, Sandra noticed that Charlie seemed a little out of sorts. He and Amy Jo went into the office to talk. Sandra went upstairs to her room to think about the day. She decided that she was glad that she came to live with the Groves. They seemed to care about her and they trusted her. They were different from her own parents.

Amy Jo and Charlie knocked on her door. "We need to talk to you," Charlie said.

"Oh, no," thought Sandra. Things had been going so well. She wondered what she did. Sandra opened the door and they came in.

"Sandra, were you and your friends in greenhouse number one today?" asked Charlie.

"Um, yes," Sandra stammered.

"Sandra, there is quite a bit of money missing from the cash register. I'm sorry to say we think your friends may have taken it."

Sandra gulped. "But they couldn't have. I was with them the whole day. I didn't see them anywhere near the cash register."

"Sandra, your friends are from the city. They have different ways from us country folk. We need to think about how we should handle this," said Charlie.

Sandra was disappointed. She knew her friends didn't take the money. She thought it was unfair of Charlie to blame them, just because they were from the city. He hadn't seen them take the money.

"I will pay you back for what is missing," said Sandra. "I will use the money from my allowance."

Charlie and Amy Jo looked at each other. "That's not necessary, Sandra," said Amy Jo. "Besides, your allowance would take a long time to pay it off. It's time for dinner," said Amy Jo. "Let's eat and we can talk about this later."

Dinner was almost silent. Sandra was very upset. It was almost as if they were accusing her of stealing. She made it through dinner and went straight to her room.

Student page 147

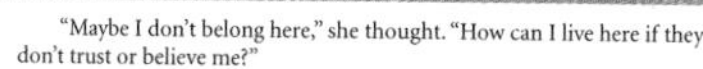

"Maybe I don't belong here," she thought. "How can I live here if they don't trust or believe me?"

The incident passed and nothing more was said. Sandra continued with her greenhouse duties. She didn't feel quite the same as before though.

One day a few weeks later, Sandra walked up to Greenhouse #1 from the field. She thought she noticed someone inside. She peered through the window through the leaves of a hanging fern.

Sandra was amazed to see Ray at the cash register. He was taking money out of it and stuffing it into his pockets! She was shocked. She couldn't move. Her **heart was racing.**

Sandra backed away from the greenhouse. She had to find Charlie. She ran as fast as she could. She found him in one of the rows in the field.

"Charlie," she panted, "I know who did it! I know who took the money! It was Ray!"

Charlie stared at her.

"I just saw him take money out of the cash register. He didn't know I was watching."

Charlie paused for just a second. "Come on." They went together to Greenhouse #1. Ray was standing outside. "Charlie, there you are. I was just getting ready to leave."

Charlie looked at Sandra, who returned his look with **pleading eyes.**

"Ray, I think we better have a talk." They went into the house and shut the door to the office. They came out ten minutes later. Ray walked to his car and left without looking back.

"What was that all about?" asked Amy Jo.

"I'm terribly sorry, Sandra," said Charlie. "Can you forgive us for accusing your friends of stealing? Ray told us that he saw your friends near the cash register. We've known Ray a long time, so I believed him. He won't be coming around here anymore. I'm sorry I was so quick to judge your friends."

"Thank you for believing me," said Sandra. She felt like **a great weight was lifted from her shoulders.** "Thank you," she said again.

That night, as she was preparing for bed, Charlie and Amy Jo walked down to say good night. "Good night, Sandra," said Charlie.

"You can call me Sandy," said Sandra.

In bed, she listened once again to the quiet sounds of the country. She smiled as she thought about herself as a country girl. The crickets and Jasper's quiet barks lulled her to sleep.

◆

Student page 148

After Reading "Foster Child"

Personal Response: You Be the Judge

Read aloud the question under **You Be the Judge** on Student Worktext page 149. Ask students to think about what it would be like to be taken away from their family. Tell them to think about having a family that couldn't take care of its members. Then have students answer the question.

Think About the Story: Reading Comprehension

Have students complete the remaining items on Student Worktext pages 149–150 independently or in pairs. Check their responses to help you assess their story comprehension. If students' responses indicate that they did not understand story events, reread the story aloud, pausing to discuss key events.

Reading Comprehension Skill: Draw Conclusions

Invite a volunteer to share his or her answers to **What's the Big Idea?** on Student Worktext page 150. Write the three sentences on the board and read them aloud. Tell students that when they draw conclusions, they take information about a character or event from the story and use the information to make a statement about the character or event. Explain:

- Conclusions are not stated directly but are supported by information in the story.
- Reasons should be available for the conclusions that are drawn.

Read aloud the answer to **What's the Big Idea?** ("Experiences help people to overcome their fears.") Tell students that this main idea was developed by drawing conclusions about the entire story. Ask:

- Is the main idea directly stated? (no)
- What details led you to believe that fears about people and places were overcome? (Sandra's enjoyment of working in the greenhouse and feeling responsible; Charlie's realizing his quick judgment of Sandra's friends)

Ask students to draw conclusions about specific passages in the text. You can model this skill by saying these examples.

The story says that Sandra's family didn't go on vacations. That may mean that they could not afford to go or that they didn't do things together as a family.

Susan tells Sandra to "give it a chance," meaning that she should try the new living arrangements without making a judgment first. When Susan says that, she is assuming that Sandra has automatically decided that she won't like the new situation.

Focus on LD

Help students draw conclusions by giving them clues from the story. For example, you might say, *The Groves have a system that waters the plants in the fields automatically. Why would this be a good system to have?* (to save time and energy) Guide students with prompts like this so that they will get into the routine of thinking about the story so that they can draw their own conclusions.

LESSON 2 *After Reading "Foster Child"*

You Be the Judge

1. Sandra's caseworker took her away from the city to a new home in the country. Do you think taking a foster child to a different home is a good idea? Why or why not? Write what you think on the lines below.

   Answers will vary.

Think About the Story

Use Story Words

Directions: Look at your list of story words on page 141. Write a story word on each line.

2. A caseworker is a social worker who works with foster children.
3. Lucy peered around the corner timidly.
4. An education is necessary in order to get a job.
5. Duane used his allowance to buy a new skateboard.
6. My father was always accusing me of making the family late.
7. I was in the routine of waking up early every Saturday and going for a five-mile run.

Write Sentences About the Story

Directions: Use words from the story to answer these questions.

8. Why couldn't Sandra live with her own family?

   Sandra couldn't live with her own family because her father and mother had problems and neither could care for her.

9. When Sandra met Mr. and Mrs. Grove on their farm, why did Sandra just stare at them?

   She didn't know what to say to country people. She was nervous.

10. At the end of the story, why does Sandra say to Charlie, "You can call me Sandy"?

    Sandra now feels comfortable enough living at the farm to allow her foster parents to call her by the name only her parents and friends may use for her.

Student page 149

What's the Big Idea?

11. Which sentence tells what the whole story is about? Circle it.
    a. Foster children need special attention.
    b. Experiences help people to overcome their fears.
    c. Farms in the country are nurturing places.

Words and Meanings

Directions: Think about how the **bold** words are used in the story. Then circle the answer that shows the meaning of each word or phrase.

12. Sandra decided that she wouldn't melt in the greenhouse, although **the air seemed sticky**. What does this mean?
    a. The air was moist and humid.
    b. The greenhouse was sticking to her.
    c. The air was dry.
13. He tried to **strike up a conversation** with her. This means he tried to _____.
    a. hit her
    b. talk to her
    c. avoid talking to her
14. Ray and Charlie went into the house to discuss the **books.** This means _____.
    a. the novels on Charlie's bookshelf
    b. the gardening books that Ray brought
    c. the accounting records
15. Her **heart was racing.** What does this mean?
    a. Her heart was beating slowly.
    b. She was having a heart attack.
    c. Her heart was beating very quickly from excitement or nervousness.
16. Charlie looked at Sandra, who returned his look with **pleading eyes.** What does this mean?
    a. She asked him to believe her.
    b. Her eyes gave the impression that she was asking him to believe her.
    c. She looked down at the ground and hoped he would believe her.
17. She felt like **a great weight was lifted from her shoulders.** What does this mean?
    a. She was relieved.
    b. She felt like she was being pushed down.
    c. She felt happy.

Student page 150

Reinforce & Extend

SPELLING: Job-Related Words Frequently Misspelled

1. occasion **3.** appointment **5.** experience **7.** references **9.** signature
2. business **4.** application **6.** interview **8.** resign **10.** punctual

Write each word on the board and go over its meaning. As you write each one, point out the difficult spelling patterns in each word. For example, the double-*c* in *occasion.* Then cover the words and have students number a sheet of paper 1–10. Dictate the words above, one at a time, pausing for students to write them. Next, uncover the words on the board and have students check each word, making corrections as needed.

Reading and Writing Practice Activity 85 provides additional practice with job-related words.

LANGUAGE: Compound Sentences

Write these sentences on the board:

People in Brazil speak Portuguese.

Presidents Washington and Lincoln were born in February.

The people in France speak French, and the people in Sweden speak Swedish.

Basketball was invented in 1891, but it was not a professional sport at that time.

Read the first sentence aloud. Tell students that this is a simple sentence because there is a complete subject and a compete predicate, and it expresses a complete thought. Ask a volunteer to come to the board and underline the complete subject, or what the sentence is about. (people in Brazil) Do the same for the second sentence, which is also a simple sentence. (Presidents Washington and Lincoln) Explain that this sentence has a compound subject, but that it is still a simple sentence.

Tell students that some sentences are not simple, but are compound. Explain:

- A compound sentence is made of two or more simple sentences that are put together.
- A coordinating conjunction connects the sentences.
- A comma usually comes before the conjunction.
- Examples of coordinating conjunctions are *and, but, or, so,* and *yet.*

Read the third sentence. Ask a volunteer to circle the conjunction (and), and then to underline the two simple sentences (The people in France; the people in Sweden). Point out the two subjects and two predicates. Repeat with the final sentence.

Reading and Writing Practice Activity 86 provides additional practice with compound sentences.

WRITING: A Persuasive Paragraph

Explain to students that persuasive paragraphs are written to convince the reader to think or act a certain way. The writer tries to get the reader to agree with the ideas he or she presents. Explain to students:

- When you persuade, you give your opinions. (*I think everyone should recycle.*)
- You must provide facts and examples to back up your opinions. (*Recycling helps the environment by saving electricity. Recycling helps to save other natural resources, such as trees.*)

The format for a persuasive paragraph is:

- Topic sentence (states the opinion)
- Body (states the reasons)
- Closing (restates the opinions)

Show students a short editorial from a magazine or newspaper. Have students analyze it, tell the topic (opinion), and give the supporting reasons. Then have them choose their own topic and write a persuasive paragraph that attempts to convince the reader of his or her ideas.

Reading and Writing Practice Duplicate and distribute Activities 87 and 88 on writing a persuasive paragraph. Then have students complete the activities in pairs.

Lesson at a Glance

Chapter 3, Lesson 3 "Our Nation's Capital"

Preview: This lesson presents a nonfiction selection about the history of Washington, D.C.

Objectives

- to read a nonfiction selection
- to read and spell homophones with *r*-controlled vowels
- to decode multisyllabic words with affixes
- to categorize details in a nonfiction selection
- to identify complex sentences
- to write a research report

Student Worktext Pages 151–161

Story Words

America, democracy, mansion, citizens, supervise

Reading and Writing Practice Activities 89–95

Before Reading "Our Nation's Capital"

Letters and Sounds

Homophones with *r*-Controlled Vowels

Write the words *soar, deer, stair,* and *morning* on the board. Pronounce each word for students. Tell students that each of these words has a homophone, or a word that sounds the same but is spelled differently. Ask students to spell a homophone for each word. (sore, dear, stare, mourning) Write the homophones together on the board. Say the word as you point to its spelling so that students can hear that they sound exactly the same. Go over the meaning of each word, making it clear that the homophones have completely different meanings.

Then have students complete Student Worktext page 151.

Reading and Writing Practice Activity 89: Homophones with *r*-Controlled Vowels.

Story Words

Read aloud these words: *America, democracy, mansion, citizens, supervise.* Tell students that these words are important in the next story they will read. Then write the words on the board and point to each one as you say it aloud a second time. Have students follow the ❑ *Read* ❑ *Say* ❑ *Write* sequence by completing **Story Words** on Student Worktext page 152. Remind students to write the story words in the Word Bank at the back of their Student Worktext. To introduce the words in context, write these sentences on the board:

- America was named after an Italian explorer.
- In a democracy, every citizen can vote.
- The wealthy businessman lives in a mansion.
- The citizens of a country vote on its leaders.
- The manager's job is to supervise employees.

Have students make a word card for *America*. Ask a volunteer to read the first sentence aloud. Then have students copy the sentence onto the back of the word card. Follow the same procedure for the remaining words. To assess students' abilities to read each new word, listen as individual students read the sentences on the board aloud.

Reading and Writing Practice Activity 90: Reading Story Words.

More Word Work

Have students work in pairs to complete **More Word Work** on Student Worktext page 152. After explaining an affix is a word part on the beginning or end of a word, have students identify affixes in words you write on the board.

Reading and Writing Practice Activity 91: Decoding Multisyllabic Words with Affixes.

LESSON 3 ▶ *Before Reading "Our Nation's Capital"*

Letters and Sounds

Directions: Though the following words are pronounced alike, they have different spellings and meanings. Read the words. Write them on the lines.

1. wear ___wear___
2. where ___where___
3. ware ___ware___

TIP: Words that are pronounced alike but have different spellings are called **homophones.**

Directions: Read the words. Connect the words that sound alike.

4. herd	whether
5. stare	hare
6. air	border
7. hair	heir
8. weather	borne
9. boarder	heard
10. coarse	core
11. corps	stair
12. born	course

Directions: Circle the word that correctly completes each sentence.

13. Her eyes met his with a cold (stair/stare).
14. He was (born/borne) in a log cabin.
15. (Where/Wear) are you going?
16. He was the (heir/air) to a large fortune.
17. She was going to the movies (weather/whether) he liked it or not.
18. They raised a (herd/heard) of cattle.
19. She was taking a chemistry (coarse/course) in college.
20. We crossed the (border/boarder) of Mexico.

Student page 151

Story Words

Directions: Read each word to yourself. Then say the word out loud. Write the word on the line. Check the box after each step.

21. America (A|mer|i|ca) Read ☑ Say ☑ Write ☑ ___America___
22. democracy (de|moc|ra|cy) Read ☑ Say ☑ Write ☑ ___democracy___
23. mansion (man|sion) Read ☑ Say ☑ Write ☑ ___mansion___
24. citizens (cit|i|zens) Read ☑ Say ☑ Write ☑ ___citizens___
25. supervise (su|per|vise) Read ☑ Say ☑ Write ☑ ___supervise___

More Word Work

Directions: Many words are changed by adding a suffix such as **able, less,** or **ing.** The suffix **able** means "capable of" or "likely to." The suffix **less** means "without." Read the word. Write it on the line.

26. unbearable ___unbearable___
27. thoughtless ___thoughtless___
28. declining ___declining___

TIP: Another word for a suffix is **affix.** In grammar, affix means a suffix or prefix added to a base word.

Directions: Write the word on the line. Circle the affix on each word.

29. comfortable ___comfortable___
30. emotionless ___emotionless___
31. understandable ___understandable___
32. unappealing ___unappealing___
33. tireless ___tireless___

Student page 152

Reading "Our Nation's Capital"

Preview and Predict

- Tell students that they are going to read a nonfiction selection about our capital, the city of Washington, D.C. Ask students whether they know what the *D.C.* stands for. (District of Columbia) Have a volunteer read the title of the selection on Student Worktext page 153 aloud.
- Ask students to predict the kinds of things the selection will tell about. (buildings, people, government, history)
- Point out the picture of the White House on page 155. Ask students whether they have seen the White House in person or on TV. Invite volunteers to describe what they saw.
- Read aloud the sentence and question under **Use What You Know** at the top of page 153. Ask students to work in pairs to write what they know about Washington, D.C.
- Tell students to preview the selection by reading the first two paragraphs on page 153. Invite students to tell why it is important that a country have a capital.
- Ask students to tell why the Revolutionary War was fought. Encourage them to share what they know about the war's importance to our country's history.

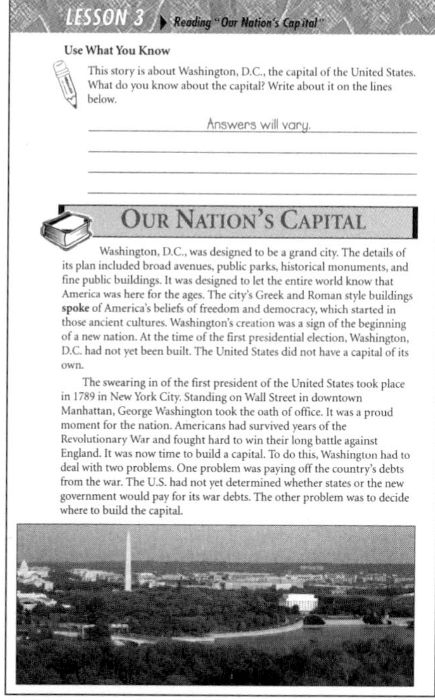

LESSON 3 ▶ Reading "Our Nation's Capital"

Use What You Know

This story is about Washington, D.C., the capital of the United States. What do you know about the capital? Write about it on the lines below.

Answers will vary.

OUR NATION'S CAPITAL

Washington, D.C., was designed to be a grand city. The details of its plan included broad avenues, public parks, historical monuments, and fine public buildings. It was designed to let the entire world know that America was here for the ages. The city's Greek and Roman style buildings **spoke** of America's beliefs of freedom and democracy, which started in those ancient cultures. Washington's creation was a sign of the beginning of a new nation. At the time of the first presidential election, Washington, D.C. had not yet been built. The United States did not have a capital of its own.

The swearing in of the first president of the United States took place in 1789 in New York City. Standing on Wall Street in downtown Manhattan, George Washington took the oath of office. It was a proud moment for the nation. Americans had survived years of the Revolutionary War and fought hard to win their long battle against England. It was now time to build a capital. To do this, Washington had to deal with two problems. One problem was paying off the country's debts from the war. The U.S. had not yet determined whether states or the new government would pay for its war debts. The other problem was to decide where to build the capital.

Student page 153

Have students finish reading Student Worktext pages 153–154 to learn more about our capital.

In the late 1700s, there were two very different ways of life in America. In the North, there were many cities. Banking and factory jobs were important. The South was mainly made up of farms and cotton plantations worked by slaves. The location of the capital was important to the North and the South, since both wanted the capital built in their own area. What is true of politics today was true of politics in President Washington's day. He knew that a compromise would be necessary. As a result, an agreement was made that the capital would be built in the South. The North would then have some of its war debts dropped.

Congress told Washington to select a place for the capital. It was to be no larger than ten square miles along the Potomac River. The President chose a spot where the Potomac and the Anacostia rivers meet. He named the area the District of Columbia after the explorer Christopher Columbus. This site was close to President Washington's home in Mount Vernon, Virginia. It was also a good spot for a seaport. This was important, since water travel was popular at that time.

Once the capital's location was decided upon, it was time to plan and build the city. A French engineer named Pierre L'Enfant was hired to complete the design. Washington, D.C., was one of the few cities planned before it was actually built. L'Enfant was thrilled to create an entirely new city.

He designed the city as a grid divided into four areas. The four areas of the grid were labeled for northwest (NW), northeast (NE), southeast (SE), and southwest (SW). Over this grid L'Enfant laid broad avenues that crossed each other at circular points. The highlight of the city would be the Capitol building at the city's eastern end. At the western end of the city would be the Mall where the Washington and Lincoln memorials are now located. In addition, the president's mansion, now called the White House, would have an important place. Throughout the city, L'Enfant planned circles and squares with small green parks. He wanted the city to be as beautiful as Paris in his French homeland.

L'Enfant was a talented but disagreeable man who angered many people. He would not give maps to city officials. He was afraid that before he could finish building his city, the land would be sold for profit. In fact, he took the lands of many rich and powerful men to build roads for the capital. Eventually, L'Enfant upset so many people that he was **fired.** A disappointed man, he took all his maps and plans with him. His two assistants replaced him. They were African American Benjamin Banneker and Irishman Andrew Ellicott. Between the two of them, they were able to put together L'Enfant's plans from memory.

Student page 154

Focus on ESL/LEP

Invite students who are from other countries to tell about their country's capital. Have them describe the buildings and history of the city. Help students use necessary vocabulary in English.

Learning Styles

Visual/Spatial Bring in a map or have students go to *www.washington.org* to find a map of Washington, D.C. that shows buildings, monuments, and streets. First give students an orientation to the city using the map. Be sure to show students the quadrants. Then point out the items that the text names.

Strategy Modeling

Access Prior Knowledge Tell students that they can make connections between ideas in the selection and things they already know. In order to make these connections, students should think carefully about the ideas in the selection. To model this process, you might say:

> *In 1814, the British set fire to the White House. Dolley Madison refused to leave the house before rescuing the portrait of George Washington. I have always been warned to get out of a building if there is a fire. Madison risked her life to stay in the building and save the portrait because she thought it was so important.*

Have students finish reading Student Worktext pages 155–156 to find out more about Washington, D.C. Point out that they should pause at the top of page 156 to make a prediction before reading on.

Focus on LD

There are several cause and effect relationships in the selection. To consider the relationships as they read, allow students extra time. For example, because Andrew Jackson's swearing-in guests were so rowdy, they damaged White House furnishings. Students should think about the causes in order to understand the effects they had.

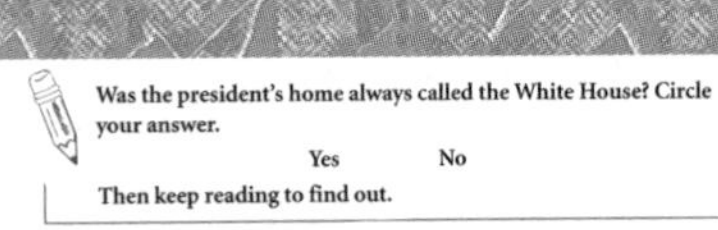

Was the president's home always called the White House? Circle your answer.

Yes No

Then keep reading to find out.

After the city's streets were planned, it was time to construct the buildings. The White House is probably the most famous building in Washington, D.C. The search for the person who would design the buildings began as a contest in newspapers across the country. The winner would receive $500 and the honor of designing the president's home. Many Americans believed the president's home should not look like a palace. The U.S. was a nation that had rejected kings and believed in the rule of the people. Americans wanted a home for their president that reflected this belief. But they also wanted the president to have a home where he would be proud to receive foreign officials. With this in mind, the simple and beautiful design of James Hoban was selected.

The building of the president's mansion began on October 13, 1792. It took many years to complete. President Washington never lived in it. After eight years of work, President John Adams and his wife, Abigail, became the first residents in November of 1800. Even after all that time, the house was still not completed. It was a cold place to live.

One year later, our third president, Thomas Jefferson, moved into the house. He was a man of fine tastes, and he began the task of decorating his new home. He wanted the best furnishings he could find. He ordered fine wallpaper and furniture from France. By 1801, most of the outside of the house was finished. It was the largest home in America.

Student page 155

During James Madison's presidency, the U.S. was once again at war with England. This was the War of 1812. In 1814, British troops attacked Washington, D.C. They set fire to the president's home. The First Lady, Dolley Madison, refused to leave the burning house. She insisted on rescuing the famous painting of George Washington. Because of her bravery, we still have this important painting. It is the only thing in the White House that was there when the house first opened. After the war, the damage to the house was repaired. However, the outside was still blackened by smoke marks. To cover the damage, the house was painted white. It was then that people began to call the president's house the White House.

The White House is the only private home of a head of state that is open to the public free of charge. In 1805, Thomas Jefferson held the first open house. It was a party to celebrate Jefferson's second presidential swearing-in ceremony. After his swearing in at the U.S. Capitol, the president greeted guests in the Blue Room. Jefferson also invited guests to the White House on New Year's Day and the Fourth of July.

In 1829, at the seventh presidential swearing in, President Andrew Jackson's celebration got a bit out of hand. Twenty thousand thoughtless guests tracked muddy boots through the White House. They stood on chairs and broke vases and lamps. Fearing for the president's safety, Jackson's aides moved him to a hotel. To get the guests out of the White House, the guards placed washtubs filled with orange juice and strong drink on the lawn.

By the time Grover Cleveland took office in the late 1800s, swearing-in crowds had become too large to bring to the White House. President Cleveland decided to set up a grandstand in front of the White House. Sitting in front of a large crowd, he watched the soldiers passing by. This practice has become a tradition of swearing-in parades. However, in 1993, President Bill Clinton brought back the tradition of inviting guests into the White House for a swearing-in party. That year 2,000 citizens were selected to be guests at the White House. The President, Mrs. Clinton, Vice President Gore, and Mrs. Gore greeted them.

Equally famous as the White House is the United States Capitol building. In addition to planning the city of Washington, L'Enfant was hired to design this building and to supervise its building. But L'Enfant refused to make any drawings for the building, saying that he carried the design in his head. This was one more reason why L'Enfant was fired.

The people still needed a Capitol, so another contest was held. Once again the prize was $500. The winner would design the Capitol that houses the Senate and the House of Representatives. A Scottish doctor named William Thornton won the contest. He designed a building made up of three sections. A low dome topped the center section. On each side were two rooms. One was to house the meeting chamber of the Senate. The other would house the meeting chamber of the Representatives.

Student page 156

Have students read Student Worktext pages 157–159 to finish the selection.

Ask students the following questions about the selection:

- How did the tradition of swearing-in parades begin? (Grover Cleveland set up a grandstand in front of the White House to watch uniformed soldiers pass by.)
- What is the Capitol? (the building in which Congress meets)
- What is Congress? (People who make up the legislative branch of government. Congress is made up of the Senate and House of Representatives. Congress's function is to make laws.)
- What is a veto? (the president's refusal to sign a bill into law) Can a bill become a law if the president vetoes it? (Yes, if two-thirds of Congress vote to pass it.)
- What does the judicial branch of government do? (reviews laws passed by Congress)
- Why did the nation's founders think we needed a system of checks and balances? (to keep the government strong and the people free)
- Why did the foreign visitors poke fun at Washington, D.C.? (It had no houses and people. People were disgusted with the sale of humans as slaves, which went against the ideals upon which the nation was founded.)
- What is Washington, D.C., like today? (It is a lively city filled with government buildings, museums, theaters, businesses, homes, and parks.)

Learning Styles

Auditory/Verbal Have students create a song or poem about Washington, D.C. They can include any of the details discussed or read in class. Students can use percussion to tap out the rhythm.

The Capitol took many years to build. During the War of 1812, the English set fire not only to the White House but also to the Capitol building. If it were not for a sudden rainstorm, the Capitol would have burned to the ground. But once again, America defeated the English. The war was ended and repairs were made to the building. As the nation grew, so did the Capitol. Additions were made to the building. Soon steam heat, electricity, elevators, and air conditioning were added.

The Capitol building has been the home of Congress for over 200 years. Congress is made up of the Senate and the House of Representatives. This is the legislative branch of the government. The United States Constitution gives Congress the power to write the laws of our country. Elected by Americans, members of Congress write ideas for laws to the president. Before they officially become laws, these ideas are called "bills." The president, who makes up the executive branch of government, can do two things about a bill. If he likes the bill sent to him by Congress, he can sign it, making it a law. If the president does not like the bill, he can refuse to sign it. This is called a veto. If the president vetoes a bill, Congress can still pass it into law. After a revote, if at least two-thirds of Congress votes to pass the bill, it becomes a law. This is called overriding the president's veto.

The third branch of our government is the judicial branch. This is our federal court system. The highest court in our land is the Supreme Court. The judges of the federal courts review the laws passed by Congress. They make sure that the laws do not break any rules of the United States Constitution. If the judges believe that a law goes against the Constitution, they can reject it.

Student page 157

The founders of our country created the government so that no one branch would have too much power. The ability of one branch of government to undo the work of another branch is called checks and balances. The founders believed that this system would keep the government strong and the people free.

It took many years to build the nation's capital. At first, Washington, D.C., was a coarse, rugged town. In the early course of its history, it had many problems. Built on swampy land, it was full of mosquitoes. It was not a place where elected officials wanted to bring their families. There were few homes and the men lived in uncomfortable boardinghouses. Another problem was the slave trade. Washington was a port city and slave ships unloaded their human cargo daily. Foreign officials were disgusted by the terrible practice of selling human beings. The U.S. claimed to be a land of freedom and equality for all. However, it allowed slaves, who were without rights. This situation would haunt the city of Washington and the entire country until the Civil War.

Though there were many slaves in early Washington, D.C., there was also a group of free African Americans. Most of them lived in the northwest area of Washington in what is known today as Georgetown. Long ago, Georgetown's port handled large shipments of the area's tobacco crop. Most of the people worked in the warehouses and on the wharves along the waterfront. But a few famous African Americans lived there also. While helping Pierre L'Enfant to build Washington, D.C., Benjamin Banneker made the neighborhood his home. Another famous resident was Yarrow Mamout. This African American arrived in the U.S. as a slave. In spite of this, during the course of his long life he gained his freedom and owned his own home. He was one of the most popular figures in Georgetown. Another Georgetown success story was Joseph Moor. He also had been a slave. Like Mamout, Moor gained his freedom. An owner of a grocery store, Moor was a well-known and well-liked businessman.

Georgetown was safe for its free African-American residents, but they still faced problems. They were not allowed out on the streets after a certain hour at night. They were not allowed to walk together in groups of more than five or six. Even in church they faced unfair treatment. African-American members of a local church were not allowed to use the main stair to the church balcony. They were forced to enter the balcony by way of a separate stairway. Many churches forced their African-American members to sit in separate areas. Finally, in 1814, 125 African Americans in Georgetown formed their own church. Today it is the oldest African American church in Washington, D.C.

Student page 158

Strategy Modeling

Access Prior Knowledge Remind students to use what they already know to make connections with what they are reading. Model an example by saying:

> *The selection makes a reference to the end of slavery after the Civil War. I know that Abraham Lincoln was president during the war and that he believed the country should stay together. To do this, he believed slavery should be abolished.*

Ask students to think about what they already know about other portions of the text. Ask them to tell what they know about government, inaugurations, slavery, or the Civil War.

Focus on LD

Explain and discuss the difference between *Capitol* and *capital. Capitol,* with a capital *c,* is the name of a building. Because it is a proper name, it is capitalized. A *capital* is the seat of government for a state, province, or country. It is a common noun and is therefore not capitalized.

In addition to building their own churches, Georgetown's African Americans began to get schooling. They began by meeting in each other's homes to learn to read and write. In 1810, an English woman named Mary Billings opened the first school for African Americans in Georgetown. Her student, Henry Smothers, opened another school for the neighborhood's African-American children. In 1823, a church opened a school for both children and adults who wanted to learn to read and write. By 1827, a school for girls was opened by an African American woman named Maria Becraft.

Though there were bright spots like Georgetown in early Washington, D.C., the city was still a rough place. Because of its problems, visitors loved to poke fun at it.

Charles Dickens, the famous English writer, visited in 1842. He wrote that the city's large avenues started with nothing and led nowhere. He said that the mile-long streets had no houses and no people. Dickens claimed that the city felt like a **ghost town.** He wrote, "Such as it is, it is likely to remain." But Dickens was mistaken.

The U.S. had the vision to create a nation of laws based on freedom. The nation had the courage to move closer to the ideals that the country was founded upon. To celebrate those ideals, America created a beautiful capital for its citizens. Today, Washington, D.C., is a great city filled with government buildings, museums, theaters, businesses, homes, and parks. People come from all over the world to visit Washington and admire the beauty of America's capital.

Student page 159

After Reading "Our Nation's Capital"

Personal Response: You Be the Judge

Read aloud the question about Pierre L'Enfant under **You Be the Judge** on Student Worktext page 160. Ask students to think about how they deal with difficult people. Do they know anyone who always wants to get his or her way? Then have students answer the questions.

Think About the Story: Reading Comprehension

Have students complete the remaining items on Student Worktext pages 160–161 independently or in pairs. Check their responses to help you assess their story comprehension. If students' responses indicate that they did not understand story events, reread the story aloud, pausing to discuss key events.

Reading Comprehension Skill: Categorize

Explain to students that putting things into categories can help them understand what they read. When they put similar ideas together, they can better understand the relationships that the author creates. Tell students that they already put things into categories all the time. (Grade levels, food groups, and sports are all categories.) Students also may have seen categorization on the Internet in World Wide Web directories, where Web sites are organized into thousands of categories.

Write these categories on the board: *buildings, people, branches of government,* and *wars.* Under *people* write *architects, presidents,* and *other.* Ask students to name the buildings that the selection tells about. (White House, Capitol) Write them on the board under *buildings.* Repeat with the other categories on the board, as shown below:

People

presidents: George Washington, John Adams, Thomas Jefferson, James Madison, Andrew Jackson, Grover Cleveland, Bill Clinton

architects: Pierre L'Enfant, Benjamin Banneker, Andrew Ellicott, James Hoban, William Thornton

other: Christopher Columbus, Abigail Adams, Dolley Madison, Mrs. Clinton, Vice President Gore, Mrs. Gore, Charles Dickens

branches of government: legislative, executive, judicial

wars: Revolutionary War, War of 1812, Civil War

Ask students to think of categories that the "other" people could go in. (for example, *explorers or first ladies*)

Categorizing can help students see the comparisons in text. For example, when the selection tells about the Civil War, students can remember the other wars that were already discussed and can then begin to make those connections into a concept of American wars.

LESSON 3 After Reading "Our Nation's Capital"

You Be The Judge

1. Pierre L'Enfant was a talented but difficult man. Though his employers liked his designs for the capital, L'Enfant often angered them. Do you think L'Enfant should have been fired? Why or why not? Write what you think on the lines below.
Answers will vary.

Think About the Story

Use Story Words

Directions: Look at your list of story words on page 152. Write a story word on each line.

2. The executive mansion is the home of the president and his family.
3. Pierre L'Enfant was hired to design and supervise the building of the new capital.
4. Americans believe in freedom and democracy.
5. Foreign guests and American citizens visit Washington, D.C., every day.
6. The capital was built to celebrate America and its ideals.

When Did It Happen?

7. Write a number from 1 to 4 in front of each event to show when it happened.
4 The Capitol building is finished.
1 George Washington is elected president.
2 President Washington selects a site for the new capital.
3 The White House is set on fire.

What Were the Facts?

8. Why was Pierre L'Enfant fired? Circle the reasons.
a. He was late for work every day.
(b. He took valuable land to build roads.)
c. He didn't finish the White House on time.
(d. He refused to provide maps or drawings to city officials.)

Student page 160

Write Sentences About the Story

Directions: Use words from the story to answer these questions.

9. When the White House was being built, what kind of home did Americans want for their president?
Many Americans felt the White House should not look like a palace, but suitable for receiving foreign officials.

10. In 1814, when the British burned the White House, who saved the only object that survived the fire and what was it?
The First Lady, Dolley Madison, saved the famous painting of George Washington.

11. In its early stages, why was Washington, D.C., thought by some to be a coarse town?
Washington, D.C., in its early days, was considered a coarse town because it was built on a swamp, full of mosquitoes, and had an active slave marketplace.

Words and Meanings

Directions: Think about how the **bold** words are used in the story. Then circle the words that show the meaning of each word or phrase.

12. When the English writer Charles Dickens called Washington, D.C., a **ghost town,** he meant ____.
a. it was full of cemeteries
(b. there were only a few people living there)
c. it was filled with ghosts

13. Pierre L'Enfant angered so many people that he was **fired.** To be fired means ____.
a. L'Enfant got very angry
b. L'Enfant was set on fire
(c. L'Enfant was let go from his job)

14. When it was designed, Washington, D.C.'s buildings **spoke** of America's beliefs of freedom and democracy. Spoke means that it ____.
a. sounded like a good place to live
(b. was a sign of the young country's beliefs)
c. was inspired by palaces in Europe

Student page 161

Reinforce & Extend

SPELLING: Homophones with *r*-Controlled Vowels

1. poured **2.** pored **3.** bare **4.** bear **5.** fare **6.** fair **7.** you're **8.** your **9.** serf **10.** surf

Write the words on the board and go over the meaning of each. Cover the words and have students number a sheet of paper 1–10. Dictate the words above, and use each in a sentence. For example, *Jennifer pored over her test results.* Have students write the correct homophone.

Reading and Writing Practice Activity 92 provides additional practice with homophones with *r*-controlled vowels.

LANGUAGE: Complex Sentences

Write this sentence on the board:

When I visit Washington, I want to see the Capitol.

Read the sentence aloud. Ask a volunteer to tell what the subject is. (There are two subjects: Washington, Capitol.) Invite another volunteer to tell what the verb is. (There are two verbs: visit, see.) Tell students that this is an example of a complex sentence.

Explain:

- A main clause can stand alone as a sentence.
- A complex sentence is a main clause and one or more subordinate clause put together to form one sentence.
- A subordinate clause has a subject and verb but no complete thought. It cannot stand alone as a sentence.
- Subordinate clauses begin with *subordinating conjunctions.* They are called subordinating conjunctions because they make the clause subordinate, or less than, the main clause. Common examples include: *after, although, because, before, if, since, unless, until, while,* and *when.*
- If the subordinate clause comes before the main clause, put a comma after the subordinate clause. No comma is needed when the main clause comes before the subordinate clause.

Reading and Writing Practice Activity 93 provides additional practice with complex sentences.

WRITING: A Research Report

Explain to students the steps of writing a research report.

Step 1: Prewriting (Plan the Report)

- Select a topic. Make sure it is not too broad or too narrow.
- Research your topic at the library. Find multiple sources.
- Take notes. Think about what will be important to your audience. Use your own words.
- Write down the title and author of each source. If you have used a Web site, write the URL, or Web address.
- When you have all of your information, organize it.

Step 2: Drafting (Write the Report)

- Write an interesting opening.
- State the topic of your report.
- Explain your topic by writing about your subtopics. Support your ideas with facts and examples.
- Write a conclusion to summarize what you learned.

Step 3: Revising (Change Your Report to Make It Better)

- Make sure you thoroughly covered your topic. Ask yourself if the reader will get the whole picture.
- Clarify any points that may be confusing to your reader. Add or delete information as necessary.

Step 4: Final Draft (Finish Your Report)

- Write your report onto nice paper or type it on a computer. Make sure it is nicely formatted and easy to read.
- Check it one last time for mistakes.

Reading and Writing Practice Duplicate and distribute Activities 94 and 95 on research reports.

Lesson at a Glance

Chapter 3, Lesson 4 "Sally Ride"

Preview: This lesson presents a nonfiction selection about astronaut and physicist Sally Ride, the first American woman in space.

Objectives

- to read a nonfiction selection
- to decode multisyllabic words with unusual spellings for consonants
- to understand the use of adverbs
- to note the sequence of events in a selection
- to spell words that end in *able* and *ible*
- to identify and correct fragments and run-on sentences
- to complete a job application

Student Worktext Pages 162–173

Story Words

physicist, communications, simulations, mechanical, satellite, engineer, external, weightlessness

Reading and Writing Practice Activities 96–102

Before Reading "Sally Ride"

Letters and Sounds

Decoding Multisyllabic Words with Unusual Spellings for Consonants

Write the words *chaos, Chicago, cherubic, scenario,* and *philosophy* on the board. Pronounce each word for students. Have a volunteer come to the board and circle the *k* sound in *chaos.* Have another volunteer circle the *sh* sound in *Chicago.* Circle the *ch* sound in *cherubic.* Tell students that most *ch* spellings are pronounced *ch.* Point out the *ch* spelling in each word, and explain that the letters *ch* can be pronounced three different ways. Next, have a student circle the *s* sound in *scenario.* Ask students if they can name any other words with an *s* sound spelled *sc.* (science, scenery) Tell students that *sc* can have an *s* sound when the letters are followed by *i* or *e.* Have another student come to the board and circle the *f* sounds in *philosophy.* Tell students that the letters *ph* always have the *f* sound. Then have students complete Student Worktext page 162.

Reading and Writing Practice Activity 96: Decoding Multisyllabic Words with Unusual Spellings for Consonants.

LESSON 4 ▸ Before Reading "Sally Ride"

Letters and Sounds

Directions: These words have the hard sound of **k** in **task.** Write the word on the line. Circle the letters that make the hard **k** sound.

1. mechanical mechanical 3. technical technical
2. unscheduled unscheduled 4. chorus chorus

Directions: These words have the sound of **s** in **sun** or **sh** in **fish.** Write the word on the lines. Circle the letters that make the **s** or **sh** sound in each word.

5. scientists scientists
6. parachute parachute

Directions: These words have the sound of **f** in **fish.** Write the word on the line. Circle the letters that make the **f** sound.

7. geography geography
8. physical physical

TIP: The letters **ch** often make the **k** sound. Sometimes they make the **sh** sound. The letters **sc** can make the **s** sound when followed by **i** or **e.** The letters **ph** make the **f** sound.

Directions: On the lines below, write the letter or letters for the sound that the underlined consonants make.

9. photograph f, f 13. ascend s
10. scented s 14. headache k
11. architect k 15. alphabet f
12. machine sh 16. chromosome k

Directions: Write letters on each line to correctly spell a word.

17. sc ientific (**s** sound) 20. de sc end (**s** sound)
18. tele ph one (**f** sound) 21. Mi ch igan (**sh** sound)
19. me ch anic (**k** sound) 22. ph antom (**f** sound)

Student page 162

Story Words

Read aloud these words: *physicist, communications, simulations, mechanical, satellite, engineer, external, weightlessness.* Tell students that these words are important in the next story they will read. Then write the words on the board and point to each one as you say it aloud a second time. Have students follow the ❑ *Read* ❑ *Say* ❑ *Write* sequence by completing **Story Words** on Student Worktext page 163. Remind students to write the story words in the Word Bank at the back of their Student Worktext. To introduce the words in context, write these sentences on the board:

- The physicist works in the lab.
- Advances in communications have made the world a smaller place.
- The flight simulations were almost like the real thing!
- The plane had mechanical problems.
- The satellites sent messages to Earth.
- An engineer knows how mechanical, structural, chemical, or electrical things work.
- The car had external damage.
- When I float in the swimming pool, I get a feeling of weightlessness.

Have students make a word card for *physicist.* Ask a volunteer to read the first sentence aloud. Then have students copy the sentence onto the back of the word card. Follow the same procedure for the remaining words. To assess students' abilities to read each new word, listen as individual students read aloud the sentences on the board.

Reading and Writing Practice Activity 97: Reading Story Words.

More Word Work

Have students complete **More Word Work** on Student Worktext page 163.

Reading and Writing Practice Activity 98: Adverbs.

Story Words

Directions: Read each word to yourself. Then say the word out loud. Write the word on the line. Check the box after each step.

23. physicist (phys|i|cist) Read ☑ Say ☑ Write ☑ physicist
24. communications (co|mu|ni|ca|tions) Read ☑ Say ☑ Write ☑ communications
25. simulations (sim|u|la|tions) Read ☑ Say ☑ Write ☑ simulations
26. mechanical (me|chan|i|cal) Read ☑ Say ☑ Write ☑ mechanical
27. satellite (sa|tel|lite) Read ☑ Say ☑ Write ☑ satellite
28. engineer (en|gi|neer) Read ☑ Say ☑ Write ☑ engineer
29. external (ex|ter|nal) Read ☑ Say ☑ Write ☑ external
30. weightlessness (weight|less|ness) Read ☑ Say ☑ Write ☑ weightlessness

More Word Work

You can use adverbs to describe verbs, adjectives, and other adverbs. Adverbs often tell **how.** They can also tell **where, why,** or **when.**

Examples: She could barely hear the voices over the engine's roar.
You must study very hard to be a successful scientist.
Her pillow is particularly soft.

Directions: Write an adverb to describe each word.

31. landed safely 34. spoke clearly
32. talked loudly 35. laughed merrily
33. walked slowly 36. looked everywhere

TIP: Many adverbs end with **ly.**

Student page 163

Reading "Sally Ride"

Preview and Predict

- Tell students that they are going to read a nonfiction selection about Sally Ride, who was the first American woman in space. Have a volunteer read the title of the selection on Student Worktext page 164 aloud.
- Ask students to tell what they know about an astronaut's job in space. Some astronauts operate the controls of the space shuttle, while others conduct experiments and operate other equipment.
- Read aloud the sentence and questions under **Use What You Know** at the top of page 164. Ask students to think about what astronauts have explored and to name any famous astronauts. Then have students write on page 164 about what they know.
- Ask students to preview the selection by reading the first paragraph. Ask students to tell whether they think they would like being an astronaut, like Sally Ride did. Encourage students to think about all sides of the issue, including the danger involved. Ask students to think of specific activities they would perform if they flew on a space shuttle mission.

Have students finish reading Student Worktext pages 164–165 to learn about Sally Ride.

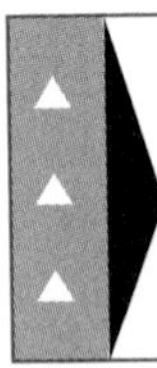

Focus on ESL/LEP

Take time to help students with some of the more difficult words in the selection: *professor, counselor, astronomy, Ph.D.,* and *NASA.*

Focus on LD

Help students understand Sally Ride's training activities by rereading the paragraph describing the activities. Reread the paragraph aloud, line by line, explaining the more difficult concepts as you go. For example, have students think about high gravity and weightless environments, which are direct opposites.

LESSON 4 ▸ *Reading "Sally Ride"*

Use What You Know

Sally Ride was an astronaut on the space shuttle. Do you know of any space shuttle missions? What did they accomplish? Write what you know about a space mission on the lines below.

Answers will vary.

SALLY RIDE

"When you're getting ready to launch into space, you're sitting on a big explosion waiting to happen," says Sally Ride, the first American woman in space. For Ride, the launch was an exciting part of her space shuttle flight. She believes that space travel is different from any experience on Earth.

Ride was born on May 26, 1951, in Encino, California, near Los Angeles. Her father was a teacher at a college. Her mother was a teacher and counselor. Ride had several heroes while growing up. One was a high school teacher who encouraged her to study science. Early astronauts, such as John Glenn and Neil Armstrong, were also heroes. Her favorite subject in high school was math. She was also interested in astronomy and physical science.

As a child, Ride enjoyed sports. She was very good at tennis. She played at a national level and spent her weekends

Student page 164

playing matches. After trying to play tennis as a pro, she decided that she was not good enough to continue as a professional tennis player. Instead, she went to Stanford University, where she earned degrees to become a physicist.

As Ride was finishing her studies in 1977, she read that NASA needed astronauts. Their job would be to conduct experiments in space. Ride decided that she wanted to see Earth from outer space, so she applied for the program. More than 8,000 people applied to NASA's space program that year.

Ride was tested and interviewed by experts at the Johnson Space Center in Houston, Texas. Afterwards, she returned home and awaited the results while finishing work on her Ph.D. in physics.

In 1978, she learned that she had been selected for the job at NASA. Of the 8,000 people to apply, only 35 were accepted for the program. Only six of those were women.

Ride had much training after she entered NASA. She learned many things. Among them were parachute jumping, water survival, radio communications, and navigation. She also had training in high-gravity and weightless environments. She had to learn all about the space shuttle, even though she would not fly it. Her training included flight simulations. These match space flight and help astronauts prepare for the actual mission. Ride enjoyed flying so much that she took lessons **on her own time** and became a pilot.

In 1979, Ride became an astronaut. This meant that she could be assigned to a space flight. Before going into space herself, she assisted on the ground with other space shuttle missions. As communications officer for flights of the space shuttle Columbia, she sent radio messages from mission control to the shuttle crews. Ride was expected to understand everything about a mission and stay calm no matter what happened. During this time, Ride also helped to design a mechanical arm for releasing and getting satellites in space.

In 1982, NASA chose Ride to serve as a crew member for the space shuttle's seventh mission. The flight needed a lot of preparation. She studied the flight manuals, step-by-step directions for every part of the flight, and practiced in the simulator. Computers make the simulator behave like an actual shuttle flight. Emergency situations are written into the computer's programs. This is done so that the crew learns how to handle the many things that might go wrong.

Ride became famous as she prepared to be America's first woman in space. Since she didn't want people to think she was chosen just because she was a woman, Ride disliked the attention and the many questions by reporters.

Student page 165

Strategy Modeling

Summarize Explain to students that they can informally summarize the text as they read to help them understand what they have read. This will enable students to remember the key ideas so that they can continue to read and understand the upcoming text. To model summarizing, you might say:

So far, I have learned that Sally Ride was studying physics when she applied to become an astronaut. She was accepted into NASA's space program and went through extensive training. In 1982, she was chosen as a crewmember for a space shuttle mission.

This summary will help students follow the rest of the selection, which tells more about Ride's missions.

Have students finish reading Student Worktext pages 166–167 to find out more about Ride's experiences in space. Point out that they should pause at the top of page 167 to summarize before reading on.

Learning Styles

Visual/Spatial Draw a diagram of the space shuttle according to the text. It will help students to understand more about Sally Ride's mission, the flight of the space shuttle, and the later explosion of Challenger. Make sure to label the orbiter, the external fuel tank, and the solid rocket boosters. Explain the function of each part as you go.

For her first space shuttle flight, Ride was given the job of flight engineer. This meant that she, the commander, and the copilot of the shuttle were responsible for the launch and re-entry of the shuttle. During takeoff and landing, she sat behind the commander and copilot. She helped them **to keep track of** thousands of dials and blinking lights on the control panel. During the flight, she and another astronaut conducted experiments. They also tested the new robotic arm.

There are three parts to the space shuttle. The part of the space shuttle that carries the astronauts is called the "orbiter." It is the part that has wings. The largest part of the shuttle is the external fuel tank. It is 18 stories high and 28 feet wide and holds the fuel used during liftoff. Solid rocket boosters are the third part of the shuttle. They are located on the sides of the external fuel tank and provide more power for liftoff. A lot of power is needed during liftoff for the space shuttle to escape the pull of Earth's gravity.

Ride and the Challenger crew took off from Kennedy Space Center in Cape Canaveral, Florida, on June 18, 1983. As the space shuttle took off, its engines roared and the shuttle vibrated. The noise was so loud that Ride could barely hear the voices from launch control through her headset. Ride is often asked if she was afraid during liftoff and the space flight. She says that there is no time to fear anything because a flight is so busy and exciting.

Student page 166

If you were an astronaut, how would you feel at liftoff? Write what you think on the lines below. Then keep reading to find out what takes place.

Answers will vary.

After two minutes, the solid rocket boosters had used up all of their fuel. They were released and dropped into the Atlantic Ocean. The orbiter became much quieter inside.

As the orbiter went up, Ride felt a great weight pushing against her chest and **pinning her to her seat.** This force was seven times greater than the force of normal gravity.

After eight and a half minutes, the external fuel tank was empty. It was later detached and burned up in space before it reached Earth. Smaller engines on the orbiter helped move the space shuttle into its orbiting position 184 miles from Earth. At that time, communication with the crew was switched to mission control in Houston, Texas.

Ride enjoyed the weightlessness of space travel. Astronauts floated from place to place in the orbiter. Ride even went to sleep while floating. She later enjoyed the view of Earth. The shuttle had windows that she could look through to see Earth and space. From the shuttle, she could actually observe cities and countries on Earth.

Challenger took 90 minutes to orbit Earth. It made 97 orbits. During the trip, Ride helped to launch satellites for other countries. The satellites weighed more than 7,000 pounds. During the next several days, Ride ran experiments. The experiments included work for companies and for schools. Ride and another crewmember, John Fabian, were the first astronauts to retrieve a satellite from space.

On board were 22 experiments created by high school and university students, a private company, and government groups. One of the experiments was created by high school students from Camden, New Jersey. It studied the effects of gravity and weightlessness on 150 carpenter ants.

When Ride was asked by mission control what it felt like to be up in space, she replied, "Have you ever been to Disneyland?" When the astronaut at Mission Control said yes, she said, "This is definitely an 'E' ticket." The more exciting rides at Disneyland once required a special "e-ticket" to ride.

Student page 167

Have students read Student Worktext pages 168–171 to finish the selection.

You might ask students the following questions about the selection.

- Was Sally Ride afraid during the liftoff and flight of the space shuttle? (No. There is no time to fear anything because a flight is so busy and exciting.)
- What happens two minutes into a space shuttle flight? (The solid rocket boosters are released because the fuel is used up.)
- Why is so much fuel used in the first two minutes? (It takes a lot of energy to get out of Earth's gravity pull.)
- What could Ride see from the window of the space shuttle? (a view of Earth and space; cities and countries on Earth)
- How long did it take Challenger to make one orbit of Earth? (90 minutes)
- What did Ride do during the trip? (She helped to launch satellites for other countries and ran scientific experiments.)
- What fun things did the crew members do in space? (They had races and caught floating jellybeans.)
- Why did the crew have to land Challenger in California on Ride's first mission? (Weather conditions did not allow them to land in Florida.)
- Who was the first woman to walk in space? (Kathryn Sullivan)
- Why didn't Ride go on her scheduled third mission? (Challenger exploded.)
- Why did Challenger explode? (It had a part on the solid rocket boosters that did not work correctly.)
- What did Ride do right after the explosion? (She went to Washington, D.C., to investigate the accident.)
- Why did Ride leave the space program? (She wanted to be a physics teacher and conduct physics research.)
- What does Ride recommend that you study if you want to become an astronaut? (math and science, beginning in middle school)

Learning Styles

Logical/Mathematical Have students use the rate of 90 minutes per orbit to figure out how many orbits the shuttle could make in 24 hours. (16)

Temperature in space ranges from minus 200 degrees Celsius to plus 200 degrees Celsius. However, inside the orbiter, the temperature remained between 70 and 75 degrees Fahrenheit. The astronauts wore light clothing, such as short-sleeved t-shirts and gym shorts.

From the window, Ride could see Oregon as they flew over Los Angeles and New York as they flew over Florida. She could see dust storms blowing over deserts and storms raging over the ocean. In space, she could see billions of lights from stars, planets, and other galaxies.

The astronauts were very busy almost all of the time they were in space. All of their activities were scheduled and controlled by NASA engineers.

The first satellite that Ride helped to release was the Anik C-2 communications satellite for Canada. This satellite would provide North America's first direct satellite-to-home pay-TV service. The release of the satellite marked the beginning of NASA's plan to use the space shuttle for profit work. This would earn NASA millions of dollars.

Ride took the controls. She watched the satellite spin in place at a rate of 50 spins per minute. The satellite would continue to spin when it was in place to keep it at its correct orbit. If the satellite didn't spin right, there was a chance the solar panels could melt. The astronauts felt a slight shake of the shuttle as the satellite was released from the cargo bay. Then they moved the orbiter away from the spinning satellite. It would take four days for the satellite to reach the planned orbit position.

Student page 168

The astronauts had to make changes to being weightless. Eating and cooking were tough. Floating pieces of food or water drops could cause the shuttle's equipment to break. Meals were cooked by two people and served in the shuttle's galley, or kitchen. The astronauts could choose from 25 different drinks and more than 75 kinds of food. A typical menu for a day included scrambled eggs, peaches, and orange drink for breakfast; hot dogs, almond crunch bars, bananas, and an apple drink for lunch; and shrimp cocktail, beef steak, broccoli au gratin, grape drink, and butterscotch pudding for dinner. Sticky foods like macaroni and cheese and peanut butter were easier to keep on a spoon.

The astronauts used a spoon and a pair of scissors to eat. They used the scissors to cut open the packages of food. They made the food by adding water into the package and waiting a few minutes for the food to mix. Some foods, such as ham, were cooked before the launch and reheated in a microwave. Nuts and cookies were kept in their original form.

The food packages were attached to trays. The astronauts strapped the trays to their legs or to tables that were mounted inside the shuttle. Sometimes they ate while floating! The astronauts usually ate together since it was more relaxing.

The crew had to make sure everything was completely clean when they finished eating. There was plenty of water on board. It was produced as a by-product by the fuel cells that made electricity for the shuttle.

The shuttle had bathrooms where Ride and the other astronauts could wash and brush their teeth.

Throughout the flight, the astronauts conducted the experiments on one another. They measured eye movements, vision, and more. With these tests, NASA hoped to solve space sickness, which affected many astronauts.

The astronauts did try to have some fun while in the orbiter. They had a race to see who could travel across the cabin the fastest. They pushed themselves off the wall in the direction they wanted to go. They also released a jar of jellybeans in the cabin. The jellybeans had been a gift from President Ronald Reagan. As the jellybeans floated around the cabin, the crew chased them and caught them in their mouths.

After six days in space, it was time to return to Earth. Because of weather conditions in Florida, the shuttle had to change its course and land in California. The commander, Robert Crippen, landed Challenger successfully at Edwards Air Force Base. Even though the landing was unscheduled, Ride had a small crowd of fans waiting for her.

Ride said of this flight, "The thing that I remember most about the flight is that it was fun. In fact, I'm sure it was the most fun I'll ever have in my life."

Student page 169

◆ *Strategy Modeling*

Summarize Remind students that summarizing text will help them remember the key points in the text. Model summarizing by saying:

I have now read about Sally Ride's first flight in space. She enjoyed her flight, from the takeoff to the trip in space. She was the flight engineer and conducted experiments on board. She also helped release satellites. During the flight she experienced weightlessness and enjoyed views of Earth and space.

Have students summarize orally what Ride did after she left the space program.

Focus on LD

Help students discern key points in the text as they summarize Sally Ride's actions after leaving the space program. Skim a paragraph chosen from the selection with students and pick out the main idea. Move on to the next paragraph and do the same.

Application

Career Connection Have students research a career in science by going to the library or using the Internet. Students could also interview a person who has a science career they find interesting. Have them find out how much education is needed, as well as the skills required. Tell them to find information about a specific career within the field of science. Have them tell why the career appeals to them. A good source to use is the *Occupational Outlook Handbook.*

Ride went on her second mission in 1984. This time there was another woman on board, Kathryn Sullivan. She became the first woman to walk in space. Ride was a flight engineer for the mission again. This mission had a lot of problems. The first came when Ride tried to release a satellite. Two of the satellite's solar panels wouldn't open because the hinges were frozen. Ride solved the problem by using the robot arm to turn the satellite so that the sun could warm the hinges. Another problem was the loss of communications. However, the crew continued to work and solve problems as they arose. At the end of the eight-day mission, the shuttle landed safely at the Kennedy Space Center.

Ride's third flight into space was scheduled for 1986. However, her training was **put on hold** when Challenger exploded only minutes after liftoff for another mission. Everyone on board was killed. Ride was put on a special team to study the accident in Washington, D.C. The team found that the explosion was caused by a faulty part located on the solid rocket boosters. NASA has since changed the design.

Ride created NASA's Office of Exploration. She was also in charge of developing a long-range plan for future space travel. Her report on America's space program is known as the "Ride Report." The report recommended setting up a base on the moon. Scientists could then live and work in space at the same time. The report also suggested conducting a detailed look at Earth, using robots to explore space, and plans for a trip to Mars. While there are no plans to send people back to the moon, NASA is thinking about sending astronauts to Mars.

Student page 170

Ride had always wanted to return to Stanford University. She left NASA in 1987 to work for Stanford's Center for International Security and Arms Control. In 1989, she accepted a position as a physics professor at the University of California, San Diego. She also served for a short period as director of the California Space Institute. Another of her projects involved working with companies to develop products for space travel.

Her students may one day become astronauts and scientists. She shares her experiences with younger children as well. She has written several books for them about space and space travel. Her writing encourages students to follow their dreams. Ride also works to improve science education. She has received many awards for her efforts, including the National Spaceflight Medal. As Professor Ride, she enjoys her job at the University of California, San Diego. She does not want to give it up for more space travel. She enjoys teaching and finds it very rewarding.

Ride is an inspiration to many young people. Because of her hard work, she continues to serve as a role model for students interested in science and space travel. For students hoping to be scientists or astronauts, Ride has some advice. She believes the most important thing is to begin studying math and science in middle school. She encourages students to take an interest in an area of science, and then to work very hard. She believes there are many exciting careers in science for both men and women.

Student page 171

After Reading “Sally Ride”

Personal Response: You Be the Judge

Read aloud the questions under **You Be the Judge** on Student Worktext page 172. Ask students to think about what Sally Ride experienced on her missions—what she did, as well as how she felt. Invite students to share some of their ideas aloud. Then have students answer the questions.

Think About the Story: Reading Comprehension

Have students complete the remaining items on Student Worktext pages 172–173 independently or in pairs. Check their responses to help you assess their story comprehension. If students' responses indicate that they did not understand story events, reread the story aloud, pausing to discuss key events.

Reading Comprehension Skill: Note Sequence

Write these sentences on the board.

- Sally Ride left NASA to become a researcher and teacher.
- Sally Ride played tennis.
- Sally Ride became the first American woman in space.
- Challenger exploded.
- Sally Ride was tested and interviewed for a position in the space program.

Tell students that the order in which events take place is called the sequence. Explain:

- You should pay attention to how the sequence is written.
- The writer may tell everything in the order that it happened.
- The writer may present the sequence using transition words such as *first, then, next,* and *last.*
- The writer may skip back and forth, going out of actual time sequence from beginning to end.

Ask students to review the first paragraph of the selection on Student Worktext page 164. Have them compare the paragraph to what they know about how the rest of the selection was written. Ask them if the second paragraph tells about something that happened after the details in the first paragraph.

Have students put the sentences on the board in sequence. Have a volunteer write *1* next to the event that happened first. Repeat this until you have sequenced all the lines. (5, 1, 3, 4, 2)

Ask students to write a sequence of events about either history or a personal experience. Have them mix up the events and then trade papers with another student to decode the sequence.

Focus on LD

Help students sequence events by asking them questions to help them remember the order of events. For example, say, *“When did Ride play tennis?”* (as a teenager) *“Could she have entered the space program as a teenager?”* (no) *“Is there anything else on this list that could have happened before she was a teenager?”* (no)

LESSON 4 ▸ *After Reading “Sally Ride”*

You Be the Judge

1. If you had been in the NASA space program, would you ever have been ready to leave like Ride did? Write what you think on the lines below.
   Answers will vary.
2. What do you think your favorite part of a space flight would be?
   Answers will vary.

Think About the Story

Use Story Words

Directions: Look at your list of story words on page 163. Write a story word on each line.

3. A physicist is someone who studies matter and energy.
4. Ride learned parachute jumping, water survival, radio communications, and navigation.
5. Satellites are launched into space and used to communicate around the world.
6. Ride helped to design a mechanical arm for releasing and retrieving satellites in space.
7. The largest part of the space shuttle is the external fuel tank.
8. When the conditions of space are imitated on Earth, these are called simulations.
9. One kind of engineer drives a train; another is trained to work with science and technology.
10. Because there is no gravity in outer space, people experience weightlessness and can float in the air.

Student page 172

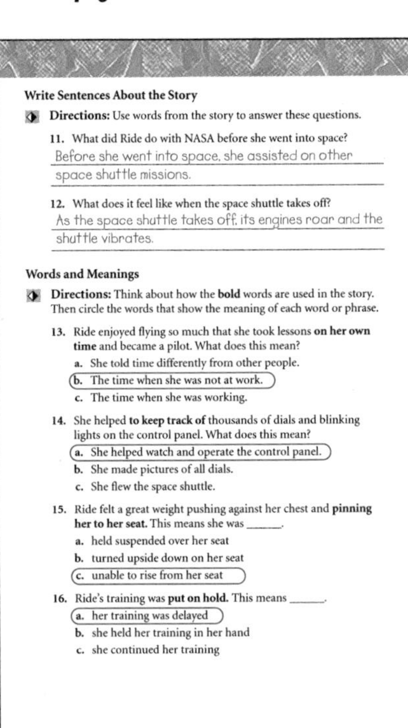

Write Sentences About the Story

Directions: Use words from the story to answer these questions.

11. What did Ride do with NASA before she went into space?
    Before she went into space, she assisted on other space shuttle missions.
12. What does it feel like when the space shuttle takes off?
    As the space shuttle takes off, its engines roar and the shuttle vibrates.

Words and Meanings

Directions: Think about how the **bold** words are used in the story. Then circle the words that show the meaning of each word or phrase.

13. Ride enjoyed flying so much that she took lessons **on her own time** and became a pilot. What does this mean?
    a. She told time differently from other people.
    b. The time when she was not at work.
    c. The time when she was working.
14. She helped **to keep track of** thousands of dials and blinking lights on the control panel. What does this mean?
    a. She helped watch and operate the control panel.
    b. She made pictures of all dials.
    c. She flew the space shuttle.
15. Ride felt a great weight pushing against her chest and **pinning her to her seat.** This means she was ______.
    a. held suspended over her seat
    b. turned upside down on her seat
    c. unable to rise from her seat
16. Ride's training was **put on hold.** This means ______.
    a. her training was delayed
    b. she held her training in her hand
    c. she continued her training

Student page 173

Reinforce & Extend

SPELLING: Words with the Suffixes *able* and *ible*

1. edible **2.** valuable **3.** reliable **4.** avoidable **5.** credible **6.** likable **7.** sensible **8.** predictable **9.** permissible **10.** peaceable

Write *expandable, movable, visible,* and *knowledgeable* on the board. Explain the suffixes *able* and *ible* mean "able or capable of being." It is not always possible to know when to add *able* or *ible.* Many times *ible* is added to words that cannot stand alone (visible). The suffix *able* is usually added to words that can stand alone (expandable, movable, knowledgeable). Sometimes the base word must be changed in order to add the suffix (movable). Cover the words and have students number a sheet of paper 1–10. Dictate the words above, one at a time, pausing for students to write them. Next, write the words on the board and have students check each word, making corrections as needed.

Reading and Writing Practice Activity 99 provides additional practice of the suffixes *able* and *ible.*

LANGUAGE: Fixing Fragments and Run-On Sentences

Write these sentences on the board.

Walking down the street.

Yes, I like corn, I like peas.

Read the first sentence aloud. Ask students to tell what the subject is. (The sentence has no subject.) Tell students that it is a fragment.

Explain:

- A fragment is not a sentence.
- A fragment does not express a complete thought.
- It may be missing a subject, a predicate, or both.

Read the second sentence. Ask students what the subject is. (There are two subjects: corn, peas.) Tell students that this is a run-on sentence. Explain:

- A sentence should have only one thought.
- A run-on sentence is two or more sentences written as though they were one. The sentences have no end marks between them.
- Run-on sentences need to be separated by end marks and have capital letters at the beginning of new sentences, or they need to have punctuation or wordings to make them complete sentences.

Reading and Writing Practice Activity 100 provides additional practice with fragments and run-on sentences.

WRITING: A Job Application

Explain to students that job applications usually ask for the following information:

- Name, address, and phone number
- Education information
- Past employment history

Sometimes applications ask for previous wages and references.

Explain to students that the job application gives an employer his or her first impression of a job-seeker. Tell students that in order to make a good impression, they should remember these points when they fill in an application.

- Write legibly.
- Complete every line on the application. Don't leave key information blank.
- Make sure the information is correct, including names, addresses, and phone numbers.
- Make sure all words are spelled correctly.
- Sign the application.

Reading and Writing Practice Duplicate and distribute Activities 101 and 102 on completing a job application. Then have students complete the activities in pairs.

Lesson at a Glance

Objectives

- to complete a trade book successfully
- to practice the word study and phonics skills learned in Chapter 3
- to practice reading the high-frequency and content words learned in Chapter 3
- to build reading fluency

Recommended Books

Shipwreck at the Bottom of the World by Jennifer Armstrong
The Pinballs by Betsy Cromer Byars
Freedom Crossing by Margaret Goff Clark
Missing May by Cynthia Rylant
Sarah Bishop by Scott O'Dell
What Do You Mean I Have Attention Deficit Disorder? by Kathleen M. Dwyer
Virtual War by Gloria Sakurzynski
Waiting for the Rain by Sheila Gordon
The Watsons Go to Birmingham by Christopher Paul Curtis
Within Reach, My Everest Story by Mark Pfetzer and Jack Calvin
The Cay by Phillip Enright
All-of-a-Kind Family by Sydney Taylor
Homecoming by Cynthia Voight
I'm Deaf and It's Okay by Lorraine Aseltine, Evelyn Mueller, and Nancy Tait

Before Reading

Introduce the Book

Display some of the books from the recommended trade book list. (Or, if the whole class will read the same book, display just that book.) Tell students that they will read a chapter book. Explain that these books use words that are the same as or similar to the words in Chapter 3, and that they will read the book for fun; they will not be expected to learn new skills.

Clarify

Tell students that by rereading a paragraph to clarify, good readers make sure they understand the facts. Remind students that when they come to a sentence or idea that they find confusing, they should stop to solve the confusion before reading on. To solve the confusion, they should reread to see if that helps them to understand. Another tactic is to read ahead as a way to increase comprehension. Tell students that they should come to a conclusion about the meaning of the sentence or idea before they continue to read.

Use Context Clues

Remind students that when they come to a word or phrase that they do not know, they should look at the words and sentences around the word or phrase to help figure out the meaning. Tell students that they should try to come to a conclusion about the meaning of the word or phrase before they continue to read.

Reading

Summarize

Explain to students that a summary contains the most important ideas of a story without including all the details. Explain that, in order to remember them, they can summarize things they have to read. To write a summary, students should state the main idea, write the key points, arrange the points logically, and use their own words. Have students select and read one of the books from the list, then summarize the most important events in the story.

Draw Conclusions

Tell students that conclusions are not stated directly but are supported by information in the story. Remind them that the main idea is developed by drawing conclusions about the entire story. Ask students to meet in pairs to draw conclusions after reading a passage from a book in the list. Have the pairs present their conclusions in an oral report.

After Reading

Evaluate/Make Judgments

Tell students to choose an action by a character in the story. Ask them to tell if they think the character made the right choice and to explain why or why not.

In nonfiction, tell students to choose a topic in the story and give their evaluation of some aspect of the topic.

Author's Purpose

Ask students to try to put themselves in the author's shoes and to think why the author wrote the story. (For example: To entertain? To inform? To surprise? To prove a point? To scare?)

Extension Activities

Reading

For their own personal interests, suggest that students read other books from the recommended list.

Writing

Suggest that students complete one of these activities:

- Write a description of one of the characters in the book.
- Write a marketing piece for the book to advertise it to potential readers.

Research

Suggest that students choose a part of the book that interests them. Students can then find out more information about the topic by using an encyclopedia, searching the Internet, or by interviewing a person who knows more about the topic.

Chapter 3 Review

The Chapter Review on Student Worktext pages 174–182 will help students review and practice the skills presented in Chapter 3. The review is divided into four parts, A–D.

Suggestions to help students complete the Chapter Review:

- Make sure that the students understand that the Chapter Review is not a test. You may have students work in pairs and then compare responses, or you may work through the review as a class.
- Read the instructions for each part aloud.
- Have students complete one part of the review at a time. Pause to go over the answers and have students mark corrections using a second color.

Chapter Test

Reproducible blackline masters of the Chapter 3 Test can be found on pages 135–137 of this book. Use the test to assess students' comprehension skills taught in the chapter.

Additional Practice

Reading and Writing Practice Activities 75–102 can be used to reinforce the skills taught in Chapter 3.

Level E Test

Reproducible blackline masters of the Level E test can be found on pages 138–140 of this book. Use the test to assess students' comprehension of the skills taught in Level E.

Part A

Part A reviews the phonics skills taught in the chapter. Read aloud the summaries presented in the tip boxes before each exercise. Then have the students complete the items. If students show difficulty understanding and using the new letters and sounds, review individual lessons or assign the corresponding Reading and Writing Practice Activities: 75, 82, 89, and 96.

Part A

Summing It Up: Letters and Sounds

- The letters **ough, augh,** and **aw** can all stand for the **broad o** sound in **wrong.**

Directions: Read each word. Circle the words that have the **aw** sound in **saw.**

1. pawn 4. laugh 7. fought 9. caught
2. tough 5. bought 8. lawn 10. rough
3. sought 6. taught

Directions: Write each word below on the lines. Circle the letters that stand for the **aw** sound.

11. pawn pawn 15. lawn lawn
12. sought sought 16. caught caught
13. bought bought 17. fought fought
14. taught taught

- The letters **ear** and **or** can stand for the sound of **ar** in **barn.**
- The letters **ear** and **ere** can stand for the sound of **ar** in **share.**
- The letters **ear** and **ere** can stand for the sound of **ir** in **irritate.**
- The letters **ear** and **or** can stand for the sound of **ur** in **fur.**

Directions: These words have the sound of **or,** as in **fortunately.** Write the word on the line. Circle the letters that stand for the **or** sound.

18. fluoride fluoride 21. fluorish flourish
19. coarse coarse 22. boarder boarder
20. fortune fortune 23. important important

Directions: These words have the sound of **ar,** as in **part.** Write the word on the line. Circle the letters that stand for the **ar** sound.

24. harp harp 27. smart smart
25. carted carted 28. partner partner
26. heart heart 29. darted darted

Student page 175

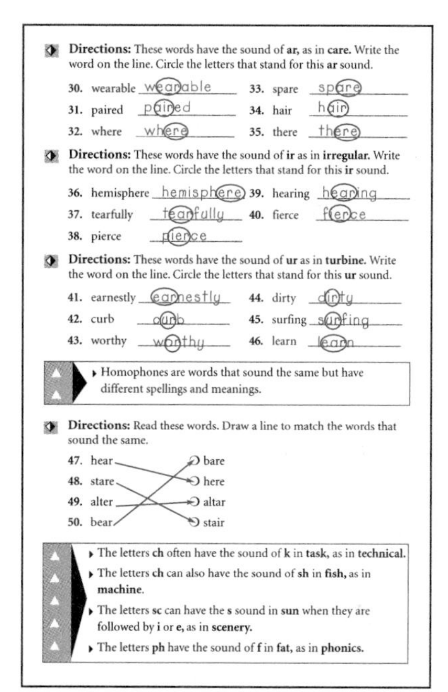

Directions: These words have the sound of **ar,** as in **care.** Write the word on the line. Circle the letters that stand for this **ar** sound.

30. wearable wearable 33. spare spare
31. paired paired 34. hair hair
32. where where 35. there there

Directions: These words have the sound of **ir** as in **irregular.** Write the word on the line. Circle the letters that stand for this **ir** sound.

36. hemisphere hemisphere 39. hearing hearing
37. tearfully tearfully 40. fierce fierce
38. pierce pierce

Directions: These words have the sound of **ur** as in **turbine.** Write the word on the line. Circle the letters that stand for this **ur** sound.

41. earnestly earnestly 44. dirty dirty
42. curb curb 45. surfing surfing
43. worthy worthy 46. learn learn

- Homophones are words that sound the same but have different spellings and meanings.

Directions: Read these words. Draw a line to match the words that sound the same.

47. hear — bare
48. stare — here
49. alter — altar
50. bear — stair

- The letters **ch** often have the sound of **k** in **task,** as in **technical.**
- The letters **ch** can also have the sound of **sh** in **fish,** as in **machine.**
- The letters **sc** can have the **s** sound in **sun** when they are followed by **i** or **e,** as in **scenery.**
- The letters **ph** have the sound of **f** in **fat,** as in **phonics.**

Student page 176

Part B

Part B reviews the word study and structural analysis skills taught in the chapter. Read aloud the summaries presented in the tip boxes before each exercise. Then have the students complete the items. You may want to review the skills by looking back at individual lessons, presenting examples on the board, or assigning the corresponding Reading and Writing Practice Activities: 77, 84, 91, and 98.

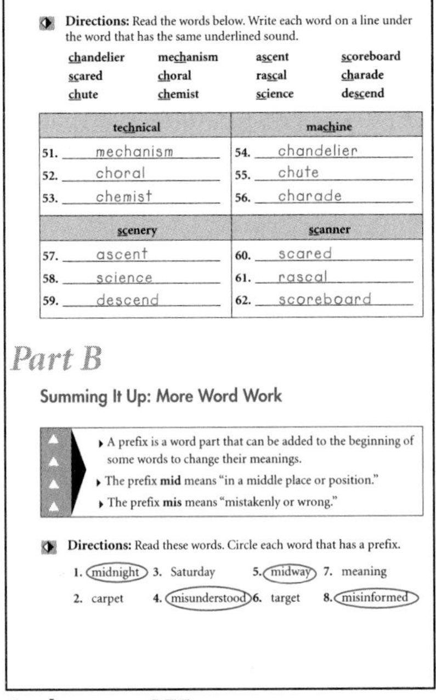

Directions: Read the words below. Write each word on a line under the word that has the same underlined sound.

chandelier	mechanism	ascent	scoreboard
scared	choral	rascal	charade
chute	chemist	science	descend

technical	machine
51. mechanism	54. chandelier
52. choral	55. chute
53. chemist	56. charade
scenery	**scanner**
57. ascent	60. scared
58. science	61. rascal
59. descend	62. scoreboard

Part B

Summing It Up: More Word Work

- A prefix is a word part that can be added to the beginning of some words to change their meanings.
- The prefix **mid** means "in a middle place or position."
- The prefix **mis** means "mistakenly or wrong."

Directions: Read these words. Circle each word that has a prefix.

1. (midnight) 3. Saturday 5. (midway) 7. meaning
2. carpet 4. (misunderstood) 6. target 8. (misinformed)

Student page 177

Directions: Write on the lines each word you circled. Then write the prefix and base word that make it up.

9. midnight = mid + night
10. misunderstood = mis + understood
11. midway = mid + way
12. misinformed = mis + informed

- The prefix **trans** means "across or beyond."
- The prefix **sub** means "under."

Directions: Read these words. Circle each word that has a prefix.

13. (subway) 14. (transplant) 15. travel 16. (substandard)

Directions: Write each word you circled on the lines. Then write the prefix and the base word that make it up.

17. subway = sub + way
18. transplant = trans + plant
19. substandard = sub + standard

- The suffix **able** means "capable of" or "likely to."
- The suffix **less** means "without."

Directions: Read these words. Circle each word that has a suffix.

20. (breakable) 21. pattern 22. (careless) 23. garbage

Directions: Write each word you circled on the lines. Then write the base word and suffix that make it up.

24. breakable = break + able
25. careless = care + less

- Adverbs describe verbs, adjectives, and other adverbs.
- Adverbs can often tell how, where, why, or when.
- Many adverbs end in **ly**.

Student page 178

Part C

Part C reviews the story words from each story in the chapter. Students are asked to recognize story words and their meanings, and to place them in sentences. Have students review the story words in the Word Bank at the back of their Student Worktext or refer to the stories in the chapter to help them complete the review. For additional practice and word recognition, assign the corresponding Reading and Writing Practice Activities: 76, 83, 90, and 97.

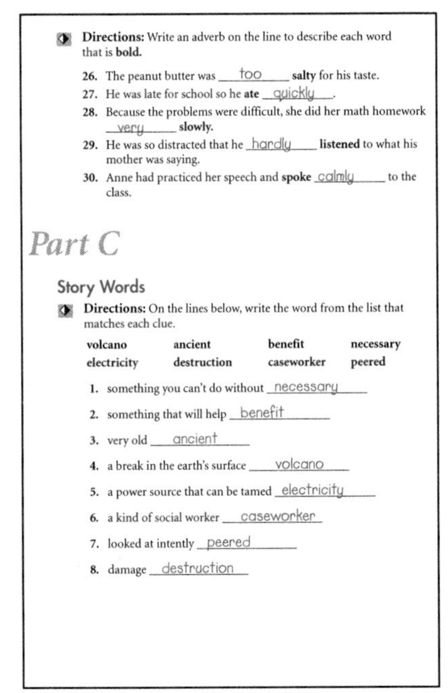

Directions: Write an adverb on the line to describe each word that is **bold**.

26. The peanut butter was too **salty** for his taste.
27. He was late for school so he **ate** quickly.
28. Because the problems were difficult, she did her math homework very **slowly**.
29. He was so distracted that he hardly **listened** to what his mother was saying.
30. Anne had practiced her speech and **spoke** calmly to the class.

Part C

Story Words

Directions: On the lines below, write the word from the list that matches each clue.

volcano	ancient	benefit	necessary
electricity	destruction	caseworker	peered

1. something you can't do without necessary
2. something that will help benefit
3. very old ancient
4. a break in the earth's surface volcano
5. a power source that can be tamed electricity
6. a kind of social worker caseworker
7. looked at intently peered
8. damage destruction

Student page 179

Directions: On the lines below, write a word from the list to finish each sentence.

routine	accusing	democracy	supervise
allowance	citizens	mansion	America

9. They were accusing her of theft.
10. He always wanted to live in a mansion.
11. His routine was to do his homework before watching television.
12. The official name of our country is the United States of America.
13. The U.S. government is a democracy.
14. All citizens should vote.
15. It was her job to supervise the workers.
16. He wanted a raise in his allowance.

Directions: On the lines below, write the word from the list that matches each clue.

physicist	mechanical	weightlessness	engineer
simulation	communications	external	satellites

17. defying gravity weightlessness
18. not the real thing simulation
19. made of machines mechanical
20. moons satellites
21. a system for talking to others communications
22. on the outside external
23. a person who plans or designs things engineer
24. a student of the laws of nature physicist

Student page 180

Part D

Part D reviews the content of the stories in the chapter. Students are asked to identify fiction and nonfiction, story characters, details, and cause and effect. If students are having difficulty remembering story details, have them reread stories they have trouble recalling and work in pairs or as a class to complete Part D again.

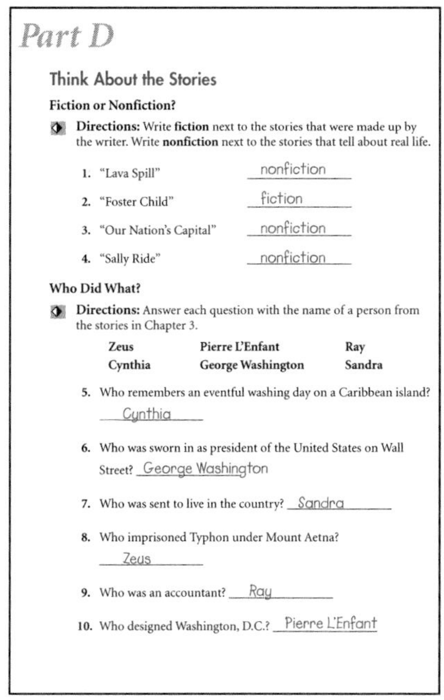

Part D

Think About the Stories

Fiction or Nonfiction?

Directions: Write **fiction** next to the stories that were made up by the writer. Write **nonfiction** next to the stories that tell about real life.

1. "Lava Spill" nonfiction
2. "Foster Child" fiction
3. "Our Nation's Capital" nonfiction
4. "Sally Ride" nonfiction

Who Did What?

Directions: Answer each question with the name of a person from the stories in Chapter 3.

Zeus	**Pierre L'Enfant**	**Ray**
Cynthia	**George Washington**	**Sandra**

5. Who remembers an eventful washing day on a Caribbean island? Cynthia
6. Who was sworn in as president of the United States on Wall Street? George Washington
7. Who was sent to live in the country? Sandra
8. Who imprisoned Typhon under Mount Aetna? Zeus
9. Who was an accountant? Ray
10. Who designed Washington, D.C.? Pierre L'Enfant

Student page 181

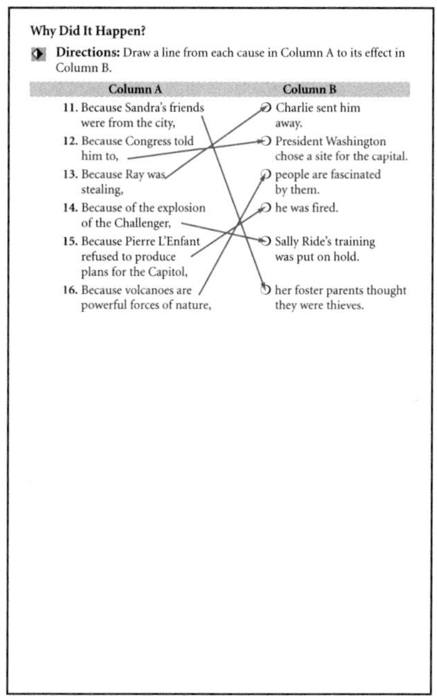

Why Did It Happen?

Directions: Draw a line from each cause in Column A to its effect in Column B.

Column A	Column B
11. Because Sandra's friends were from the city,	Charlie sent him away.
12. Because Congress told him to,	President Washington chose a site for the capital.
13. Because Ray was stealing,	people are fascinated by them.
14. Because of the explosion of the Challenger,	he was fired.
15. Because Pierre L'Enfant refused to produce plans for the Capitol,	Sally Ride's training was put on hold.
16. Because volcanoes are powerful forces of nature,	her foster parents thought they were thieves.

Student page 182

◆ Individual Record Form

Level E

Name ______________________ Period __________ Date __________

Skill Level at Beginning ______________

Student Worktext

Chapter 1	Before	During	After	
1 It's Never Too Late, 1	____/45	+ ✔ -	____/17	Chapter Review ____ out of 153
2 It's Never Too Late, 2	____/36	+ ✔ -	____/17	
3 Birthday Party	____/43	+ ✔ -	____/14	Chapter Test ____ out of 51
4 Oprah Winfrey	____/37	+ ✔ -	____/16	
5 Role Models	____/51	+ ✔ -	____/15	Independent Reading + ✔ -
6 Against All Odds	____/45	+ ✔ -	____/15	

Chapter 2	Before	During	After	
1 Finding New Friends, 1	____/47	+ ✔ -	____/15	Chapter Review ____ out of 124
2 Finding New Friends, 2	____/46	+ ✔ -	____/16	
3 Second Sight	____/37	+ ✔ -	____/14	Chapter Test ____ out of 42
4 Student Volunteer	____/39	+ ✔ -	____/17	
5 Blood Brothers, 1	____/35	+ ✔ -	____/16	Independent Reading + ✔ -
6 Blood Brothers, 2	____/40	+ ✔ -	____/15	

Chapter 3	Before	During	After	
1 Lava Spill	____/48	+ ✔ -	____/15	Chapter Review ____ out of 132
2 Foster Child	____/43	+ ✔ -	____/17	
3 Our Nation's Capital	____/33	+ ✔ -	____/14	Chapter Test ____ out of 49
4 Sally Ride	____/36	+ ✔ -	____/16	
				Independent Reading + ✔ -
				Level E Test ____ out of 36

◆ Individual Record Form

Level E

Name ______________________ Period __________ Date __________

Skill Level at Beginning ______________

Reading and Writing Practice

Chapter 1	Phonics	Story Words	Word Work	Spelling	Study Skill	Lang. Arts	Writing	Literary Appreciation
1 It's Never Too Late, 1							+ ✔ -	
2 It's Never Too Late, 2								
3 Birthday Party								
4 Oprah Winfrey								
5 Role Models							+ ✔ -	
6 Against All Odds							+ ✔ -	

Chapter 2	Phonics	Story Words	Word Work	Spelling	Study Skill	Lang. Arts	Writing	Literary Appreciation
1 Finding New Friends, 1							+ ✔ -	
2 Finding New Friends, 2								
3 Second Sight							+ ✔ -	
4 Student Volunteer							+ ✔ -	
5 Blood Brothers, 1								
6 Blood Brothers, 2							+ ✔ -	

Chapter 3	Phonics	Story Words	Word Work	Spelling	Study Skill	Lang. Arts	Writing	Literary Appreciation
1 Lava Spill							+ ✔ -	
2 Foster Child							+ ✔ -	
3 Our Nation's Capital							+ ✔ -	
4 Sally Ride							+ ✔ -	

◆ Class Record Form

Reading Skills for Life

Chapter ______________ Level ______________

	Story																				
	Student	Before	During	After	Before	During	After	Before	During	After	Before	During	After	Before	During	After	Before	During	After	Chapter Review	Chapter Test
1																					
2																					
3																					
4																					
5																					
6																					
7																					
8																					
9																					
10																					
11																					
12																					
13																					
14																					
15																					
16																					
17																					
18																					
19																					
20																					

Name ______________________ Date __________ Period __________

Chapter 1 Test

Letters and Sounds

◆ Read these words. Circle each word that has a long vowel sound. Then write the words you circled in the chart where they belong.

slime	sleigh	boat	key	great	though
pie	cool	tread	slight	moon	bunt
conceit	bomb	swoon	prey	dean	poem

long *a* as in *grate*	long *e* as in *greet*	long *i* as in *wife*	long *o* as in *comb*	long *u* as in *cute*
1. ________	4. ________	7. ________	10. ________	13. ________
2. ________	5. ________	8. ________	11. ________	14. ________
3. ________	6. ________	9. ________	12. ________	15. ________

◆ Read these long vowel words. Write them in the chart where they belong.

robin	format	laser	snicker
private	parent	combine	weather

V/CV as in pilot	VC/V as in planet	VC/CV as in magnet	VCC/V as in wither
16. ________	18. ________	20. ________	22. ________
17. ________	19. ________	21. ________	23. ________

◆ Read each word below. On the lines, write hard *c* or soft *c* to tell the sound made by the consonant *c*.

24. subscribe ____________________ **26.** ceiling ____________________

25. spice ____________________ **27.** college ____________________

Name ______________________________ Date __________ Period __________

Word Work

◆ Add *s* or *es* to each word to make it plural. Write the new word on the line.

1. video ____________________

2. father ____________________

3. quiz ____________________

◆ Circle the correct word for each sentence.

4. The three (hero's, heroes') friends admired them.

5. The (runners', runner's) time was slow.

6. Both (student's, students') assignment were surprises.

◆ Add the suffixes to each word. Write the word on the line.

7. swim + er = ____________________ **9.** cry + ed = ____________________

8. dim + ed = ____________________ **10.** beg + ar = ____________________

◆ Read each word below. On the lines, write the prefixes and the smaller words that make up each word.

11. unusual = ________________ + ________________

12. preview = ________________ + ________________

13. design = ________________ + ________________

14. import = ________________ + ________________

Story Words

◆ Read these words. Write each word on the line next to each clue.

humble awkward memories admire improve

15. look up to ____________________

16. to get better ____________________

17. modest ____________________

18. uncomfortable ____________________

19. remembered moments ____________________

Name Date Period

Read and Think

◆ This is part of "Role Models," a story you read in Chapter 1. Read the passage. Then answer the questions.

The person I most admire is my mother. I don't know anyone who works harder. She works all day long in an office. Then she goes to school at night. Yet she still manages to keep the house and our clothes clean, and to cook our meals. My mom didn't finish college because she had to take care of me when I was a baby. I am glad she is going back to school now. She is doing it for herself because she likes to learn and wants to get an interesting job. But she is also doing it for us. She wants me to have a better future. My mom is a good person. She is the best person I know. I love her.

Carol read what she had just written. She liked it. She decided to show it to her mother when she got home. "No," Carol changed her mind. "I'll show it to her tomorrow, after she's taken her test."

Write Sentences About the Story

◆ Use words from the story to answer these questions.

1. Why is her mother the person Carol most admires?

____

____

____

2. Why does Carol decide not to show her mother what she has written until after her mother's test?

____

____

____

Why Did It Happen?

◆ Draw a line from each event to the reason it happened.

3. Carol's mother didn't finish college.	❍ She wants to learn and to get an interesting job.
4. Carol's mother is also going back to school because of her family.	❍ She was taking care of baby Carol.
5. Carol's mother is going back to school for herself.	❍ She wants Carol to have a better future.

Name ______________________________ Date __________ Period __________

Chapter 2 Test

Letters and Sounds

◆ Read these words. Write each word in the chart where it belongs.

larger	original	gem	tiger
organize	ground	great	agenda

has the soft *g* sound	has the hard *g* sound
1. ____________	5. ____________
2. ____________	6. ____________
3. ____________	7. ____________
4. ____________	8. ____________

◆ Read these words. Write each word in the chart. (Four words do not belong.)

person	boney	supposes	hangar	portable	bale	fitted
soccer	frigid	seed	cereal	axis	sincere	hasten

schwa plus *l* sound	schwa plus *r* sound	schwa plus *s* sound	schwa plus *n* sound	schwa plus *d* sound
9. ________	11. ________	13. ________	15. ________	17. ________
10. ________	12. ________	14. ________	16. ________	18. ________

Word Work

◆ Write a contraction for each set of words below.

1. you + will = ____________ 3. do + not = ____________

2. he + had = ____________ 4. will + not = ____________

◆ Circle each compound word and write its parts on the line.

5. network ____________ 7. barnyard ____________

6. fishing ____________ 8. wristwatch ____________

◆ Add the given prefix or suffix to each word. Write the new word on the line.

9. port + able = ____________ 10. thorough + ly = ____________

Name ______________________ Date __________ Period __________

Story Words

◆ Read these words. Write each word on the line next to its meaning.

Paris   observe   trophy   cultivate   pedestrian

11. someone who walks ____________________

12. capital of France ____________________

13. develop or grows ____________________

14. to study ____________________

15. award ____________________

Read and Think

◆ This is part of "Blood Brothers," a story you read in Chapter 2. Read the passage. Then answer the questions on the next page.

Well, everybody finally stopped gushing over John. Then we made our way out to the parking lot. As we got closer to the car, I noticed John was walking kind of fast. I figured he was trying to get to the car first and get a window seat. And I knew my parents would make me let Karen have the other window. That would mean I'd be stuck in the middle. No way, I thought. I'm not being crushed to death all the way to the ice cream parlor. So I started walking faster, too. John sped up. He was just about to reach the car door when I sped up and brushed past him. I guess it had rained during the game because the ground was wet and slippery. I swear I didn't touch John. But just as I got ahead of him, I heard a loud thump. I turned around and there was John on the ground. He was hollering like a baby. Everybody made a huge fuss over him. Mom said, "Todd, give your brother a hand."

Name ______________________ Date ______ Period ______

Write Sentences About the Story

◆ Use words from the story to answer these questions.

1. How does Todd explain John's falling down?

____

____

____

2. How can you tell Todd's feelings about John?

____

____

____

When Did It Happen?

◆ **3.–7.** Write a number from 1 to 5 next to each sentence to show the order of events.

____ John is on the ground and is hollering.

____ John is just about to reach the car door; Todd brushes past.

____ Todd notices John is walking fast.

____ Their mother says, "Todd, give your brother a hand."

____ Todd starts walking faster.

Why Did It Happen?

◆ Draw a line from each event to the reason it happened.

8. John was walking fast.	❍ Todd does not want to be stuck in the middle seat.
9. Todd walks faster.	❍ John wants to get a window seat.
10. John has fallen on the ground.	❍ John slipped on wet ground; Todd brushed by him.

Name ______________________ Date ________ Period ________

Chapter 3 Test

Letters and Sounds

◆ Read these words. Write each word in the chart where it belongs.

atmosphere uncertainty soaring contrary Pawnee sorrowful

articulate fluorescent traumatic disturbance legionnaire wearily

has the *aw* sound as in *awful*	has the *or* sound like *format*	has the *ur* sound like *turbine*	has the *ar* sound like *heartless*	has the *ir* sound like *tear*	has the *ar* sound like *unfairness*
1. ________	3. ________	5. ________	7. ________	9. ________	11. ________
2. ________	4. ________	6. ________	8. ________	10. ________	12. ________

◆ Read these words. Write each word in the chart where it belongs.

physical scenic parachute architect

technical alphabet scented chandelier

k sound as in *task*	*s* sound as in *sun*	*sh* sound as in *short*	*f* sound as in *fast*
13. ________	15. ________	17. ________	19. ________
14. ________	16. ________	18. ________	20. ________

◆ Read these words that each have an *r*-controlled vowel sound. Circle the six words that make part of a homophone pair.

21. bears **23.** boars **25.** course **27.** cars **29.** stairs

22. stares **24.** coarse **26.** bores **28.** choirs **30.** stars

Word Work

◆ Add the given prefix or suffix to each word. Write the new word on the line.

1. sub + tract = ________________ **4.** repeat + able = ________________

2. sleep + less = ________________ **5.** mid + stream = ________________

3. mis + taken = ________________ **6.** trans + fer = ________________

Name ____________________ Date __________ Period __________

Chapter 3 Test, page 2

Story Words

◆ Read these words. Write each word on the line next to its meaning.

weightlessness   mansion   peered   volcano   routine

7. looked carefully ____________________

8. usual, everyday ____________________

9. large, formal house ____________________

10. not having gravity ____________________

11. mountain that erupts ____________________

Read and Think

◆ This is part of "Foster Child," a story you read in Chapter 3. Read the passage. Then answer the questions on the next page.

The next morning Sandra was up early, at least for her. She found Charlie and Amy Jo already hard at work in the **greenhouses.** Amy Jo was cutting back some of the plants and removing dead flowers. Charlie was spraying something on the leaves of some of the plants. He said it was a mix to help the plants grow. He said it would also keep some of the insects away. He handed Sandra a watering can. He pointed out the hose to her. She must have stared blankly at him because he told her to fill the watering can. After she filled it, she came back, and he told her which plants to water. Sandra did as she was told.

This became the morning routine. Each day she would spend the morning watering the plants. Sometimes she used a hose and sometimes she used the watering can. Sandra didn't realize that she would have to work for her foster parents. She wasn't happy about this at all. During summers at home, she hung around with her friends all day. In the city she didn't have to work.

Write Sentences About the Story

◆ Use words from the story to answer these questions.

1. How was Sandra's morning routine on the farm different than her life in the city?

____

____

____

2. Why does Sandra look blankly at Charlie when he hands her the watering can?

____

____

____

When Did It Happen?

3.–7. Write a number from 1–5 next to each sentence to show the order of events.

_____ Sandra watered the plants.

_____ Charlie told Sandra he was spraying a mix on the plants.

_____ Amy Jo was cutting back some plants.

_____ Sandra woke up early, at least for her.

_____ Sandra filled the watering can.

Words and Meanings

◆ Think about how the **bold** word is used in the story. Circle the meaning of the bold word.

8. Charlie, Amy Jo, and Sandra work in **greenhouses,** which are ______.

a. energy-conserving houses painted green

b. buildings with controlled climate for raising plants

c. barns where animals are kept

Name Date Period

Level E Test

◆ Read this story. Then answer the questions.

"It looks like you have all you need, Chris. If you need something, go next door and see Hardy. Well, don't paint yourself into any corners."

I laughed as my father headed for the door. My parents and my brother were going to help Grandma and Grandpa with spring cleaning. I wanted to finish before they returned.

I'd watched Dad and my brother paint, so I was ready to try painting for myself. It was my room, so I had a personal interest in doing the job. Just to be safe, I had my own instruction book. My big brother, Larry, had reminded me of everything I should do. I had folded some paper into a little book and wrote my notes inside.

"Chris, all the real work will be in the preparation," Larry had said. "If you do everything right, the painting part is easy."

I spent a day washing the walls and filling in old cracks. Then I painted with primer. I knew I had to do that so the paint would stick. I kept pencilling checkmarks into the book.

Larry was right about the preparation. But I did have one bad moment. I began with the ceiling. A few spots needed touching up, so I took a brush and climbed the stepladder. My head must have been a little too close to the ceiling, because I felt two hairs pulling up. They were sticking to fresh paint. I climbed down and wiped away the paint. "And that," I said aloud, "is why painters wear hats." I made myself a hat out of paper.

Just then, I heard someone at the door. I pushed it open. It was Hardy.

"Hi! I just got a call from Larry. He couldn't remember if he had given you a painter's hat. He asked me to bring you this." In his hand was a hat. "But I see you have taken care of yourself. Mmm." He looked around. "Nice job, Chris. It looks like you've done everything else **by the book**."

I just smiled at Hardy and patted my pocket.

1. What is this story mostly about? Circle the sentence that best sums it up.

   a. Hardy comes to the rescue when Chris needs help.

   b. Larry has told Chris everything necessary for doing the job.

   c. Chris's organization and quick thinking make a big job go smoothly.

2. Do you think Dad or Larry expects Chris to be painted into a corner or to have any trouble with this painting job? Explain your answer.

   ____

   ____

Name ______________________ Date ____________ Period ____________

Level E Test, page 2

◆ Draw a line from each event to the reason it happened.

3. Chris cleaned the walls.	❍ He wanted to see if Chris had a hat.
4. Chris made a paper hat.	❍ He wanted to protect his head from paint.
5. Larry asked Hardy to see Chris.	❍ He needed to prepare them for painting.

6. What does **by the book** mean in the story? Circle the correct answer.

a. The bookshelves were carefully painted.

b. Every step was followed in the correct order.

c. Chris should have read up on painting before starting the job.

◆ Find a sentence fragment in the story. Write it on the line below.

7. ____

◆ Fix the fragment. Write your answer on the line below.

8. ____

◆ Reread the story. Find a sentence written in the present tense. Write it on the line below.

9. ____

◆ Find a sentence written in the past tense. Write it on the line below.

10. ____

◆ Find a sentence written in the future tense. Write it on the line below.

11. ____

◆ Find a sentence written in the past perfect tense. Write it on the line below.

12. ____

Name ______________________ Date ________ Period ________

Level E Test, page 3

◆ Read these words. Write each word under the word with the same vowel sound in the chart.

toughen	hawk	wait	arrow	earning
though	weight	dirty	enough	they
roughness	automobile	sought	turkey	dough

gate	slow	cuff	taught	gather
13. ________	14. ________	15. ________	16. ________	17. ________
18. ________	19. ________	20. ________	21. ________	22. ________
23. ________	24. ________	25. ________	26. ________	27. ________

◆ Fill in this chart by adding suffixes to the base words.

Base Words			
bear	**28. able** ________	**29. ing** ________	**30. er** ________
sense	**31. ible** ________	**32. less** ________	**33. or** ________
right	**34. eous** ________	**35. ly** ________	**36. ful** ________

◆ Test Answer Key

Chapter 1 Test

Letters and Sounds

Circled: slime, sleigh, boat, key, great, though, pie, cool, slight, moon, conceit, swoon, prey, dean, poem,

1. sleigh
2. prey
3. great
4. conceit
5. key
6. dean
7. slime
8. slight
9. pie
10. boat
11. though
12. poem
13. moon
14. swoon
15. cool
16. private
17. laser
18. parent
19. robin
20. format
21. combine
22. weather
23. snicker
24. hard *c*
25. soft *c*
26. soft *c*
27. hard *c*

Word Work

1. videos
2. fathers
3. quizzes
4. heroes'
5. runner's
6. students'
7. swimmer
8. dimmed
9. cried
10. beggar
11. un + usual
12. pre + view
13. de + sign
14. im + port
15. admire
16. improve
17. humble
18. awkward
19. memories

Read and Think

1. Carol most admires her mother because she works so hard, yet also manages to go to school, keep house, wash clothes, and cook meals.
2. Possible answers include: Carol does not want to distract her mother from studying; she wants to surprise her mother later, when her mother can relax.
3. She was taking care of baby Carol.
4. She wants Carol to have a better future.
5. She wants to learn and to get an interesting job.

Chapter 2 Test

Letters and Sounds

1. original
2. agenda
3. larger
4. gem
5. organize
6. ground
7. great
8. tiger
9. cereal
10. portable
11. soccer
12. hangar
13. supposes
14. axis
15. person
16. hasten
17. fitted
18. frigid

Word Work

1. you'll
2. he'd
3. don't
4. won't
5. circled, net + work
6. not circled
7. circled, barn + yard
8. circled, wrist + watch
9. portable
10. thoroughly
11. pedestrian
12. Paris
13. cultivate
14. observe
15. trophy

Read and Think

1. Todd says John slipped on the rain-soaked ground. Todd also says he brushed by John, but didn't touch him.
2. Todd uses strong words that reveal his resentful feelings: everybody is "gushing over John" and making "a huge fuss over him" while John was "hollering like a baby."

3–7. 4, 3, 1, 5, 2

8. John wants to get a window seat.
9. Todd does not want to be stuck in the middle seat.
10. John slipped on wet ground; Todd brushed by him.

◆ Chapter 3 Test

Letters and Sounds

1. traumatic
2. Pawnee
3. fluorescent
4. soaring
5. disturbance
6. uncertainty
7. articulate
8. sorrowful
9. atmosphere
10. wearily
11. contrary
12. legionnaire
13. architect
14. technical
15. scenic
16. scented
17. parachute
18. chandelier
19. alphabet
20. physical
21. not circled
22. circled
23. circled
24. circled
25. circled
26. circled
27. not circled
28. not circled
29. circled
30. not circled

Word Work

1. subtract
2. sleepless
3. mistaken
4. repeatable
5. midstream
6. transfer
7. peered
8. routine
9. mansion
10. weightlessness
11. volcano

Read and Think

1. On the farm, each day she spent the morning watering the plants. In the city, she didn't have to work and in the summer could hang around all day with her friends.
2. Sandra did not expect to have to work for her foster parents. She also may be unfamiliar with a watering can.

3–7. 5, 3, 2, 1, 4

8. b. buildings with controlled climate for raising plants

Level E Test

1. c. Chris's organization and quick thinking make a big job go smoothly.
2. Answers will vary: No, because Chris has watched his father and brother paint before and has gone over the process with his brother; yes, because his father mentions that Hardy is next door in case Chris needs any help.
3. He needed to prepare them for painting.
4. He wanted to protect his head from paint.
5. He wanted to see if Chris had a hat.
6. b. Every step was followed in the correct order.
7. Possible answer: "Nice job, Chris."
8. Possible answer: "You've done a nice job, Chris."
9. Possible answer: "But I see you have taken care of yourself."
10. Possible answer: I wanted to finish before they returned.
11. Possible answer: "Chris, all the real work will be in preparation," Larry had said.
12. Possible answer: Just to be safe, I had my own instruction book.
13. wait
14. arrow
15. toughen
16. sought
17. earning
18. wait
19. though
20. roughness
21. automobile
22. turkey
23. they
24. dough
25. enough
26. hawk
27. dirty
28. bearable
29. bearing
30. bearer
31. sensible
32. senseless
33. sensor
34. righteous
35. rightly
36. rightful